MW01194306

Advance Praise for *Succeeding*

"*Succeeding* is a beacon of hope. It's a must-read for all successors, predecessors, and anyone involved in the succession process, offering a comprehensive roadmap for those stepping into the shoes of a predecessor, guiding them through every step with clarity and confidence."

—**Jason Leck**, president and successor, Leck Waste Services

"An insightful guide that explores succession as a two-way street, where both current and next-gen leaders play pivotal roles. Full of real-world stories, this book is essential for anyone involved in a business transition."

—**Bud Dunn**, president, VXP and surviving family successor

"Having worked closely with Albert in our leadership development program at one of our portfolio companies, I can attest to the power of his insights. The practical advice and strategic wisdom he shares are invaluable for every leader. It's a must-read for those preparing to pass the torch, especially in a steadily growing worldwide business like ours."

—**Steve Townes**, CEO & founder, Ranger Aerospace LLC and vice chairman, ACL Airshop LLC

"Make time to read this book. Albert does a wonderful job distilling the principles of succession for business owners and rising leaders alike. You'll get answers to the questions you've been too busy or too afraid to discuss."

—**Laurie Barkman**, business transition advisor
and Amazon best-selling author of *The Business Transition Handbook*

"Albert's practical wisdom and easy-to-follow strategies were instrumental in helping us through a difficult transition, following the unexpected death of our CFO. The guidance and insights in *Succeeding* make it a must-read for any leader managing a senior team or preparing to step into a new role. It offers a roadmap that balances emotional intelligence with practical steps and key strategic insights."

—**Lisa Tepper Bates**, president & CEO, United Way of Connecticut

"*Succeeding* brilliantly combines emotional intelligence with practical advice, making it an accessible and actionable guide for anyone stepping into a leadership position. Highly recommended for successors ready to take the helm."

—**Matt Wineinger**, president & CEO. United Sugar Producers & Refiners

"Albert's book is a must-read for all newly minted successors. Whether leading through the multifaceted challenges of succession within a business unit of a high-tech corporation or taking the helm of a founder-led organization, *Succeeding* provides a clear, actionable framework for navigating these transitions."

—**Todd Stirtzinger**, CEO, Galvion

"Albert and his work provide a great pathway to business and personal success. Succession planning and leadership development are essential for business for not just survival, but long term success through the next generation. While automation will continue to be an important part of the business space, most companies are still in the 'people' business. As President/CEO of a 4th generation family-run trucking company, the continued development of our talented team is my most important goal. Albert is a huge help to me with this and his insights in this book are impactful."

—**Bill Ward, Jr.**, president/CEO, Ward Transport and Logistics

"Albert's book is a refreshing take on business leadership. It is tightly written and cuts through the usual business book fluff to deliver practical, actionable advice. This 'how-to' guide to success is a must-read for rising leaders and those developing into executives."

—**Jeff Lefebvre Ph.D.**, president and founder, PriSim Business War Games Inc.

"Ciuksza's thoroughly researched book leaves little to the imagination for a successor going through a transition. No book I've read on the subject so carefully deals with the topic from the successor's point of view. Kudos to the author! His playbook is filled with triumphant and cautionary tales of transitions, guiding our successors on everything from handling the different personalities (archetypes) of predecessors to the traps (quicksand) that can undermine your success."

—**Jonathan Goldhill**, founder, Goldhill Group
and author of *Disruptive Successor: A Guide for Driving Growth in Your Family Business*

"In an industry where we often rely on tried-and-true methods, Albert pushed me to rethink what it means to pass the baton. *Succeeding* goes beyond the basics and forces you to confront the biases that could hold your business back."

—**Frank Piedimonte**, retired president and COO,
current external board member, Brayman Construction Corp.

"Succeeding is a must-read for business owners navigating a generational transition, offering valuable insights for any executive, manager, or employee involved in this critical process. The book lays out a comprehensive framework for planning, executing, and keeping your transition on track, ensuring that every step is handled with precision and care."

—**Braden Wagner**, president, Wagner Equipment

"This book speaks to the heart of leadership in a way that crosses borders and cultures. It's a must-read for anyone ready to embrace the complexities of modern leadership in a world that has constant change."

—**Luis Rodriguez**, president, FC Juárez

"The transition process requires meticulous planning and execution, with countless variables to consider from both sides. Albert's advice was an invaluable guide as I navigated this entirely new experience. I highly recommend this book to anyone in a leadership role—these concepts are essential for anyone facing the complexities of succession."

—**Daniel M. Coast**, managing director of property & casualty, Henderson Brothers

"*Succeeding* is an insightful and timely read as we experience the mass retirement of the Boomer generation. As a predecessor and Boomer who is currently amid succession planning, this was a real eye opener. This information would have been invaluable to me as a successor and will shape the way I interact with my successor during this process."

—**Thomas E. Bates, Jr.**, president and CEO, Legends Bank

"Ciuksza's *Succeeding* is a much-needed resource for any leader, whether they are passing the torch, or taking on the stewardship of a company's legacy into the future."

—**Drew Farrar**, senior vice president, integrated communications

"Having spent the last 20+ years building the next chapter of an already successful company by pivoting to a new industry, I wish I had this book when I started. It would have helped me avoid the naïve assumption that everything should just follow the playbook that made the previous chapter so successful. New generations, new philosophies, new world. *Succeeding* illustrates clear examples and shares the wins and losses of those on this journey, giving readers a distinct advantage over the hurdles ahead."

—**Ryan Pruchnic, MS, MBA**, managing vice president, Cook MyoSite, Inc.

Succeeding

Succeeding

Stepping Up Without Stepping in It

The ultimate playbook

for successors

Albert Ciuksza Jr.

PERCHERON
PUBLISHING

PITTSBURGH, PENNSYLVANIA

Percheron Publishing
152 Wabash Street
Pittsburgh, Pennsylvania, 15220
www.percheronpublishing.com

ISBNs: 978-1-965559-01-7 (pbk); 978-1-965559-00-0 (hc); 978-1-965559-02-4 (ebk)

Front cover art and design by Percheron Publishing
Book design by Mayfly book design

Library of Congress Catalog Number: 2024917820
First Printing: 2024

Contents

Chapter 1:
The Wave We're Watching

Chapter 2:
More Than a New Job Title

Chapter 3:
Walking the Predecessor's Path

Chapter 4:
The Ultimate Reality Show

Chapter 5:
The Quicksand Survival Guide

Chapter 6:
Install a Leadership Upgrade

Chapter 7: It's Go Time

Foreword

by Buddy Hobart

Father Time is undefeated. None of us will live and work forever, and if we want to create a lasting legacy, we must accept this reality. It's inevitable.

Ultimately, Father Time will win, and we need to plan for that. As someone once said, "Only a fool fails to plan for the inevitable." Succession planning is about recognizing that inevitability and taking a thoughtful, strategic approach. Trust me, it's never too early to start.

Having been a consultant for over three decades, I've walked alongside countless business owners as they wrestled with developing their plans. One near-universal lesson I've learned is that it's never too early to start the process. And for those who have ignored the inevitable — it's never too late to start either. The key is to get started.

Now, having reached retirement age myself after leading Solutions 21 for over 30 years, I had to take my own advice. We began our plan years ago. I paid attention to what I saw elsewhere and wanted to be proactive. But I didn't fully grasp the strategic and emotional need to stay grounded and committed to the process until it was my time. I had to confront my own emotions honestly while remaining dedicated to the plan. Anything less would be hypocritical — and counterproductive.

There's a metaphor I've used with others and tried to embrace myself: passing the baton in a relay race. In track, no one gently passes the baton — they slap it into their teammate's hand. It's a hard pass, and the other person needs to feel it. Both runners need to be sure they've "got this," and no one drops the baton. During the exchange, they run a few strides together, and then the first runner lets go — completely. They don't hang on; that only slows things down. But they don't walk away either — they cheer like crazy!

A great relay team is strategically aligned. Each runner has a mission, and the next runner is often just a bit faster. Winning teams usually anchor the relay with their fastest runner. In other words, you expect the next person to be even better than you.

This, in a nutshell, is succession planning. The first runner does their best — hopefully passing the baton with a lead — and the next runner takes it without looking back. Their eyes are forward, the baton has been forcefully passed and released.

In my experience consulting on numerous leadership changes — whether in corporate mergers or family businesses — the same truth holds: It's always the leadership and people issues, not the systems, that lead to failure. Technology can be fixed, upgraded, or reprogrammed. People need to be led, and leaders need to be developed.

Leadership is needed in both directions. The runner passing the baton and the one receiving it must be in sync. They need to exert leadership not just with each other but with the organization, stakeholders, customers — everyone involved.

Albert has created a must-read for everyone, and I mean everyone, involved in the succession process. Whether you're the one passing the baton or receiving it, this book is essential reading.

My only regret is that I couldn't read this book sooner. The insights, strategies, and advice are spot on — from dealing with emotional hurdles to providing practical solutions, this book has it all.

It's never too early or too late to start the succession planning process. This book will help you get started. If you're already in the process, it will offer insights to help you run the best race possible.

When the handoffs are smooth and everyone runs their race, the results — in both track and business — are a beautiful thing to behold.

Buddy Hobart
CEO and founder, Solutions 21

Acknowledgments

When you've never written a book before, you've got a lot of people to thank.

Here goes.

Thank you to those who were willing to be interviewed for this work. Your candid and vulnerable answers shed light on the fundamentally emotional experience of succession.

I especially want to thank Bud Dunn, the first person I interviewed, and Jason Leck, Richard Willis, Ami Kassar, Marilyn Landis, Jeff Lefebvre, and Jim Futrell for lending your networks and enabling this deeply researched result. Your insights, support, and relationships had a disproportionate impact.

Thanks to Jack Adams, whose experience and storytelling led me to consider grief in the context of professional loss, a fundamental change in direction that made this work better.

I am immensely grateful to the Solutions 21 team, whose contributions have greatly enriched this book.

- ▶ To Rob Salome, Tyler Palko, Dan Kelly, Jason Davis, and Tom Shandy, your fingerprints are all over this final product. Your willingness to share your stories and ideas and listen to me "think out loud" as I framed out the various drafts and started to fill in the blanks was invaluable. You will see that result throughout the text.

▶ To Dori Carpenter, thank you for playing quarterback in making this a reality, simultaneously launching a publishing imprint and leading the marketing and promotion of the book. This wouldn't be in anyone's hands without you leading the charge.

▶ To Jacey Kennedy, thank you for turning a messy list of links into the references cited throughout. I'm not sure I would have survived getting them into Chicago style. Your keen editing eye was essential, too.

▶ To Eve Pyle and Michelle Cerqua, thank you for your encouragement and experience. Your words gave me the confidence to push forward, knowing that we'd figure out how to make it work.

A special thanks goes to Buddy Hobart, founder of Solutions 21, the author of the foreword, and the person in our organization who set the standard for authorship. Your vision laid the groundwork for much of what is in these pages, and I'm eternally grateful for your teaching and mentorship. It's hard to distinguish which of these ideas and concepts are really yours and which are merely influenced by you and your work.

To the folks who made this happen from a technical perspective:

▶ Tim Hayes and Annie Saunders, thank you for your editing and fact-checking prowess. You helped turn unintelligible ramblings — with frequent notes of "What does this even mean?" — into coherent ideas and a finished product.

▶ Julie and Ryan Scheife at Mayfly Book Design and Publishing Services, thank you for your patience with this first-time author. There's no one else I would have wanted to partner with to make this project a reality, and I appreciated your expertise and strong recommendations that tempered my wilder instincts.

▶ Thanks to Jesse Naus and Red Caiman Studios for their incredible professionalism and audiobook production expertise. Thank you for your friendship and partnership.

On the personal front, I owe my family, friends, acquaintances, and those randomly passing by on the street a huge thanks for putting up with me talking about this book for the last two years. You pretty much know everything in here by now. Consider this both a thank you and an apology.

Thanks to Mallory, my wife and lifelong project partner. There's no venture that we don't tackle together, this one included. Thank you so much for letting me lament my frustrations, celebrate the (sometimes) small steps forward, and allow this project to consume so much time and energy. I love you so much.

The last thank you is to you, the reader. Not everybody wants to get better, and even fewer want to engage in hard emotional conversations around grief and conflict. Congratulations on being one of the few (based on projected book sales, ha!) willing to give it a go.

Introduction

Why bring a knife to a gunfight?

The Story

Succession is existential.

Beyond the balance sheets, profit and loss statements, valuations, cap tables, and key performance indicators are people — individuals with experience, agency, and ego. Those people want their careers, legacy, and *lives* to mean something.

An emotional time requires an emotion-aware approach. Instead of discussing succession from an operational lens, I'm writing this as a coach, helping you navigate the natural highs and lows, hopes and fears, and successes and failures of an organizational transition.

Who is experiencing this emotional turmoil? Everyone — the predecessor, employees, stakeholders, board members, customers and clients, suppliers, and *you.*

I wrote this book about you. Maybe not you yet, but the you that you're about to become — or just became — living in the world where you're the head honcho. You're *El Jefe.* You're **the boss**. You're the one who makes the decisions. The corner office, the parking spot — whatever symbols come to mind that tell the world you're the person who makes the hard calls.

Yet, it's just out of your grasp. Maybe you're talking about transitioning into that role, planning it, or just about to take over. Perhaps you've taken over, even with the title, but it feels incomplete — the role isn't yet *yours*. It's time to take a more emotionally aware approach.

Background: I began writing this when my coaching and consulting conversations were about succession conflicts. Hours of searching for resources — books, articles, research, blog posts, anything, really — came up empty. What I *did* find fell into two categories:

1. Condescending articles written by Boomer-aged consultants whose message boiled down to "shut up and listen to your elders."
2. Books, courses, webinars, consultants, trade organizations, accountants, lawyers, financial advisors, breakfast groups, accreditations, and (deep breath for another list of "stuff") that exist to support the exiting owner or outgoing executive.

My conclusion? Predecessors have the power. They are in the driver's seat and have the resources to get the advice they need to achieve their goals.

Successors are at a disadvantage. At best, you've got:

1. A network of mentors and peers.
2. A coach or consultant paid for by the predecessor.
3. A trusted relationship with the predecessor.

Successors are bringing a knife to a gunfight. I didn't think that was fair.

Getting Personal: Good coaches are impartial. Yet, as I spoke with successors, I identified with their frustrations. I, too, was looking for help.

So, I did the only thing I knew how to do: I started talking to predecessors, successors, and experts in exit planning and family businesses. Was I trying to solve the problem for our clients (research)? Or was I trying to get to the bottom of what I was experiencing (*me*search)?

What you're about to read is a product of that effort: hundreds of hours of interviews, thousands of hours of consulting, and a whole lot of time coaching clients worldwide on building succession experiences that reduce the emotional impact so all involved can get what they need out of the experience.

Bottom Line: While this research isn't a double-blind, p-value, statistically significant, peer-reviewed study, it is the collection of much research, experience, reading, and conversation. Contained herein are some of the most vulnerable discussions most successors and predecessors — by their admission — have ever had. In exchange, I gave them confidentiality. I hope you find value in it. I certainly have.

A Note About our Robot Overlords

Welcome to the era of authorship and readership in the age of artificial intelligence.

Instead of ignoring or dodging the question, I wanted to talk directly about how I used technology when writing this book. In addition to the obvious — Google Docs and Microsoft Word — and a few different search engines for research, I used two tools to sharpen my writing:

- ▶ **Grammarly:** As a paid subscriber to Grammarly for almost a decade, I don't write anything without it. In addition to the obvious (spelling and grammar), it helps me to write more concisely in the tone I hope to achieve.

- ▶ **ChatGPT:** ChatGPT became an essential tool. I was able to query it to provide feedback. It helped me shorten longer stories to their most important parts and gave me bullet points to help me understand the reader's takeaways. It was a research partner and editor and collaborator, all at once.

I used these within the bounds of three principles:

1. **I write it first:** These tools helped summarize and reframe my writing, but they did not generate it. The source material is mine.
2. **Shorten and simplify:** As a consultant, I sometimes need to write in the passive voice or with words like "tend to be" or "oftentimes," which is torture to read in this format. ChatGPT can help identify those tendencies and fix them.
3. **Call out the gaps:** ChatGPT doesn't care about the emotion of the writing, which helped uncover where there was too little information to be helpful.

Lastly, this book was a distinctly human effort. In addition to writing it, I had the help of my editors, Tim Hayes and Annie Saunders, and many others who gave me helpful critiques along the way.

Bottom Line: This book was authored by me. Yet, without the help of humans and robots, you would have hated it.

How to Read This Book

A friend of mine hates business books.

"They're 300 pages of fluff with 10 pages of useful content."

That was ringing through my ears the entire time I was writing. Thanks, Jeff.

Borrowing heavily from *Smart Brevity*, the book by the folks from Politico and Axios, I found a format that was compatible with what I wanted to say and how I wanted to say it. Some of the layout even looks the same. Imitation is the sincerest form of flattery.

The result? A book with a bunch of big ideas broken down into bite-sized chunks, with all the bullet points and numbered lists you can handle. Need a little more context? Most concepts include stories from interviews and other sources that reinforce why it matters.

While I'm not going to tell you how to read this — you're on your own journey — I thought I'd share a few intentions I had as I was writing:

- ▶ **Read what matters, skim the rest:** The short paragraphs and bulleted copy is designed for you to flip through and find what matters most to you. My goal was for you to understand 80% of the point by just skimming the content.

- ▶ **Don't feel bad about skipping chapters:** Don't care why we're in the situation we're in? Then skip Chapter 1. Not worried about developing your leadership skills (yikes!)? Don't worry about Chapter 6. If you need to learn something from a previous page, you'll see references and page numbers (like my much-beloved *Choose Your Own Adventure* books as a kid).

- ▶ **Don't stop at this book:** There are many, many concepts that could be books, and maybe libraries, in and of themselves. Want to learn more about Emotional Intelligence? Feel free to dig into the many theories and structures that are out there. Think the Cynefin Framework is something that you could really sink your teeth into? Go nuts. My goal was to introduce the concepts that I've seen change people and organizations for the better.

Bottom Line: Don't feel the need to treat this like other books you've read. What matters most is how you apply what you've learned.

CHAPTER 1

The Wave We're Watching

Why we're surprised by what we saw coming, and how what we didn't predict made it worse.

The Silver Tsunami

The upcoming generational transition is ripe for disaster, but demographics don't have to be our destiny.

Since 2011, 10,000 Baby Boomers have been hitting the traditional retirement age (65 years old) daily, a trend that will continue through 2030[1] and peak between 2024 and 2027.[2]

That's 3,650,000 retirements a year. Let's consider the scale of that number. The entire workforce in the state of Arizona is only 3,260,000.[3] One year's worth of Baby Boomer retirements would wipe out every job in that state before the end of November. That's a massive number of experienced professionals about to hit the exits.

We're not prepared. Only 14% of leaders think their organization does succession well,[4] and only 35% of organizations are engaged in a formal process at all.[5] By my math, that means fewer than 5% of organizations are any good at succession.

Part of the challenge is the predecessor. Many predecessors think they'll live forever. Some want to spend that time working, some want to travel, and others want to spend time with their families. Almost all want to live their retirement years on their terms. They'll get to do that because they own (businesses and real estate) and "own" (positions of power, community leadership, elected roles) a lot of stuff. The Boomers have the gold.

You know the Golden Rule, right? Not that one. The other one.

"They who have the gold make the rules."

Why It Matters: Retirement age doesn't mean retirement. Baby Boomers want to continue to contribute. That is, if they retire at all; 71% want to work past 65 in at least a part-time capacity. They're rewriting the rules, and the abrupt full-time-work-to-relaxation model is no longer in vogue.

Here's why Baby Boomers say they are sticking around:

- ▶ **Financial:** 83% of those who want to continue to work are doing so because they're concerned about their financial situation.
- ▶ **Health:** 77% want to stay active, keep their minds alert, enjoy what they do, or have a sense of purpose.

Despite wanting to contribute in at least some capacity, Baby Boomers still present three realities companies must face:

1. Someone needs to be accountable to do that full-time job.
2. Those exiting workers have a ton of knowledge and relationship capital.
3. Life comes at you fast, and plans can fall apart.

The Big Picture: That wave of retirements or ramp downs? That's the Silver Tsunami — the coming demographic disaster likely to accelerate over the next decade. While no one can agree on when Gen X ends and Gen Y/Millennials start, there's one absolute truth: There are not enough experienced professionals to assume roles that Baby Boomers are vacating.

Here's the 2023 population data per the U.S. Census Bureau based on the definitions Solutions 21[i] uses:

- ▶ **Baby Boomers (1946-1964):** 67.8 million
- ▶ **Gen Xers (1965-1979):** 60.8 million
- ▶ **Millennials/Gen Y (1980-1997):** 81.3 million

---

i. Solutions 21, a national consulting firm specializing in leadership, is my employer. We've been around for more than 30 years, and researching generational dynamics for more than two decades.

Figure 1.1

U.S. Population by Generation, in Millions (2023)

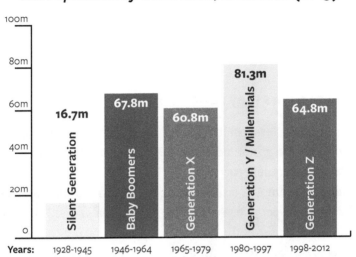

The ranges I used align with Solutions 21's past work to improve inter-generational relations. Adjusting birth years slightly doesn't change the core idea: Younger leaders must take on decision-making roles earlier than our predecessors due to the sheer number of workers walking out the door. Debates about individual years, or even sub-generations (such as Xennials), distract from the core point — there's an experienced leadership chasm.

If we lived by the old rules, where the next generation filled in for the previous one-for-one, we're 7 million workers (or more than two Arizonas) short.

Bottom Line: Time isn't standing still, and neither are the Baby Boomer leaders vacating their jobs. We must decide who will step in.

What's My Age Again?

That 7-million-person shortfall assumes Gen Xers are in the running.

A lot of data shows they're not. Consider:

- ▶ 79% of Gen Xers feel like they're overlooked in the workplace.[6]
- ▶ Gen Xers are promoted at 20-30% slower rates than their Millennial counterparts.[7]
- ▶ Gen X is promoted less for going the extra mile and averages 1.2 promotions per five years vs. 1.6 (Millennials) and 1.4. (Baby Boomers)
- ▶ Leaders default to elevating the "long runway" Millennial.

The decision to elevate Millennials relies on the assumption that Gen Y wants work as long as their Baby Boomer predecessors, when Millennials actually want to retire at 59.[8]

Go Deeper: Skipping over Gen X puts even more pressure on Millennials to step up.

The problem? A communication gap prevents Baby Boomers and Millennials from successfully executing knowledge transfer. Here's a quote from a paper digging into intergenerational interactions:

> *". . . younger generation employees reported difficulty interacting with older generations as one of their major workplace challenges [while] older generations avoid working with younger generations who, as a result, might be under-prepared for leadership roles due in part to lack of mentoring."[9]*

At a time when Baby Boomers and Millennials need to be connected, there's conflict. And Gen X is too frustrated to bridge the gap.

Bottom Line: Baby Boomer predecessors are conflicted. Yet, they're skipping over Gen Xers, who are perceived as overripe, and picking a generation (Millennials) who aren't as committed to the long-term as assumed.

Wealth Transfer

Baby Boomers have lived through the greatest economic expansion in human history and have expectations to match.

As recently as 1840, 90% of the world existed on what it grew, farmed, or hustled to sell or trade. Fast-forward to today and reverse those numbers — only 10% of the world's population lives in extreme poverty.

Guess when those numbers flipped? Around the time Baby Boomers heard Ovaltine commercials on the radio.

By the Numbers: Here are two ways to look at growth — worldwide GDP overall and per capita. Let's look at 50-year chunks:

- ▶ Before 1850 (including only a tiny part of the Industrial Revolution) worldwide GDP growth hovered between 25% and 50%, correlated to population growth.
- ▶ Between 1851 and 1900, GDP growth exceeded 120%, significantly outpacing population growth.
- ▶ From 1901 to 1950, growth was north of 150%, with post-war expansion just beginning to be visible in the last few years of that stretch.
- ▶ Between 1950 to 2000, worldwide GDP growth exceeded 600%.[10]

If that doesn't move you, worldwide GDP per capita paints a stark picture. Here are the numbers in 2023 dollars[11]:

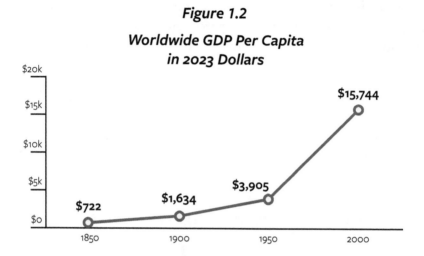

Figure 1.2

Worldwide GDP Per Capita in 2023 Dollars

In the U.S. alone, Baby Boomers have lived through seven multi-year economic growth spurts of greater than 4% per year and two stretches of 2% annual growth that lasted at least a decade.[12] "But," the Baby Boomers might retort, "we suffered through tremendous economic challenges." True enough. Eight significant recessions occurred over the career of Baby Boomers (1969 onward)[13]:

▶ The guns and butter recession and energy shocks of the '70s (11 months and 16 months, respectively).
▶ The "double-dip" inflations of the '80s (22 total months).
▶ The Gulf War recession of the early '90s (8 months).
▶ The dot-com bubble burst and 9/11 (8 months).
▶ The Great Recession (18 months).
▶ The COVID pandemic (2 months).

Even with those downturns, if you invested $100 in the S&P 500 when the oldest Baby Boomer turned 18 (1964) you would have about $35,716 at the end of 2024, at an average growth rate of 10.31% per year,[14] compared to an annual inflation rate of only 3.9%.[15]

A Little More Context: Before the Baby Boom generation, there wasn't much to inherit. Succession, as it existed, was limited to royalty or the very wealthy. If you were born before 1946, your grandparents likely left behind little of value.

The Greatest Generation first experienced accelerated economic expansion, a welcome change from their earlier years of recovering from the Great Depression and the Second World War. With newfound disposable income, they bought "stuff" — symbols of middle-class success — like china, dining room sets, and upright pianos. That "stuff" became "family heirlooms" and "antiques." It also became stocks and cash stuffed in mattresses. For the first time, there was something to hand down to the next generation.

Fast-forward to today, wealth transfer numbers are economy-changing.

- Baby Boomers hold about half of the United States' wealth, about $78 trillion in assets.
- The disproportionate growth of real estate drove much of that wealth, followed by the stock market, and equity in their businesses.
- Boomers will hand down about $53 trillion in assets through 2045 to Gens X, Y, and Z.[16]
- The management of those assets became professionalized, starting in 1972 when the Certified Financial Planner designation was born.[17]

Even More Context: So what about the businesses that Baby Boomers own? The numbers are overwhelming:

- Nearly 3 million businesses owned by age 55+ generate $6.5 trillion annually.
- 32.1 million employees (about twice the population of New York) representing $1.3 trillion in payroll are employed by those companies.
- 60% of business owners are looking to sell/transition in the next decade.

What It Means: The Baby Boomers who are transitioning their roles and businesses:

- ▶ Are part of the first generation to have been raised by a generation that, at least in allied countries, achieved middle-class lifestyles en masse.
- ▶ Lived through the most remarkable economic expansion in human history.
- ▶ Had access to professionals that, for the first time, could solely focus on the expansion of their wealth.
- ▶ Own more than half of all wealth in the United States.

For those who have had enough financial success to be part of a growing business to sell or transition, their expectation is success. Save for a couple of significant bumps in the road, nothing in their history suggests the future should be any different.

Bottom Line: There's a lot of gold. Be ready for a bumpy ride.

Oh, THAT Pandemic

All those trends would have happened. COVID was the accelerant.

Check out this data from the U.S. Census Bureau:

From January 2000 to March 2020, the Census predicted with near perfection the number of retirements. Then the pandemic hit.

What happened? Baby Boomers who could get out of the workforce bailed at unforeseen numbers. In some metros, that represented tens of thousands of experienced workers. If that wasn't enough, parents who relied on daycare started to do the math and realized the financial equation didn't add up, leading to a large exit from the workforce, as well.

Figure 1.3
Not in the Labor Force and Retired (16+), Actual & Expected

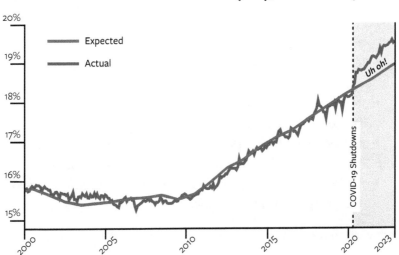

That giant sucking sound? Capacity in the form of human capital from both older and younger workers.

Then there's working from home.

At the end of 2022, the CEO of LinkedIn, Ryan Roslansky, shared some data about the state of talent attraction.

- ▶ Pre-pandemic, about 1% of all jobs posted on LinkedIn were remote. As of the end of 2022, that number was about 14%. (Not surprising.)
- ▶ More than 50% of all job applications on LinkedIn go to that 14% of remote jobs. (Shocking.)

While it seems that many companies are pulling back on fully remote hiring, it's clear that the same-old, same-old isn't coming back. Even Zoom, which was a lifeline to those who were forced out of their offices in early 2020, has brought employees back to a hybrid schedule.[18]

The workforce won't be the same. McKinsey[19] found that there are now five labor pools:

- ▶ **Traditionalists:** the "classic" worker, which makes up most of the labor force, but is shrinking.
- ▶ **Do-it-yourselfers:** everyone from entrepreneurs to gig economy workers.
- ▶ **Idealists:** those motivated to work for a specific cause or broader end goal.
- ▶ **Caregivers and others:** people who have responsibilities to take care of children or family members in addition to their work.
- ▶ **Relaxers:** retirees and those who have the resources to avoid returning to a traditional job.

And what do the non-traditionalists prize? Flexibility and meaning.

The Big Picture: An entire book could be written on how COVID changed work (and we don't have time for all of that). Here's what you need to know:

1. The idea of work has been permanently changed and we're still defining what that means.
2. The models the predecessor used to make people decisions are unlikely to work today.
3. There will be a generation of workers who will be professionally behind because of the developmental and experiential delays caused by shutdowns.
4. Pendulums tend to swing to the extremes, and organizations that approach the workforce with creativity are likely to be the most successful.

Why It Matters: The successors of today are in a bind. On one end of the workforce spectrum is a generation of live-to-work Boomers who will need significant support to transition their organizations successfully. On the other is a generation of younger, less-experienced employees who had their career development marred by the pandemic and, in general, are unsatisfied and disengaged.[20] All of this comes with entirely new definitions for what "work" means for much of the workforce.

Successors — largely made up of late Xers and Millennials — are stuck in the middle of two monster leadership challenges, both made worse by COVID.

In other words, get ready to lead in an environment of changing and uncertain norms.

Bottom Line: Succession is never a straight line, but workforce dynamics have made the puzzle even more complicated.

No One Washes a Rental Car

This book relies on one significant assumption:
You care.

In every positive succession process I have seen, the successor cares. They care about the business, the predecessor, the vision, the team, the industry, the clients, the relationships, the product, the strategy, the legacy — you name it, it matters.

Because they care, they're willing to make sacrifices. They're eager to take the harder way out — running the next leg of a race they didn't start — rather than do something else that would be easier and, in many cases, more financially gratifying. Great successors are unusual. They wash the rental car.

A Story: Years ago, I coached a woman in her early 30s. She was intelligent, well-educated, and quickly climbed the career ladder. When I met with her, she had just accepted a new job working with an impressive Executive VP at a big, tightly regulated company. Sold the new role as a potential successor to the VP and the opportunity to skip a rung or two on that ladder, she discovered that the VP had been relegated to an inconsequential corner of the business and brought her in as a glorified gofer.

Recognizing her as a potential talent in the organization, the company hired me to demonstrate their commitment to her and help prepare her for a different role when she was ready. Leadership was most interested in assessing her commitment to the organization. No matter how much I poked and prodded to get her to see it differently, she only worried about her title and salary.

She would *never* wash the rental car.

A few years later, I ran into her at an event and asked about her progression. She was with the same organization, stalling out. Within a minute or two of talking, she expressed her frustration that she had only had one small promotion and cost-of-living pay raises. She complained that no one in the business would meet her near-constant requests for more.

She *still* wouldn't wash the rental car.

Why It Matters: Sure, the successors can earn a good living, be anointed the leader of an organization, and stand among peers in the communities in which they operate. Yet, all those trappings of success tend to be lagging indicators rather than leading ones.[ii]

The hard work comes first. If you view succession only as a career development play, much of this book will likely seem empty. That's okay — to each their own — though I'd prefer you learn that after you've already paid for the book.

For the rest of you, from fully bought-in to commitment-curious, you're in luck. In car ownership, there's a worthy debate between owning and leasing, and whatever your speed, you're likely to be in a mindset — and willing to act with emotional intelligence — to be a worthy successor.

---

ii. I talk more about lagging vs. leading indicators on page 164.

Regardless of your position on the owning/leasing debate, one thing is sure: No one washes a rental car.

Bottom Line: There are more straightforward, less stressful, and lower-risk ways to earn a living than to be a successor. If you want to wash the car, you've come to the right place.

The Bottom Line on Chapter 1: The Wave We're Watching

TL;DR:[iii]

You're not crazy. The inevitable wave of Baby Boomer retirements, accelerated by the pandemic, is indeed reshaping the workforce. While Gen X would have been the natural next generation to lead, the demographic deck is stacked against them, putting Millennial-aged leaders in succession roles. Since Boomers have so many resources—and half the wealth—successors are in a dance not just to save their organizations but ensure a smoother economic transition.

The Hits:

▶ **Silver Tsunami:** The mass retirement of Baby Boomers is creating significant gaps in the workforce that need immediate attention.

▶ **Pandemic Push:** COVID-19 has accelerated retirements, making the need for effective succession planning more urgent than ever.

▶ **Overlooked Gen X:** Gen X leaders often get bypassed in favor of Millennials, leading to a potential loss of valuable experience.

▶ **Boomer Wealth:** Baby Boomers control a significant portion of wealth and leadership roles, requiring careful transition planning.

▶ **New Work Norms:** The rise of remote work and changing job definitions complicate the traditional approaches to succession.

---

iii. TL;DR is internet slang for 'Too long; didn't read."

Thought-Starter Questions:

- ▶ What do the demographics look like in your organization and how many leaders are looking for the exits?
- ▶ How has the pandemic reshaped the way your organization has talked about the workforce?
- ▶ Who are the experienced leaders in your organization who could provide a steady hand in a time of change?
- ▶ How can you build stronger relationships with key stakeholders in your organization?
- ▶ What actions can you take to demonstrate your commitment and readiness as a successor?

Successor Strategies for Success:

- ▶ Deepen your understanding of business transactions and exit planning by researching industry standards and terminology.
- ▶ Engage a financial advisor early in your planning process, preferably one experienced in organizational transitions.
- ▶ Strengthen relationships with key stakeholders and potential successors.
- ▶ Stay informed about industry trends and changes affecting succession; ideally engage in industry groups to learn more.
- ▶ Regularly review and update your own professional development goals.

On Deck:

The successor role is more than just a title change, there's a lot to do to be ready for the work ahead. You'll read about the transaction and what you're *really* transitioning when you're stepping in as the next leader.

The Bottom Line

CHAPTER 2

More Than a New Job Title

There's more than meets the eye when you're taking over. Here's what to know.

Understanding the *Real* Transition

Predecessors have dominated the landscape for so long that they don't know what they're handing off.

Why It Matters: For founders and long-time leaders, what they did to run the business was just "their job." The organization once relied on *one person* to do things *so well* that it now seems impossible to split the tasks into discrete roles.

Thankfully, we've got ideas.

There are five things the organization needs to transition. The first three are universally known, which you'll find in most books about transitioning a company:

1. **Ownership:** The legal ownership of the business.
2. **Governance:** The process used to make big decisions.
3. **Management:** The way the organization runs day-to-day.

The next two are huge. They're almost always overlooked until it's too late:

4. **Leadership:** The culture and strategy driving the organization's success.
5. **Brand:** The people and relationships that create enterprise value.

The Big Picture: One predecessor was talking about his transition when he said, "We started the business 15 years ago, then one day we looked up and realized it was worth something." Part vulnerability, part humble-brag, his experience is common.

They don't even know what they know or do. They just do it.

Enter the cadre of experts to help the predecessor solve the equation. Here's the kind of stuff they're talking about with their advisors.

Transition Factor #1: Ownership

As Jay-Z said, it's best to "own your own product."

Why? Then you're in control. That's why you need to think like your predecessor. What motivates them? What do they want? Scrooge McDuck money? A legacy? To be a hero to their employees? Enter exit planning.

The Process: According to the Exit Planning Institute, more than 4,000 certified exit planning advisors[21] are available to identify predecessors' goals and help get them there. Here's what they're telling the predecessor they can do:

1. **The owner sells to an acquirer.** An acquirer can buy the business in a transaction that leverages any value, such as cash, debt, or stock, to buy the company.
2. **The owner sells to an individual or the management team.** The owner sells the business to the management team, which takes control of the business.
3. **The owner sells to an ESOP (Employee Stock Ownership Plan) or similar entity.** An ESOP is a tax-advantaged ownership transfer that allows employees to have a stake in the business.[iv]
4. **The owner liquidates the business' assets.** Like in the old Steve Miller Band song — sells the business for parts, takes the money, and runs.

If we're selling an asset, how much is it worth? Enter the valuation.

---

iv. If you see a company advertised as an "employee-owned business," it's usually an ESOP.

Since you're unlikely to be transitioning a public company, which has a share price on a public market, you must take a guess. There are plenty of professionals who can help with the process, and they'll tend to look at the following factors:

▶ Financial performance.
▶ Future opportunity.
▶ Strength of the management team.
▶ Transactions of other similar businesses.

From there, they'll use various tools to figure out the value. A few options.

▶ **Multiple:** Applies some multiplier to a financial metric, like revenue, gross profit, EBITDA, etc. A more complicated measure is SDE (Seller's Discretionary Earnings), which captures what the seller *actually* makes from the business, including salary, benefits, and offset expenses like a cell phone bill.
(Example: a $10 million business with a 3.5x multiple would be worth $35 million)

▶ **Income approach**: This approach considers the business' current structure and the expectation of future earnings. A valuation pro will calculate the present value of those earnings based on a few assumptions.

▶ **Asset-driven approach**: This approach examines the business' assets and determines how much they would sell for today. Essentially, it's the value if the business was sold for parts.

▶ **Market approach**: This approach scans the landscape for the sale of similar businesses in similar markets and determines how closely this business could mimic those transactions. It works a bit like real estate, where the value will be determined by recent transactions involving similar houses.

Then there might be agreements with individual employees that are treated like stock. The two most common:

1. **Synthetic equity, shadow shares, or phantom stock**: An agreement between the owner and an individual that treats the non-owner like they had equity in the business at a certain point, usually a sale.

2. **Stock appreciation rights or equity appreciation units**: Like phantom stock, these rights pay out only on the increase in value of the equity rather than the equity as a whole.

No matter the approach, getting familiar with the language of buying and selling businesses is crucial to ensure you're in the best position you can be. Yet, there's a dirty little secret.

> *The transaction details are only a symbol.*

The Big Reveal: The transaction details are only a symbol. There are a whole lot of variables — the money involved and percentages of ownership being the two big ones. How they get put together makes everyone feel better. Don't believe me? Here are a few stories:

- ▶ A businessperson who, instead of going on the promised succession path of having his daughter take over the company, decided to sell the business for $100 million so, in his words, "I could brag to my childhood friend who sold his for $80 million." While he walked away with a wad of cash, he lost the relationship with his daughter and the respect of the 75 employees who had tirelessly worked for him. "It was the dumbest, worst decision I've ever made in my life, and I regret it every day."

- ▶ An entrepreneur who built her business from the ground up wanted to sell and retire, so she invested in an executive team to double the company and share in the riches of its growth. At the precipice of the sale, she napalmed the entire plan, stepping back into the CEO role and firing the executive team. "I couldn't handle being retired or seeing their success with my name still on the building." She replaced half of her staff — and all executives

One In, One Out

Raj started his small financial advisory business 20 years ago, never imagining it would grow into a well-known and thriving boutique firm. He balanced work with family, especially caring for his two children: Priya, a high achiever with a knack for numbers, and Amir, who is neurodivergent and gravitated toward software engineering.

Priya, after gaining valuable experience at a national firm, decided to join the family business. Raj was thrilled. Her fresh ideas and enthusiasm were exactly what the company needed. After a few years, Raj asked Priya if she wanted to take over. Priya was over the moon until Raj dropped a bombshell: "You decide how to split ownership between you and Amir."

Priya was torn. She wanted to honor Amir as her brother but also wanted control over the business she'd be running. She believed Amir deserved a fair share, but she also knew he'd never work for the company. After much thought, and consulting an outside resource, Priya proposed an 81%/19% split. This would give her control while ensuring Amir's financial security.

Raj approved, naming Priya the new CEO. He still visits the office weekly, offering his wisdom and support. Priya now leads with a vision to grow the business while ensuring Amir is always cared for. Raj watched proudly as Priya navigated the challenges, confident that his legacy was in good hands. ▶

— with family and lost most of the value of the business in the process.

▶ One business owner grew a waste management business from a small trash hauler to a full-service regional one that competed with national brands. In his mid-70s and failing health, he refused to hand over even 1% of the business to the leaders who helped him grow the company. "They've made plenty of money, and they can live without this company if it folds," in a tone that was equal parts callous and delusional.

In each case, the predecessor couldn't handle what the sale represented. Whether it was bragging rights, identity, or mortality, each transaction symbolized something unrelated.

Then there's the buyer side. What do *you* want? Would you like to own 100% of the business? Are you interested in creating an ESOP? Do you want to have controlling ownership (51%)?

One Last Challenge: The seller *always* overvalues the business.

How rare is it to have alignment in sales price between buyer and seller? In a survey of those who lead transactions often, "only 1.4% indicated a frequent alignment between buyers and sellers on valuation."[22]

There are a lot of reasons why sellers overestimate the value of their business. One of the most common?

The IKEA Effect.[23]

That's the tendency for people to put more value in things they built themselves vs. the price they would pay for the finished product. In this context, the seller wants to feel competent and that all the work and sacrifice were worth it. The price is the symbol of that success.

See the tension?

The seller overvalues the business because it's a part of who they are, and you don't see that value because you're buying something already built.

Bottom Line: Don't let the mess of numbers distract you from what the transaction *really* is. Know what motivates you and the predecessor first.

Transition Factor #2: Governance

Someone must have the 51st vote.

Governance is exceptionally complicated and driven by how the business is structured. Is it a sole proprietorship? C-corp, S-corp, or LLC? Nonprofit? Is governance even relevant in your succession situation? This book won't cover *all* the nuances, but I'll give you enough to help you start asking educated questions.

In the simplest sense, governance is about how the company will make big organizational decisions. Who gets to vote? Who is the tiebreaker? And how are the rules made?

Why It Matters: In businesses with an exiting founder or a sole shareholder, Ownership, Governance, and Management are the "chief cook and bottle washer" of business. The predecessor probably blended all of those duties seamlessly for most of their career.

Then, there are other approaches to governance.

1. In closely held businesses, a board of directors, usually made up of shareholders, guides decision-making. These boards have a fiduciary duty to maximize shareholder value, meaning that they have a legal obligation to ensure and encourage the company's growth. Depending on the organization, the board could include one or more non-shareholders. Votes tend to be doled out in proportion to ownership.

2. Publicly traded companies or companies with many shareholders will have a board that is typically elected by the shareholders. These people also have a fiduciary duty, though it is to the broader group of shareholders rather than a few individuals.

3. In nonprofits, the board directs the executive director on strategy and makes decisions about how the organization will function. These individuals have a fiduciary responsibility to the organization to ensure that resources are spent in ways that are aligned with the organization's mission.

4. Advisory boards are not legal boards but an informal structure that provides feedback and analysis to any organization. Their advice is not binding in any way.

Focus On the Majority: Since most companies are closely held businesses or sole proprietorships, we'll spend our time here.

For single owners, the transition can look relatively simple — the new owner takes over decision-making for the organization since they own 100% of the business. What if the predecessor keeps ownership in the company? This is where state laws can create challenges — owning 20% to 49% of a business provides some rights that owning 19% or less does not.

The point? Ownership is king. For closely held businesses, how many owners are there? Equal ownership (50/50 with two partners, 33/33/33 among three partners, etc.) is a nightmare since it is almost impossible for the partners to contribute equally. Then there's the tiebreaker — who gets the final vote? It's better if there is an odd number of owners, but if family or other ties are involved, things can devolve quickly.

There's one other wrinkle. Governance in this conversation assumes "voting shares."

Shareholder agreements can distinguish between certain types of shareholders and shares. In an extreme example, a predecessor could own 1% of the business but retain 100% of control. There are a lot of reasons why a predecessor might retain controlling ownership as a minority shareholder, but they tend to boil down to:

The Unwanted CEO

Craig built an incredible company over 15 years, leading a significant private equity investment that fueled the organization's growth throughout his time at the helm. About three years before he exited the business, he met with the chair of the board for a pre-board meeting strategy session. "Before we get started, I'm leaving the company," Craig told the chair. After an initial panic, Craig continued. "...at some point. I want it to be an orderly, intentional transition."

The company began the search in earnest about six months before Craig's planned exit. Three candidates emerged from the executive search firm out of more than 80 interviewed. Much like the story of Goldilocks and the Three Bears, the candidates were one each of too much, too little, and just right:

▶ The too-much candidate had experience growing private equity-funded companies, meaning he was out of the price range for the business.
▶ The too-little candidate had direct industry experience but a spotty track record. Plus, he was not in the country's headquarters and preferred to stay in his home country.
▶ The perfect candidate had it all. Affordable, hungry, an entrepreneur who bought and sold multiple businesses. While he didn't have direct industry experience, his adjacent experience would be a great fit, especially under Craig's tutelage during the transition.

At the board meeting, the obvious choice, at least according to Craig, was seen as risky given his lack of industry knowledge, so they decided to hire the "too little" candidate. Craig was stunned. Publicly, he supported the board and its decision. Privately, he fumed. "You would think, for as long as I've been at this, the board would take my counsel."

Within months, Craig was struggling to withhold his opinions and the successor — Shin — had decided to freeze out Craig and reorient the company on a new axis. At an international trade show where the transition had its coming-out party, Craig watched Shin speak as if he was hired to rescue the company from distress. Clients and media alike approached Craig, wondering why the business hired Shin in the first place. At the 10-month mark, Shin told the board that he was resigning, having failed to move the needle even on the easy wins he had assumed, and accepted a reduced role at his prior company.

"I was just sick to my stomach. I've transitioned two other businesses and know that I can do it. We whiffed on our pick, and we lost at least a year in the process." Craig returned to an interim CEO role and, at the time of publishing, was pursuing a new successor for the business. ▶

> ▶ The predecessor seller is financing the transaction (known as owner financing) and wants to retain decision authority of the business until the loan is sufficiently paid off.
> ▶ The predecessor wants to see how the business functions without their hands in the day-to-day, and they want to observe the new leadership team's performance.
> ▶ They don't want to let go of control.

Bottom Line: Being the successor might mean something other than what you think it means. Make sure you understand the implications of the governance structure in which you're operating.

Transition Factor #3: Management

Not everything can be at 30,000 feet; there's an organization to run day-to-day.

Now we're getting into the nitty-gritty. Management drives the key decision-making within the organization. Governance sets the organizational direction and management handles the day-to-day execution to that end.

Bocconi University published a study about ownership, governance, and management that looked at three areas in relationship to family-owned firm performance.[24] A few significant points:

- **Education matters:** Investments in education significantly impact the success of a business, especially "when family members are strongly emotionally attached to their family firms." Education boosts performance.

- **Management skills drive success:** Ensuring that there's enough managerial skill in the organization, even if it means hiring from the outside, drives the firm to perform better. Family managers only succeeded if they were highly educated.

- **Family ownership doesn't ruin growth:** The lifestyle the family wants to live drives growth in family-owned companies. The constraint, therefore, isn't about who owns the business, but the education or skill of those in ownership and management.

The universal takeaway? Get smart. Get skilled. This is all true for closely held businesses that aren't transitioning to family, as well.

Yet, there's something that can't be overlooked. The business gets in trouble when predecessors are "strongly emotionally attached to their family firms."

Get smart. Get skilled.

Therein lies the rub. Will the predecessor let you make decisions?

Quick Story: One successor I interviewed talked about a business he stepped into as the founding owner said she wanted to step away. Reggie is a highly competent leader, but you only hire him if you're ready to make tough decisions. Ann, the predecessor, said she wanted someone to clean house, but it was clear within the first 60 days that it wasn't true. Ann stopped Reggie from making crucial people decisions, only allowing him to replace the front-desk receptionist. Her, "I agree, but. . ." approach, and ability to veto every decision Reggie made, drove him mad, and he left within a year.

The Challenge: Letting go of management is the sticking point for existing owners and outgoing executives (for many reasons we'll get to). Some are legit and business-focused, some aren't and are selfish. The rest of this book is about recognizing, adapting, managing, and guiding through the emotional experiences of both you and the predecessor.

Bottom Line: "Management" is one way of saying "making decisions." For the predecessor, giving up that control can be the hardest step in the process.

Transition Factor #4: Leadership

Who will the team follow?

Ownership, governance, and management are consensus picks for discussion in succession. With so much of the conversation about the *transaction*, leadership of the business gets lost in the noise.

The reason? My best guess is that it's too hard to define for most people. Ownership, governance, and management are concrete.

How do you measure the value of good leadership?

It isn't easy. Here's what we *do* know:

- ▶ Financial performance only accounts for about half of an enterprise's value.[25]
- ▶ The other half (strategy, brand, talent, R&D, innovation, risk, and so on) make up the rest.
- ▶ Leadership is all about that second half (and tees up the first).

▶ Long-term investors allocate about 30% of their decision-making on the quality of leadership.[26]

If so much organizational value is driven by good leadership, even if we can't pinpoint just how much, surely we can define leadership, right?

The tens of thousands of leadership books on Amazon say otherwise.

I'm fond of a model from a book called *The Work of Leaders* (more about this on page 208) which takes some of the mysticism out of leadership and focuses on what leaders actually do. In their work, it boils down to three things:

▶ Craft a **vision** for the organization to achieve something significant.
▶ Build **alignment** among the team at all levels to make it happen.
▶ Champion **execution** to ensure the organization achieves the vision.

In that model, the leadership style, method, philosophy, or approach is personal, but the steps are concrete.

Most crucial to the approach? Leadership is about creating an environment to enable others to do the work. The jack-of-all-trades approach, which was a big part of almost every predecessor's reward structure, simply doesn't work anymore.

Yet, like most other things about predecessors, their approach to leadership might not have developed intentionally.

The Challenge: Leadership as we know it today is a relatively new phenomenon.

It's hard to find a better example of how much the idea of leadership, and particularly executive leadership, has changed than by looking at the required capabilities of a CEO in job postings. Since 2007, job descriptions mentioning strength in managing financial and material resources have plummeted by 40%, while mentions of social skills and emotional intelligence have increased by almost 30%.[27]

Value placed on management and leadership skills are moving in opposite directions.[v] Yet many business owners and outgoing executives, most of whom haven't had a meaningful manager for decades, operate with a management and leadership model that hasn't evolved much in their nearly half-century careers. The result?

Modern leadership approaches are a foreign language to most predecessors, yet the organizational transition is dependent on their handing over leadership well.

Why It Matters: As the successor, it's on you to set a tone for the future of the organization. That's not choosing the coffee vendor or how to finance a new piece of equipment — management stuff — that's a leadership decision that you need to make, with whatever team you choose, as the new leader. We'll delve into how best to do it in parts three and four.

Bottom Line: There's a whole section in the book on how to approach leadership as a successor. With apologies to G.I. Joe, knowing that it needs to happen is half the battle.

Transition Factor #5: Brand

How do you keep the business going if someone else's name is on the door?

How many businesses can you think of that include the owner's name? You might know legacy brands like Westinghouse, conglomerates like Anheuser-Busch, and local holes in the wall like Bill's Pub. The

---

v. We'll revisit this on page 188 (with a chart and everything).

common thread? Much like how people who have names that sound like "doctor" are more likely to become physicians[28] (it's a bias known as implicit egotism), they're part of the 19% of companies named after their founders.[29]

The surprise? Companies named after their founders are more successful than peers that aren't. This may be attributable to entrepreneurs being motivated to work harder since their names are on the doors. Comparing the least familiar names and the most common ones, companies that bear a founder's unusual name are almost twice as likely to be successful.

If you're gutsy enough to put your name on the business, you're going to be all-in on its success. Think it's easy to let go of that? Successfully separating the person from the brand is hard even when the business *doesn't* feature the founder's name. Microsoft is (still!) Bill Gates. Tesla is Elon Musk. Amazon is Jeff Bezos. It's not Mission Impossible, but it's Mission Hard as Hell.

Brand transition creates a two-fold problem:

1. It's exceedingly tough to connect a new face to the brand.
2. Most predecessors struggle with separating themselves from the organization's brand.

Why It Matters: Transitions, especially when ownership changes hands, can generate a financial term of art known as "goodwill," defined as the value of a business over and above the book value of the company. It's the financial value of "our good name."

With a successful brand transition, the business becomes more valuable. The reverse is also true. Customers over-identify with the business owner or the family and are willing to bolt under new ownership. Employees feel loyalty to the owner rather than the organization and start exploring other options. Intentional brand transition prevents both from happening.

Digging Deeper: The brand doesn't have to be the name on the side of the building.

The Gauntlet

Anthony Jr. had worked in the business in various roles since shortly after graduating college. For the prior 10 years, he'd been learning at the hands of his father, Anthony Sr., at a $2 billion regional distribution company that Senior's father started with the family name on the building. Junior had done all he needed to for Senior — and the experienced executive team — to be confident in his son taking over. Yet, they couldn't transition the business on their terms.

The manufacturer they represented had veto power.

"It doesn't make any sense," Senior said with frustration. "He's done everything they could ask him to do. Yet, we still have to show success for two more years, hitting all of these different metrics. And even if we do that, the board must grill Anthony and pass their test. He's ready! Why are we doing all of this?!?"

Junior sees it differently. "I get that I'm not a proven commodity yet," Junior shared. "They need to make sure I won't wilt under pressure. There aren't a lot of companies in the dealer network, and if I can't drive results, they'll give the territory to someone else. I understand the stakes, and I'm happy to prove to them I can do it."

As of publishing, the transition wasn't complete, but Junior was doing everything he could to ensure he could continue as the successor. Thanks to his ability to lead his team, every member of the executive team excitedly supports him in the transition. ▶

Tom Peters, co-author of one of the seminal business books, *In Search of Excellence*, introduced the revolutionary idea of "personal brand" in a cover-story article in *Fast Company* titled, "The Brand Called You." His thesis was that brands weren't reserved for products like Tide and Coca-Cola. They were for you, too, and deserved the same level of intentional management.

As such, we created brands for all sorts of things. Employer brands. Leadership brands. Each carefully curated for maximum effect. The outgoing generation, one that has had such a vast impact on our culture, is full of individual brands. The leaders and owners of organizations have cemented themselves as high-impact legends. To borrow from Mr. Peters, each individual is "Me Inc."

This creates staggering implications for transitions.

- ▶ For predecessors, the brand presents a two-fold problem. On a personal level, it's hard to separate brand from personal identity. From a business perspective, it's tough to separate your brand from *the* brand. Disrupting that brand has a cost.

- ▶ For successors, there is only one truth: Your brand is not the predecessor's. Whether you're a known quantity, an external hire, or a next-generation successor, stakeholders affected by the transition are, at minimum, aware that things will change.

- ▶ For the enterprise, the transition from the predecessor brand (known) to a successor brand (untested) is a significant risk for the business, even if the predecessor has been known to be a roadblock to progress.

Bottom Line: For the predecessor, there's something different when your name is on the building. As the successor, you're a steward of the brand, rather than a revolutionary.

The Bottom Line on Chapter 2: More Than a New Job Title

TL;DR:

Succession is about much more than just stepping into a new role; it's about mastering the intricate dance of ownership, governance, management, leadership, and brand. Understanding these elements and how they function is a symbol that helps name and prioritize what matters to you and the future of the business. By gaining a comprehensive understanding of these areas, you'll enable a smoother transition while stepping into the job with crucial context.

The Hits:

▶ **Ownership Transfer:** Learn what it means to become an owner and take control of the financial and operational aspects.

▶ **Governance Shake-Up:** Understand the new rules and structures, and how you'll fit into the governance framework.

▶ **Management Dynamics:** Adapt to new management practices, aligning with existing systems while bringing your unique approach.

▶ **Leadership Evolution:** Develop your leadership style to fit your new responsibilities, meeting the needs of your team and role expectations.

▶ **Brand Continuity:** Ensure the company's values and image remain consistent and aligned with what your stakeholders need.

Thought-Starter Questions:

▶ What resources will you use to help you with the transition of ownership and its financial implications?

▶ How important is having decision-making control for you, and why?

▶ How can you integrate your management style with existing practices, and does it make more sense for you to adapt to the organization or the reverse?

▶ How does your leadership style mesh with the current organization and what different approaches will you need to take to be successful?

▶ How can you keep and enhance the company's brand during the transition?

Successor Strategies for Success:

▶ Plan: Consider each transition factor, identify what you want, and design an approach to achieve it.

▶ Create a personal board of advisors not connected to the organization who can provide outside feedback in all five areas.

▶ Draft a clear vision and strategy for your leadership journey, setting achievable goals and milestones.

▶ Engage with your team to get a feel for the company culture and find areas where you can make a positive impact.

▶ Prioritize open communication and consistent actions to build trust and establish yourself.

On Deck:

Whether obvious or hidden, the predecessor is experiencing grief, which explains why the interactions you're having might feel a little off. Understanding how the predecessor's emotional experience plays a role in the transition will help you minimize the conflicts that can put an organization at risk.

CHAPTER 3

Walking the Predecessor's Path

Begin by understanding where your predecessor has been and what they're going through.

Preventing Wildfires

Transitions put the organization at risk of disaster. How you manage that risk will determine the extent of the damage and what it takes to recover.

Whether a bolt of lightning, the flick of a cigarette butt, or an unextinguished campfire, one spark can cause a blaze that rages through thousands of acres of forest — or land harmlessly on wet ground.

The difference between a dodged bullet and a disaster? The conditions on which those sparks fall.

Like a particularly dry patch of brush, succession is ripe for enflamed conflict. Some of those conflicts are easily squashed. Others threaten the viability of the business.

> **Only you can prevent wildfires.**

The best approach is prevention. As Smokey Bear said, "Only you can prevent wildfires."

Why It Matters: There's a lot that can trigger angst, anger, and distrust between the successor and the predecessor. Going into the process, your goals should be to:

1. Accept that conflicts are inevitable.
2. Minimize the opportunities for conflicts to start.
3. Contain the blaze when they do.
4. Repair the damage as quickly and permanently as possible.

Wildfires are the worst-case scenario result of bad interactions between successors and predecessors. Typically, they're destructive episodes that spread throughout the organization, reducing trust and confidence that don't just impact the predecessor-successor relationships, but can consume employees, customers, and the business.

Quick Story: Jeff, a third-generation successor, grew interested his family's distribution business early in his career. While Jeff's father ran the organization day-to-day, with his mother supporting in finance and public engagement roles, his grandmother retained controlling interest and final say in organizational decisions. In his early 30s, Jeff's parents, who were now majority owners, started divorce proceedings in a public, messy way. Seeing the business at risk, Jeff was forced to step in and not just ensure the business continued to run, but mediate his parents' divorce so that all parties would be satisfied. Today, Jeff runs the thriving business, though his grandmother and father keep decision authority and he owns a minority stake knowing that, one day — through natural attrition — he will be the sole shareholder of the company.

The Conditions

Whether it's one spark or a torrent of them, the conditions determine the disaster's extent.

> *After you retire, there's only one big event left, and I ain't ready for that.*
>
> ~ Bobby Bowden

Every predecessor experiences a sense of loss independently of whether they initiated it, benefit from it, or are seemingly anticipating it.

Two things come from loss: *grief*, the internal experience of loss, and *mourning*, the external expression of that grief. It works like this:

Figure 3.1

The Grief Process

That grief experienced by the predecessor? Those are the conditions on which the sparks fall.

A Little Context: *Every* predecessor is experiencing grief. Here are some types of losses that trigger grief in retiring predecessors[30]:

- ► **Explicit loss:** On-the-table and potentially obvious:
  - › They feel like they don't have a choice or a sense of control.
  - › They feel the number of options is overwhelming.
  - › They feel a lack of purpose.
  - › They feel a lack of connection.
  - › They feel unproductive.

- ► **Ambiguous loss:** Losses that are harder to uncover and might even be unresolvable:
  - › They feel like they lost a part of themselves.
  - › They feel a conflict between the social expectations (enjoy life now that you're retired!) and the reality (I'm struggling with the transition).

You might be aware of the seven stages of grief found in the research of Elisabeth Kübler-Ross and her collaborators: shock, denial, anger, bargaining, depression, testing, and acceptance and hope. Sparks land in these conditions.

Why It Matters: Knowing the emotional context of the predecessor's decisions is the most critical data as you move through the transition. Ignoring the stages and associated dangers is a recipe for a disaster you might be unable to control.

Before we dig into each stage, there are caveats:

► You don't know when the sense of loss started or will start; predecessors typically start the grieving process long before starting the transition. In extreme situations, the transition might occur only after the predecessor has finished grieving.

► Few predecessors are self-aware enough to understand that they're actively grieving.

► The stages aren't linear, and people tend to bounce between stages, skip steps, or return to a stage previously thought to be over.

The Stages and Dangers

SHOCK

The predecessor can't process the transition, a defense mechanism against the pain of the experience. This stage is typically accompanied by behavior that can seem very high-functioning since they aren't yet engaging with their feelings of grief. The team tends to walk on eggshells as they try to figure out where the predecessor's headspace is in the moment.

Danger:

The predecessor can seem anywhere from completely clearheaded to dazed and confused. This can be uncomfortable for others since it typically goes with a disconnect between their behavior/mood and the reality around them. This disconnect could create a vacuum of decision-making that is low-impact in the short term but presents challenges in the long term if it doesn't improve. The predecessor might ignore transition decisions or milestones, complicating the process.

How it might look:

► **Pre-Transition:** A sense that it's strange that their friends/peers are retiring or moving into new life phases, but the predecessor still has a lot of runway.

- ▶ **During Transition:** Surprise when decisions are made or actions taken, even if agreed upon prior.
- ▶ **Post-Transition:** Actions that suggest the transition hasn't happened, such as getting ready or leaving for the office after the transition or attending events that are no longer appropriate.

Approaches:

- ▶ Needs a high-EQ approach; kindness and tenderness (typically) wins.
- ▶ Provide space and flexibility where possible.
- ▶ If dire or in an emergency, address directly.

DENIAL

Much like shock, denial is a coping mechanism where the predecessor pushes the negative thoughts or pain out of their minds. Denial can include everything from denying that they're experiencing any grief at all, denying that there is a reason for grief, or denying that the transition is happening. The team's reactions will share similarities with shock, though with the added frustration of believing the predecessor is actively working to stay in denial.

Danger:

Denial can look like shock, though the predecessor shows signs of awareness that the transition is happening. The disconnect between mood/behavior and the situation around them frustrates the team as they know the predecessor is actively working to stay in the denial stage. The predecessor might ignore or actively push back on transition progress.

What it might look like:

- ▶ **Pre-Transition:** A persistent belief that there's no reason to initiate a transition.

▶ **During Transition:** Might provide a continuously moving retirement window, typically three to five years.

▶ **Post-Transition:** Stepping in to make decisions after the transition has been made.

Approaches:

▶ Much like shock, this stage needs an even higher EQ approach since the predecessor is beginning to process the grief.

▶ Provide space and flexibility where possible.

▶ If dire or in an emergency, address directly.

ANGER

While denial might be used to cope with grief, predecessors will use anger to mask feelings of sadness and assign blame for those feelings to an external source. Predecessors tend to get angry at anyone in their circle — advisors, family members, successors, bosses, or other subordinates — who could be connected to the experience.

Danger:

High emotions are ripe for danger, and the diffuse reasons for anger — from perceived slights to legitimate frustrations — inflame everyone involved in the transition. Anger and resentment can easily spread throughout the organization if not addressed quickly.

What it might look like:

▶ **Pre-Transition:** Expressing anger or frustration at actions taken by people within the organization or succeeding team, even if they are correct.

▶ **During Transition:** Hoping the succeeding team fails or actively setting them up for failure; excessive criticism or lashing out.

▶ **Post-Transition:** Harboring anger and resentment toward the succeeding team; sabotaging or starting a competing effort.

Approaches:

▶ Short of abuse, it is best to allow the predecessor to emote while recognizing what triggered the anger is unlikely to be related to the situation.

▶ Reframe the experience and avoid taking it personally.

▶ Maintain appropriate boundaries.

BARGAINING

Grief can make you feel helpless, vulnerable, and out of control, experiences that most predecessors have spent their lives and careers avoiding in pursuit of success. Predecessors can respond in a variety of ways, ranging from insular and harmless (such as second-guessing decisions they made in the past) to extremely disruptive (such as taking drastic organizational action).

Danger:

Bargaining is the most extreme condition in the transition. Predecessors have achieved much of their success because of their keen gut instinct. During their careers, feeling helpless, vulnerable, and out of control were warning signs that they needed to step in and solve problems. It is easy for predecessors to self-deceive in this stage, believing that the transition plan they put in place is going off the rails. In the most extreme situations, predecessors might change the terms of the transition without "good reason."

What it might look like:

▶ **Pre-Transition:** Actively working to transition but intentionally holding onto a key piece of information.

▶ **During Transition:** Seeing errors successors make as validators of a bad decision; second-guessing decisions.

▶ **Post-Transition:** Harboring anger and resentment toward the succeeding team; sabotaging or starting a competing effort; or retaining or taking back control.

Approaches:

- ▶ Maintain a level head and focus on the big picture.
- ▶ Develop a mantra or other touchstone that allows you to remember that the other person is in active mourning and is experiencing extreme discomfort.
- ▶ Take an active role in containing the blaze (more on that shortly).
- ▶ Ensure that you always have a backup plan and maintain a sense of control.

DEPRESSION

In this stage, the reality is setting in for the predecessor, and they are experiencing a sense of sadness and resignation about the transition. The predecessors tend to be distant in this stage as they cope more actively with the loss. While they are less likely to be actively impacting decisions, their approach might slow down the team as they continue to disengage.

Danger:

In the depression stage, the predecessor is at risk for disengagement and avoidance as they continue to process their emotions. This can have a wide-ranging impact on the organization, leaving crucial tasks undone or knowledge gaps in critical areas. Their low energy can sap the energy of others in the organization and negatively impact momentum.

What it might look like:

- ▶ **Pre-Transition:** Slow or lack of response to requests for information or meetings; tasks going undone.
- ▶ **During Transition:** Disengagement, excessive time off/away, lack of follow-through.
- ▶ **Post-Transition:** Bringing down team members due to their sadness and attitude toward the transition, especially mentees or close former colleagues.

Approaches:

- ▶ Provide space for the predecessor to process emotions.
- ▶ Create accountability tools to help the predecessor stay on task.
- ▶ Recognize the predecessor's work and legacy.

TESTING

In this stage, the predecessor explores new opportunities, identities, and approaches to their work and life to find a new normal. Testing typically brings the healthiest coping mechanisms; you might see parts of the "old" predecessor coming back. Since the predecessor is in a more positive mental space, the impact on the organization tends to be minimal and positive.

Danger:

Since the testing stage is forward-looking, the predecessor isn't much of a risk. Yet, stumbling blocks remain. New identities might lead to a belief that they need more resources from the transition than previously agreed, or the predecessor might realize that they don't want things to change. Additionally, the predecessor might quit sooner than expected after finding their next adventure, leaving the team holding the bag. This stage can lull the succeeding team into a false sense of security, especially if the transition is incomplete.

What it might look like:

- ▶ **Pre-Transition:** Delegating key tasks and stepping away for more personal time; might ignore remaining duties.
- ▶ **During Transition:** Disengagement, excessive time off/away, and lack of follow-through; looking to get more out of the organization than previously agreed.
- ▶ **Post-Transition:** New identities might raise the eyebrows of stakeholders depending on the approach the predecessor takes.

Approaches:

- ▶ Create easy-to-follow accountability plans that minimize the predecessor's need to engage.
- ▶ Provide enough support that the predecessor trusts the transition is on track.
- ▶ Ensure agreements are documented in case of last-minute rethinking of the transition.

ACCEPTANCE AND HOPE

The predecessor has come to terms with the process and has not just accepted the transition but sees how their lives will look in the future. They might not be completely content, but they can act and feel more whole. Decisions are easier, and the team is more comfortable and confident in the predecessor's thought process.

Danger:

Now that the grief process has almost entirely run its course, few concerns remain in the transition. This doesn't mean that there won't be opportunities for trouble, but they're unlikely to occur or turn into something unmanageable. Their comfort might not be matched by other members of their team, however, and if they choose to continue to be present, the predecessor might inadvertently hold the organization back.

What it might look like:

- ▶ **Pre-Transition:** True comfort with the dynamics of succession; even in moments of high emotion, the trend is toward positive and healthy movement.
- ▶ **During Transition:** The predecessor actively participates in the transition where appropriate and engages when necessary.
- ▶ **Post-Transition:** The predecessor engages in other activities and often can serve as a positive sounding board or mentor for successors and others.

Approaches:

▶ Honor the legacy of the predecessor in meaningful and appropriate ways.

▶ Stay connected to demonstrate the relationship was not transactional, minimizing "buyer's remorse."

▶ Encourage conversations where mentorship would be mutually beneficial.

Figure 3.2
The Stages at a Glance

Danger level	Stage	Look out for	What to do
LOW	Acceptance and Hope	Contentment	Celebrate
MED-LOW	Testing	Exploration	Support
MEDIUM	Shock	Disconnect	Be kind
MEDIUM	Denial	Active pushback	Be patient
MED-HIGH	Depression	Distance	Allow space
HIGH	Anger	Volatility	Reframe
EXTREME	Bargaining	Whiplash	Contain the damage

One More Caution: In most cases, the successor has a close relationship with the predecessor. Watching a close mentor, friend, or family member experience the pain of grief is hard. You want them to be happy.

A dirty little secret? You might be grieving, too.

The relationship between you and the predecessor, and the context in which they are exiting, has a lot to do with how you feel about the transition. Inevitably, the nature of your relationship will change.

This dynamic — where you want to support someone you care about while you are also experiencing a sense of loss — can lead to a lot of miscommunication, confusion, and conflict.

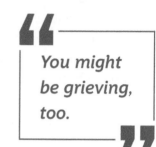

You might be grieving, too.

Those are the sparks that start the fire.

Bottom Line: You can't control the conditions, but you can know what they are and their potential risks. Minimizing those risks — the sparks — is your best shot at success.

The Sparks

No matter the conditions, you can't start a wildfire without a spark.

Humans cause nearly 90% of wildfires in the United States via discarded cigarettes, unattended campfires, burning debris, or through equipment malfunctions.[31]

Replace "humans" with "successors" in that statistic, and you're running about even with succession wildfires.

The problem with sparks is how little threat they seem to pose at the onset. It's almost unfathomable to believe that one small issue, left unattendended, can lead to such catastrophic consequences. Without an obvious sense of danger, it's easy to get careless and let sparks fly.

The following are the most common sources of dangerous sparks.

Spark #1: The Prisoner's Dilemma

There's a thought experiment called the Prisoner's Dilemma involving a tandem of criminals who must decide whether to stay silent or confess in the face of a harsh prison sentence. The description is: "a paradox in decision analysis in which two individuals acting in their own self-interests do not produce the optimal outcome." (Thanks, Investopedia!)

If you've not seen it before, here's how it works:

Figure 3.3
The Prisoner's Dilemma

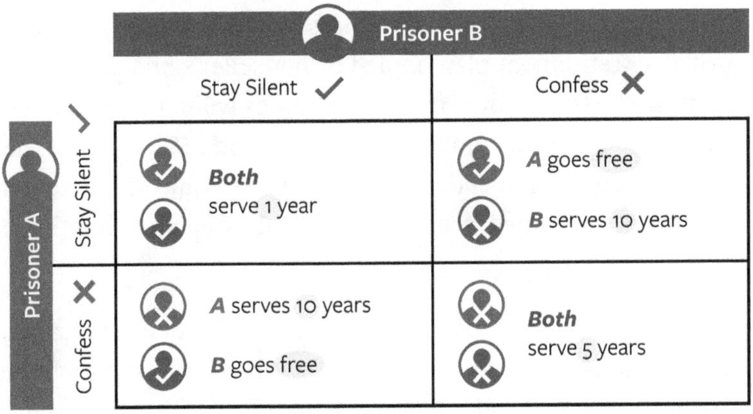

Predecessors and successors face similar punishments. The best possible outcome for each — the equivalent of the "stay silent" result — "hurts" them both. The successor and predecessor must be restrained, humble, and other-focused for the best outcome.

Easier said than done. Yet, if they both try to maximize self-interest, be it skill, ego, or financial gain, they're likely to lose, and the business will (maybe) fall apart. That's worse.

The greatest danger? When only one party plays to maximize.

Why It Matters: Transitions are emotional, and motivations aren't always transparent. It doesn't help that most successful business owners win through smarts and savvy. Setting that winning strategy aside to create a mutually beneficial transition requires a whole lot of trust and emotional intelligence.

Consider the following from this mother/son succession challenge.

▶ The 60-something mom/founder: "To be candid, I didn't trust my son to take over the business." She described how her son had extravagant tastes — acknowledging her enabling role in them — which led to company budget-busting splurges on the latest tech. She was sure that the business would implode — along with her retirement plan funded by her seller's financing — the minute she turned over the keys. She was willing to give him the CEO title but stayed on as Chairwoman and 85% owner of the company, a recommendation from her long-time accountant and confidant. "I wanted to make sure I could step back in if things went sideways."

▶ The 30-something son/successor: "I know she doesn't trust me, and it's sad because she doesn't know; she is just so out of touch with the business and industry," said the son. He viewed the proposed tech investment sprint as a down payment on getting back to being competitive after his mother decided to pocket profits rather than reinvest. "I appreciate that I have a small piece of the company now, but the constant second-guessing has been exhausting. It's gotten bad enough that I've started evaluating other opportunities to see if maybe I could be happier doing something where I had more freedom."

Both views are logical. You might have found yourself agreeing with each after you read them. Maybe, you have a strong preference for one person's argument over the other, or one of the arguments irritated you.

That is the essence of the Prisoner's Dilemma in succession. Both players are holding back power or information despite having a close (mother/son!) relationship.

Going Deeper: What's the difference between the classic prisoner's dilemma and what is at play in succession?

The Golden Rule.[vi] Predecessors have ownership, information, and access to expertise that the successor doesn't. How much, exactly?

- ▶ **Ownership:** Repeating it for those in the back, Baby Boomers own more than half, or $78 trillion, of the wealth in the United States.
- ▶ **Information:** More than 90% of companies in the U.S. are closely held,[32] and globally, about the same percentage of businesses are family-run,[33] meaning the financials are private. Shareholders can choose whether to show any information or none.
- ▶ **Access to expertise:**
  - › First, predecessors have access to thousands of lawyers, accountants, financial advisors, and other experts with experience in selling businesses.
  - › Second, it's a business expense to hire these experts (ultimately a cost, but a tax-reducing cost), while this kind of advice is paid out-of-pocket by the successor.
  - › Lastly, any resources provided to the successor are controlled by the predecessor.

This disparity creates the following dynamic:

- ▶ Predecessors tend to want to hold as many cards as possible, ensuring they make the final call on the terms of the transition.
- ▶ Successors want to trust the predecessor, but those taking over have a suspicion that there's something they don't know that will blow up in their faces.

vi. If you didn't read what I mean by that, check out page 3.

Bottom Line: Succession remains one of the few areas where knowledge can be unequal. This gap ultimately creates mistrust between predecessors and successors in the best of circumstances. It takes a lot to cut through the noise, which is why you're here, isn't it?

Spark #2: What the Light Touches

In the 1994 Disney hit *The Lion King*, Mufasa, the father lion and reigning king of the jungle, brings his son, Simba, to the top of a mountain and tells Simba he will eventually rule over "everything the light touches." Almost every succession situation starts in a similar vein.

Why It Matters: Acknowledging for the first time that a predecessor will be transitioning to a successor is one of the most significant moments in succession. It's a weighty decision, and usually, both parties understand that it is a moment of vulnerability. With such a high emotional watermark, it's impossible for the rest of the process to align with that one magical moment.

Quick Story: A second-generation owner in his early-60s, Greg grew the business 100-fold since taking over as CEO from his father three decades prior. Approaching retirement age, and wanting to focus on his community work, he decided he was ready to step aside to allow Stephanie, a longtime employee in her late 40s, to move into the CEO role.

The ask was idyllic. He invited her to his second home in Florida where he, his wife, and Stephanie had a dinner prepared on their patio looking out on the lake near their property. After a couple of glasses of wine, Greg asked Stephanie if she thought she was interested, and ready, to take over as CEO. They both were tearful and understood the heft of the conversation and that moment.

"It feels like nothing was the same after that," Stephanie said. Instead of behaving in a more trusting way, Greg began scrutinizing every decision she made. "I don't think I'm making decisions he wouldn't make; I just think he's just not the one making the decisions."

Greg saw the disconnect, too. "I didn't feel like Stephanie really understood how big of a deal it was. This business is my baby and the last remnants of my family. If she can't make decisions that will preserve that, I'm not sure she's up to the job."

Greg eventually learned to trust Stephanie — at his wife's significant urging — and focused his efforts on his philanthropic work as he had originally intended.

Digging Deeper: At its worst, the misalignment between the "everything the light touches" moment and the reality of transition turns into, itself, a point of conflict. When things go sideways, predecessors can view the succession plan as a failure, even regretting choosing the successor in the first place. The greater the disconnect, the more likely that the gap between expectation and reality causes sparks.

Digging Even Deeper: One other dynamic you can't control? ***Your ascent is their descent.***

You're excited and eager to step into what might be the role of a lifetime. You're energized by what the future holds.

The predecessor? They're mourning the closing of a chapter.

Even if you're not intentionally throwing off sparks, it's hard for predecessors to watch their successors assume a role they just recently occupied. No matter how excited they are for you to take on the challenge, or how well they've managed their grief, there is a sense of cognitive dissonance they feel when watching you do the job.

Bottom Line: Explicitly separating the "moment" from the day-to-day work takes intention, and both the successor and predecessor need to be open from the first day that there will be challenges and disagreements along the way.

Spark #3: The Exit Iceberg

Maslow's hierarchy helped frame what drives human behavior back in 1943 when he published *A Theory of Human Motivation*. Since then, the model has been used everywhere from psychology to performance appraisals.

For those who need a refresher, Maslow named a hierarchy of needs. The lowest are things that keep us alive — water, food, and shelter. Between the lowest and the highest are needs that range from safety and love to belonging and esteem. At the highest is self-actualization, which means becoming the most complete and authentic version of ourselves.

Figure 3.4
Maslow's Hierarchy of Needs

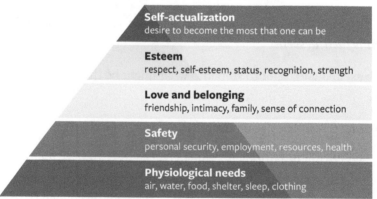

The easiest succession situations involve exiting owners who want to cash out at the highest possible value without regard for executives in the business, employees, or anyone but themselves. You know exactly what their motivations are, and you can work aggressively to get the seller a number that they can brag about to their friends. Esteem and self-actualization needs are explicitly on the table.

It's when the predecessor doesn't know, or won't communicate, those needs that sparks fly.

Digging Deeper: Esteem and self-actualization needs are individual and can be invisible. One person might define them as professional success, while others might want to go fishing more often. Self-actualization tends to be the most complex in the hierarchy — there are countless examples of people reaching for it without having their other needs met. Enter the Exit Iceberg, which explains the potential complicators that can trip up the relationship:

Figure 3.5
The Exit Iceberg

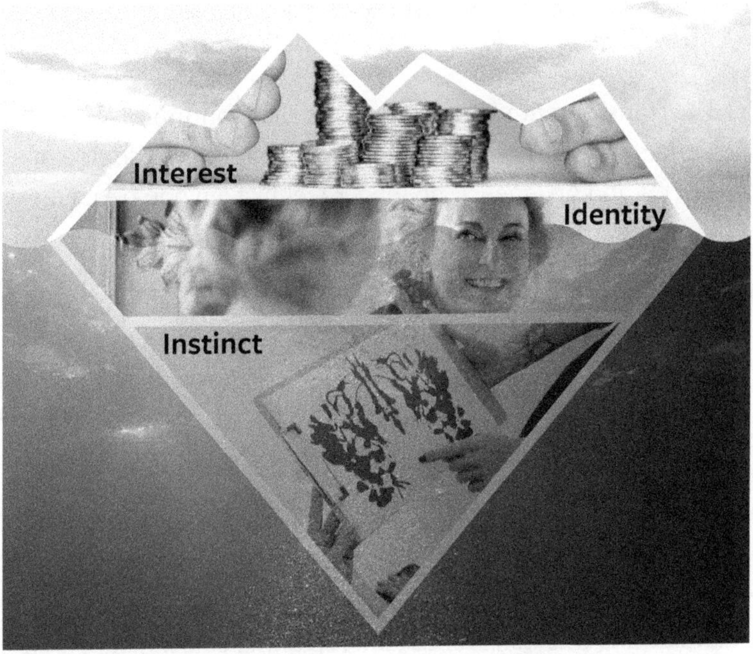

- ▶ **Interest:** These motivators exist above the surface and in full view — the self-interested resources that their prior role brought, or hope to bring, such as:
  - › Money and financial resources.
  - › Notoriety within and outside of the organization.

> Access to other resources (company event tickets or a company car).
> Board appointments, nonprofit, political, and community leadership roles.

▶ **Identity:** Let's go to the American Psychology Association for the definition of identity[34]:

"Identity involves a sense of continuity, or the feeling that one is the same person today that one was yesterday or last year (despite physical or other changes). Such a sense is derived from . . . the feeling that one's memories, goals, values, expectations, and beliefs belong to the self."

The transition fundamentally alters that continuity, which can happen in ways both obvious ("I no longer have the title of CEO") and opaque ("I no longer feel like anyone treats me with respect because I'm not the boss").

▶ **Instinct:** This one usually impacts the relationship between the predecessor and successor the most. It's below the surface and more extensive than you think; the strongest ship will sink like the Titanic if you run up against it. What makes it so challenging? You don't know it's there until you feel the jolt.

Predecessors rely more on their instincts the closer they are to the transition point (as we discussed in the section on Conditions). While their ability to connect the dots drove their success in the past, it goes on hyperdrive during this heightened time, sparking emotional responses to situations that otherwise don't have an explanation. The most common for predecessors? The feeling that they're being replaced before their time.

Bottom Line: The experience of succession feels like an emotional rollercoaster. Predecessors encounter emotions and thoughts they've largely put to bed through most of their careers.

The "New" Logo

A marketing executive, poised to take over from a successful founder CEO who had always trusted her implicitly, was directed by the CEO to "freshen up the marketing." For five years, she had been using a modified version of the company's logo for social media, since it fit modern formats better while maintaining the brand's essence.

One day, the CEO stumbled upon the modified logo and accused her of changing it without permission, seeing it as a personal affront because the original logo, one of his first significant investments in his business, had been a point of pride. She tried to explain that the logo hadn't changed and had been in use for years, but he was too upset to listen. To him, it felt like she was already trying to replace him before the transition was complete.

After he calmed down, he still didn't apologize, accusing her with, "Why didn't you tell me that in the first place?" His first reaction was driven by deeper, unseen feelings about the transition and the fear of being replaced. ▶

Spark #4: The End of Effortless Expertise

The last time you drove somewhere, you probably didn't remember much about the trip or decisions you made behind the wheel. You're more likely to remember the scenery (or the song you were singing along to). But you weren't born knowing how to drive, right?

The Model: In the 1970s, Noel Burch[35] developed the "ladder of learning" that explained the stages people go through when incorporating new information. Adapted from his work, these stages are:

> ▶ **Uninformed Ineptitude:** Summarized as "You don't know what you don't know," these are situations where you don't understand how easy — or hard — something is. In our driving example, this would be like being a child in the back seat of a car

Figure 3.6
The Learning Model

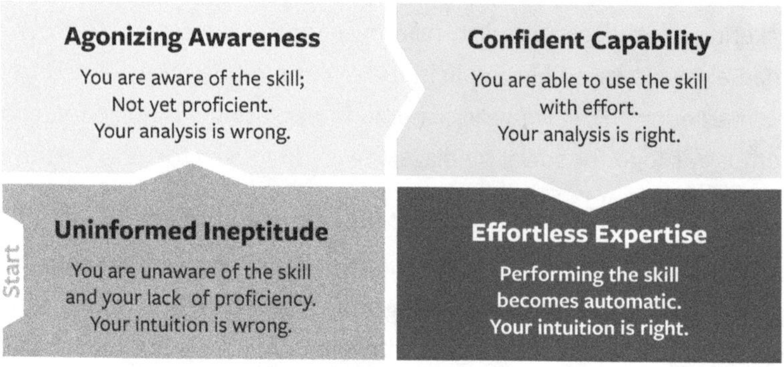

Agonizing Awareness	Confident Capability
You are aware of the skill; Not yet proficient. Your analysis is wrong.	You are able to use the skill with effort. Your analysis is right.
Uninformed Ineptitude You are unaware of the skill and your lack of proficiency. Your intuition is wrong.	**Effortless Expertise** Performing the skill becomes automatic. Your intuition is right.

Start

watching the driver and thinking, "That looks easy!" It feels great since you don't know any better.

▶ **Agonizing Awareness:** You've given something a try and become aware that you don't know what you're doing, and either need to work harder or give up. Continuing our driving story, this would be the panic you felt the first time behind the wheel, realizing it is a whole lot more complicated than you expected. It feels terrible because you're stressed and anxious about not being any good at the thing.

▶ **Confident Capability:** You know you can accomplish the task because you have practiced enough. In the driving metaphor, this would be where you are driving your friends around. It feels good to know that you can do what you need to do.

▶ **Effortless Expertise:** Not only are you confident in your ability, you're not even aware of the steps you take to achieve the results. Driving a car has become second-nature. This is the highest level of capability. It feels amazing to be able to get it done without a lot of thought and preparation.

The learning model helps to explain a major source of sparks.

- ▶ The predecessor is an Effortless Expert in the job and the successor is not.
- ▶ The predecessor has never transitioned out of the last role of their career before, and that experience puts them squarely in the middle of Agonizing Awareness.

Digging Deeper: Here's where it gets messy.

Predecessors are Effortless Experts in their role and probably have been for a long time. This level of capability is nice, but there are drawbacks:

- ▶ Effortless Expertise means the predecessor can rarely explain what they know or how they know it, making knowledge transfer frustrating at best, and impossible at worst.
- ▶ It can create tunnel-vision focusing solely on the thing we have already mastered, creating blind spots for things that change (or need to) — sometimes leading to Uninformed Ineptitude.
- ▶ It can make leaders believe their own press.
- ▶ As more things become part of our Effortless Expertise, there's a lower tolerance for Agonizing Awareness, which can affect resilience and long-term health overall.[36]

In transition, predecessors are living through Agonizing Awareness. They've never retired before and are having to rethink parts of their lives that have been on autopilot for years or decades. They *feel* like the process should be easier than it is as a result.

What is the experience of Agonizing Awareness for predecessors?

Here are some interview quotes:

- ▶ "Anxiety and depression."
- ▶ "Frustration at feeling like I don't have a handle on things."
- ▶ "This is the first time in a while that I felt stupid."
- ▶ "I haven't doubted myself like this in a long time."

Putting it plainly, Agonizing Awareness sucks.

Then there's you.

The only thing we know about you is that you're **not** an Effortless Expert and, truth be told, you're probably a little of all three others. Some elements of the job you blissfully don't know you can't do yet, some you're terrified about, and others you feel ready for.

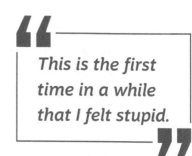

This is the first time in a while that I felt stupid.

Any of those three create friction (sparks!) with the Effortless Expert that is the predecessor. Even in the best-case scenario, where they're trying to tee you up for success, they don't even know what to tell you. That all assumes that you handle every interaction with grace, dignity, and in alignment with what the predecessor wants.

Bottom Line: Predecessors aren't used to *not* knowing how to make something happen. The result? They start seeing the transition as a form of failure and consider reversing course.

Minimize, Contain, and Repair

Where there's smoke, there's fire. How quickly and capably you respond determines whether it's a discrepancy or a disaster.

At the start of the chapter, I said that you had four goals:

1. Accept that conflicts are inevitable.
2. Minimize the opportunities for conflicts to start.
3. Contain the blaze when they do.
4. Repair the damage as quickly and permanently as possible.

Now that we understand the volatility of the situation, we can dig into what to do to make the succession process as smooth as it can be.

Minimize the Chances

The predecessor's mindset and emotional state dictate the Conditions. Sparks, sometimes in the successor's control, are external events that, when seen through the predecessor's lens, can trigger a fire. It's the interaction of the two that determines the result, which looks like this:

Figure 3.7
Sparks vs. Conditions

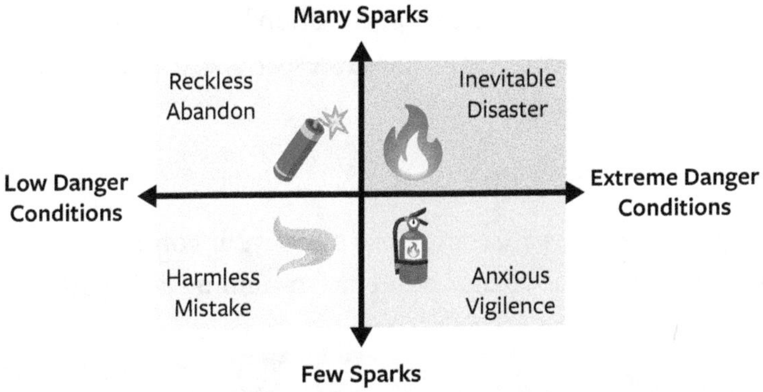

1. **Harmless Mistake:** In the best-case scenario, the predecessor works to keep conditions low-risk and you're minimizing sparks that trigger meaningful conflict. The successor and predecessor work well together through the transition, and handle the few conflicts that occur with candor, trust, and in the interest of moving the organization forward.

2. **Reckless Abandon:** While the predecessor has done the mental hard work of managing their grief, the successor isn't minimizing sparks. While unlikely to start a fire, conflicts can rage during the transition as the predecessor loses patience with

the successor or the successor ignores or misinterprets the cues to be more mindful.

3. **Anxious Vigilance:** The successor does almost everything possible to minimize sparks, but the predecessor is in high-danger grief stages. Often described as "walking on eggshells," the successor usually feels that no matter what, a fire is likely to rage. In these cases, the predecessor is making it almost impossible to avoid disaster.

4. **Inevitable Disaster:** The worst-case scenario, the conditions are ripe for a full-scale wildfire with sparks flying. The predecessor is uncontrolled, and the successor isn't adapting. It's only a matter of time, and the organization braces for impact. The predecessor struggles as the successor doesn't seem to want to prevent catastrophe.

There are two key takeaways:

- ▶ The conditions are completely out of your control.
- ▶ Minimizing the chance of fire means minimizing sparks.

THE MOST EXTREME CONDITIONS

People are terrible at figuring out why they're uncomfortable. How bad? Fewer than 36% of people can name their feelings in the moment.[37] This inability to connect the emotional dots is why *everyone* can feel crazy in succession. The predecessor feels like they've lost their "touch," and successors begin mistrusting their predecessors' decisions.

Here's what typically happens:

Figure 3.8
The Grief Wildfire Process

1 The predecessor feels the grief of transition. **Conditions worsen.**

2 The predecessor attributes that pain to an external force rather than their internal experience. **Conditions are Extreme.**

3 An interaction causes concern. **There's a spark.**

4 The predecessor's "gut instinct" kicks in and interprets the negative emotion as an indicator that the transition is off course. **Spark meets conditions.**

5 The predecessor looks at the successor under a microscope, collecting enough "evidence" to justify a new approach. **The fire intensifies.**

6 The predecessor decides to change the strategy, buoyed by the evidence. **The blaze is now a wildfire.**

What's toughest about the above? It's logical, even if the premise might be faulty.

Think about it from the predecessor's point of view. When things don't feel right, something *must* be wrong. The predecessor starts thinking about the plan and the role of the successor in it. Then, the second-guessing comes. "Is the successor the right pick? Wait, why did they make *that* decision? And, come to think of it, I don't like how they make an awkward joke in certain social situations. Plus, why do they 'umm' so much when they don't have the answer? Is that the kind of executive presence we need?"

This worsens if the predecessor-successor relationship is family or a long-time mentorship. The database of past slights and sins to use as fodder is endless.

That rabbit hole eventually leads to the risky question: "Am I making a mistake?" If the predecessor is bargaining, the answer will likely be ,"Yes." Where it goes from there is anyone's guess.

The worst part from the successor's perspective? You might not even know any of this is happening in the background. Then one day — woosh — everything's ablaze.

HOW TO MINIMIZE THE SPARKS

Since you can't control the conditions, your job is to relentlessly focus on sparks. Here's how to handle it:

1. **It's not about you:** The predecessor's response to your actions is rarely about you, even if they make it personal. Separate the emotion from the interaction to maximize your chances of engaging with a level-headed approach.

2. **Reframe:** Since you know it's not about you, rewrite the story to be calm, measured, and empathetic in your response. (There's more about how to do this on page 75.)

3. **It is about them:** Going back to the Golden Rule, they get to dictate the terms. Continuing to acknowledge, respect, and honor their work and contributions helps to reduce the chances of misperceived motivations.

4. **Focus on the relationship, not the transaction:** Grief is a lonely place, and checking in on the predecessor emotionally can pay dividends for you both. Further, minimizing the sense of transaction will help all parties feel more connected.

5. **Establish your own identity:** Identifying closely with the predecessor or the organization can mean that you're riding on their rollercoaster. Ensuring that you have an identity strong and separate enough from your current or future job will make it much easier for you to see everything more clearly.

In a particularly difficult succession challenge a few years ago, I recommended a mantra to someone I coached.

"It's not about you, and they're doing their best."

The good news in all of this? You can be proactive, instead of reactive. Chapter 7 is about the toolbox you need to take as much productive ownership and control as possible.

Bottom Line: You can only control what you can control. The conditions are what they are, but a successor can make sure the sparks don't fly.

> *It's not about you, and they're doing their best.*

Contain the Blaze

When wasps invaded a wall in my house, I needed a professional to fix the problem. When the exterminator arrived — and began cutting a hole in my interior drywall — I asked him where he thought they had come from and why they chose to nest there.

"Everyone asks me that," he said. "And I always say the same thing: I don't know, and it doesn't matter."

His point? They're there, and the problem needed to be fixed as soon as possible.

Unfortunately, when fires break out, we tend to focus on why they happened instead of solving them. That tendency wastes critical time and allows the fire to grow and spread.

> *I don't know, and it doesn't matter.*

Let's be like the bee guy and adopt his mantra: I don't know, and it doesn't matter. Then we can put our energy into containing the fire.

Some context: Conflict is inevitable, but destruction is not. It's how, and how quickly, we respond to it that determines its danger.

The Handoff

Jim, an innovation-minded business leader, had spent most of his career developing companies that provide new ideas to the construction space. Sandy had founded her modular building company in her late 50s about 10 years prior and had grown it to the maximum point of her capability. She saw the company as a diamond in the rough, but after two years of stagnation, she decided that taking on a partner, or selling outright, was the best move for her, the employees, and the company.

The match was made. Jim bought a controlling interest in the business and structured a longer-term buyout of Sandy both to keep her engaged in the business and to share in the growth. While Jim had complete control of the decision-making, he consulted Sandy on every decision during the first year. Once Sandy got more comfortable, their meetings moved to quarterly updates. While Jim and Sandy typically talk weekly, most of the conversations are updates Jim provides her rather than the dialogues and debates of the first year.

"I knew for the business to be successful, Sandy needed to be a partner. She worked hard. She deserved it. And I knew if I just walked in and took control, she'd hate that and hate me. We've built a great working relationship, and our nonexistent turnover suggests that they don't mind me being the CEO."

Sandy sold the remaining shares to Jim two years before the original agreed-upon timeline. "I trusted Jim and how he handled the business and especially our employees," Sandy said. "Sticking around was just going to get in his way, and I knew all of that work and those relationships were in good hands." ▶

To understand how it works, we'll borrow a model from cognitive behavioral psychology to help us understand how people respond to sparks. Known as the behavior chain, it works like this:

Figure 3.9
The Behavior Chain

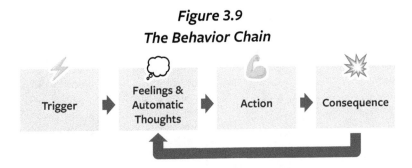

- ▶ **Trigger:** The action that sets our minds into motion, also known as an event; these can be sparks.
- ▶ **Feelings and automatic thoughts:** What goes through our mind, and courses through our veins, when we encounter the trigger and write a story; conditions are a sizable part of this for predecessors.
- ▶ **Action:** The action we take based on the story we've written, which comes from our feelings and automatic thoughts.
- ▶ **Consequence:** The result of the action, which will inform our feelings and thoughts in the future.

Let's revisit the story about the "New Logo" on page 63 and break it down using our model. We're going to make some assumptions about what the predecessor experienced in the story:

Figure 3.10
Behavior Chain Example: The New Logo

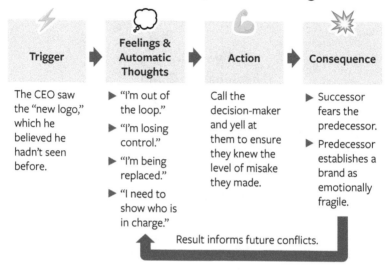

Trigger	Feelings & Automatic Thoughts	Action	Consequence
The CEO saw the "new logo," which he believed he hadn't seen before.	▶ "I'm out of the loop." ▶ "I'm losing control." ▶ "I'm being replaced." ▶ "I need to show who is in charge."	Call the decision-maker and yell at them to ensure they knew the level of misake they made.	▶ Successor fears the predecessor. ▶ Predecessor establishes a brand as emotionally fragile.

Result informs future conflicts.

Since this predecessor was processing their grief, they responded in a way that turned a harmless spark into a full-blown inferno.

As the successor, knowing the model can help to put a fire out quickly. How?

▶ Understanding the spark helps the successor to understand why the situation happened and to be more aware of how to prevent them in the future.

▶ Being aware of the conditions allows the successor to be other-focused, and think through the thoughts, feelings, and mental models the predecessor is currently using. This can inform a host of decisions and help the successor prioritize their approach.

▶ Having this context helps explain why the action makes sense and connects logical threads. This empathetic approach increases success overall.

▶ Seeing the connection to consequences allows for the consequences to sting a little less, which is crucial to the repair phase.

Digging Deeper: Since we're human like the predecessor, we too can leverage the behavior chain to both understand others' behavior and adapt our own. We have a choice in how we behave, even amid the worst sparks and in the most dangerous of conditions.

The best tool in the arsenal?

The pause button.

A study from UCLA[38] shows that taking the time to actively label the emotion you feel — a pause-button strategy — greatly lowers the negative emotional experience, and, by extension, reacting to those emotions.

When emotions are high, and the trigger has us angry, we are more willing to react without considering the potential consequences. It is exactly at this moment that we need to hit pause and separate ourselves from the stimulus (what made us upset) and our response (the action and the consequences that come after).

We get there by asking ourselves three questions:

▶ The story I'm writing: **Is it true?**
▶ Even if it's true, **am I exaggerating it?**
▶ Are there **alternate explanations I haven't considered?**

In nearly every case, the story we're telling about the situation is adding fuel to the fire rather than ramping down the emotion. Answering these questions honestly allows you to adapt more quickly and effectively.

While you can't control the predecessor, you can control whether you barrel through the stop signs to uncontrolled action or pause and reconsider the situation.

Digging Even Deeper: Controlling the impact goes beyond you and the predecessor. An untamed fire can become an inferno when it involves other team members. In the worst of examples, wildfires damage the foundation of the succession process.

To minimize the risk of the fire spreading, there are a few ironclad rules to follow:

▶ **Eliminate triangular communication:** Triangular communication is when you bring a third party into your conflict, typically through complaining or sharing unhelpful information about the other person. Instead of addressing the conflict directly with the person, this manipulative approach brings someone else into the mix. This action not only breeds distrust, but creates an additional point of relationship failure.

▶ **Limit confidants:** The succession process lends itself to our lesser selves, with juicy drama and interpersonal conflict (there's a reason an entire prestige TV show was built around it). Your brand is on the line, and the fewer people who are aware of your thought process and frustrations, the better. While you will need third-party support for everything from a pick-me-up to reframing challenges, keeping a tight inner circle will minimize opportunities for misunderstandings.

▶ **Avoid the quicksand:** You're likely to make mistakes along the way, but quicksand — outlined in Chapter 5 — is what most often makes wildfires worse.

▶ **Mind the grapevine:** When there's uncertainty, people will fill the void with conjecture. Ensure that you have a pulse on the organization and the stresses of the team and do what you can to minimize the concerns.

Bottom Line: Stay aware of your thoughts and feelings, hit the pause button when you can, and realize that wildfires can spread quickly if you lose control.

Repair the Damage

No matter how intense — from a scary near-miss to a thousand-acre wildfire — there is damage to repair.

That damage is a loss of trust.

The idea is intuitive, but the realities of trust are much more complex than what it might seem at first glance.

Digging Deeper: Let's start with getting to know the "The Trust Triangle," the result of research by Frances X. Frei and Anne Morriss.[39]

Figure 3.11
The Trust Triangle

Authenticity
I experience the real you.

Logic
I know you can do it; your reasoning and judgment are sound.

Trust

Empathy
I believe you care about me and my success.

The model acts like a three-legged stool, where each leg is crucial to your ability to create trust. It works like this:

- **Logic:** The confidence you have in another's decisions and judgment.
- **Empathy:** How much you believe the other person cares and "has your back."

▶ **Authenticity:** The extent that you know the interaction is genuine and you're experiencing the other person's vulnerability.

If there's a gap in trust, it's because of what the authors call a "wobble." You've damaged the trust of at least one of those core trust drivers.

How do you fix it?

ASSESS THE DAMAGE

Like a good forensic fire investigator, your job is to get to the truth, regardless of how you feel about the answers you uncover. Here's the process:

▶ **Start with introspection:** Instead of blaming the other person for the gap in trust, assume their analysis of you is 100% correct. Then look at the three factors of trust and ask yourself the hard questions:
  > Did I show that I'm incapable of doing the work?
  > Did I make the predecessor reconsider their own judgment?
  > Did I have my predecessor's back?
  > Have I been open and accountable, even if I've made a mistake?

▶ **Consider past wobbles:** Think back to previous trust-breaking mistakes and ask yourself:
  > What happened in my past situations?
  > Is there one of the three trust drivers where I tend to wobble?

▶ **Rethink your assumptions about the predecessor:** Since the relationship between the successor and predecessor is typically close, you might make assumptions about the relationship and decision-making that aren't true. Ask:
  > Am I taking my predecessor's trust for granted?
  > Do I assume that our relationship means there's a higher level of trust than exists?

> Do I think the predecessor might be more naturally trusting than they are?

Review the sparks. Look in the mirror. Be honest with yourself.

Once you've answered those questions, you likely know why the gap exists.

Now let's fix it.

REPAIR

Repair needs to be as swift and complete as possible.

The secret-est of secret weapons? A good apology.

Yet, it's not enough to say, "I'm sorry," and "my bad" does more harm than good.

Digging Deeper: Eric Barker, author of several books, did a fantastic rundown on apology best practices based on his review of available research. His findings?[40]

- Apologies do make a difference. People often prefer them over money, even if they're just cheap talk.
- If it's clear you intentionally did something wrong, you're probably better off not apologizing. After intentional acts, apologies tend to backfire and make things worse.
- Giving money is not an effective way to apologize but research has shown that expensive gifts can work.
- The best way to apologize is not to apologize for what you think you did wrong. Apologize for what they think you did wrong.
- Being reminded of times when they did something wrong makes people more likely to accept apologies and forgive. So, a little guilting might not be a bad idea. (Ugh.)

Like everything else, timing is everything.

On one hand, we may put it off far too long. The risk in delay? We allow the damage to linger, which creates more damage. We avoid those challenging conversations because we systematically overestimate how negatively others respond to conflict. From research[41]:

> Underestimating how positively relationship partners will respond to an open, direct, and honest conversation about relationship concerns may create a misplaced barrier to confronting issues when they arise in relationships, thereby keeping people from confronting issues that would strengthen their relationships.

On the flip side, doing it right away might not land, either. In *Wait: The Art and Science of Delay*[42]:

> "Apology timing was positively correlated with outcome satisfaction; when the apology came later in the conflict, participants reported greater satisfaction." Statistical tests showed that, the greater the delay, the more a victim felt heard and understood. With more time, there was more opportunity for voice and understanding.

Let's say you figured out when to apologize and nailed the words, tone, and timing.

Digging Even Deeper: There's still damage to repair.

The conversation helps start the repair process, but what can you do to fully fix the damage?

Given how close the predecessor/successor relationship tends to be, and especially considering how connected the fortunes are between the two, marriage can be useful when thinking about how to approach it. Dr. John Gottman, who spent a career studying successful relationships, is here to give insight.

Gottman identified "Four Horsemen" that kill interpersonal relationships (helpfully summarized by Eric Barker[43]):

▶ **Criticism:** Criticism is staging the problem in a relationship as a character flaw. People in the best relationships do the opposite: They point a finger at themselves, and they really have a very gentle way of starting up the discussion, minimizing the problem, and talking about what they feel and what they need.

▶ **Defensiveness:** A natural reaction to being criticized, it takes two forms: counterattacking or acting like an innocent victim and whining. Again, people in healthy relationships were very different even when their partner was critical. They accepted the criticism, or even took responsibility for part of the problem. They said, "Talk to me; I want to hear how you feel about this."

▶ **Contempt:** Contempt is talking down to the other; being insulting or acting superior. Not only did it predict relationships ending, but it predicted the number of infectious illnesses that the recipient of contempt would have in the next four years when we measured health.

▶ **Stonewalling:** It's shutting down or tuning out. It passively tells the other person, "I don't care."

In challenging situations, both the predecessor and successor can fall into these traps. Even if there's a well-executed apology, criticism, defensiveness, contempt, and stonewalling can creep in. You can't control the predecessor's behavior, but you can be aware of and control yours.

The way to a healthier, repaired relationship:

▶ **Know the other person:** Spend time talking about the person and their life rather than just day-to-day logistics.

▶ **Respond to (and send) "bids":** "Bids" are the small ways we engage each other's attention. An Instagram story or a text message about something familiar is a small way of connecting with the other. The more you do that, the more capital you have when there are inevitable conflicts.

▶ **Admiration works:** In the best of relationships, each person sees each other as better than they really are (and in bad ones, worse). Take time to acknowledge your predecessor's work.

Bottom Line: Conflict doesn't need to be permanent. Take ownership of your part and have the humility to recognize the predecessor's struggle.

The 13 Predecessor Archetypes

While we're all unique, we tend to behave similarly. We've found the same with predecessors, finding 13 archetypes that help explain how a predecessor acts. If wildfires are disasters, the archetypes give a hint to the type of wildfire you're fighting.

The Context: We often see others' behavior as "illogical." It's an example of our biases at play — just because we don't understand the context of the decision, doesn't make it wrong.[vii]

In other words, absent a significant mental health diagnosis, decisions aren't illogical.

While wildfires explain the types of emotions that are pulling at the predecessor's heartstrings and mind, archetypes help to explain the potential approaches a predecessor might take. You'll note that these archetypes are extreme — very few predecessors behave *exactly* this way — but they help to give context and language to some of the ways a predecessor might react.

---

vii. This is a good example of actor/observer bias. We'll talk more about biases starting on page 194.

Why It Matters: When we apply judgment to someone's behavior, we tend to see them as a caricature of themselves, shadowboxing the person we *think* they are instead of the rational (and successful) person and professional sitting across from you. Making this mistake will make you emotionally dumber. You'll react in ways that will seem illogical to them, which will trigger their biases, lowering trust and generally causing frustration and chaos for all.

In contrast, having a framework to understand why someone might make certain decisions helps you shift the frustration and focus away from a value judgment ("they're crazy") toward something more empathetic (they're being a "Proud Parent") because it makes them more confident in making this decision. Naming the archetype as it's happening is like a smoke alarm; it alerts you to possible danger and gives you time to think about how to react.

> *Shadowboxing a caricature of the predecessor will make you emotionally dumber.*

Common Reasons: Regardless of the archetype(s) the predecessor might represent, the behaviors typically stem from a standard set of stories or beliefs the predecessor holds. These tend to be:

1. **Legitimate concerns:** Their response, even if destructive, comes from a place of legitimate worry about the leadership team. Their role as existing executive or new outsider creates a context where they feel they can't express those concerns in a productive way.

2. **Smoldering:** Sometimes a wildfire only looks to be extinguished, but there's smoldering under the surface ready to reignite. This can put the predecessor on a "hair trigger" that sparks another conflict, regardless of how tiny the previous spark might be.

3. **Care and concern:** Not all predecessor motivations are wrong or selfish. The predecessor might have a paternalistic care and concern for the organization and its people and, in a time of transition and vulnerability, ends up complicating the lives of the remaining or new organizational decision-makers.

Bottom Line: Empathy is the fire extinguisher of succession wildfires. It might not save you in the worst of cases, but it can get the job done when there's a flare up.

Predecessor Archetype #1: The Zen Master

Zen Masters never (seem to) have a worried bone in their bodies. They're entirely at ease with transition, even if some evident potholes lie ahead.

Their Mantra: "It will all be just fine."

It will all be just fine.

Typical Behaviors:

- ▶ Feels completely comfortable moving onto their next step.
- ▶ Glosses over potential pitfalls and warning signs.
- ▶ Looks forward to the future without having the urgency to address loose ends.
- ▶ Expresses extreme optimism in the face of any issues discussed.

Potential Drivers:

- ▶ Prioritizes peace and comfort over addressing challenging problems or navigating conflict.
- ▶ Focuses on their future, with limited interest in solving pre-transition problems.
- ▶ Avoids the realities of the transition; reaction serves as a self-protective "front."

Transition Dangers:

- ▶ Ignores or hides potential issues.
- ▶ Remains unwilling to have hard conversations or conflict.
- ▶ Sets successor up to fail.

Approach to Succession: Assumes successor is capable and will succeed without consideration for current situation, successor readiness, or organizational dynamics.

The Zen Master in Action

A super successful female executive grew her career at a mid-sized bank in the Midwest. For the last 10 years of her career, she took a younger, high-potential professional male under her wing. Every time she got promoted, he did, too. She had such a level of confidence in his skillset that she gave a month's notice to the organization that she would be retiring. "He can handle it," she told anyone who would listen.

Janet had mentored William for the last decade, and they were close. The problem? William didn't know what he was doing. Worse, William developed an internal brand for being a product of Janet's mentorship rather than a professional. What William said didn't matter if Janet didn't co-sign. She was the brand. He was the personal assistant.

The day before Janet left, she was informed by the CEO that William wouldn't be promoted to her role. She was furious, but ultimately let it go. William struggled massively. In the end, it took two years for him to go from a shell-shocked, underprepared, high-potential employee to a well-regarded teammate in the organization. While he never got the promotion, he realized he didn't *want* it, and found a role that aligned with what he envisioned for himself.

Predecessor Archetype #2: The Proud Parent

The Proud Parent isn't just excited about handing over responsibility to the successor; they're bragging about how great the successor is and will be. Despite the predecessor's enthusiasm, the high praise for the successor becomes grating, sometimes to the point that it impacts the ability to maintain relationships with other leaders in the organization.

I have zero doubts they can make it happen.

Their Mantra: "I have zero doubts they can make it happen."

Typical Behaviors:

▶ Excessively talks or brags about the successor.
▶ Ignores the contributions of other leaders or members of the team.
▶ Develops a personal connection that can impede impartiality.

Potential Drivers:

▶ Has overly personalized the business as part of an identity.
▶ Sees leadership transition as a significant part of legacy.
▶ Wants to retain some influence through a family-like relationship.

Transition Dangers:

▶ Predecessor overconfidence in successor's ability to step into role leads to glossing over potential issues.
▶ Subversion of the successor occurs within the organization as teammates feel frustrated or neglected.
▶ Legitimate issues are kept under wraps until they grow into larger, potentially fatal, problems.

Approach to Succession: The transition becomes as much about making the Proud Parent feel good about the decision as it does about successfully ensuring a solid handoff. Anything that could be interpreted as negative about either the predecessor or successor is ignored in the transition calculus.

The Proud Parent in Action

William founded his company more than 40 years prior as a small manufacturing business. In his 70s, he had a heart attack at work and realized that, after four decades working at the business and never having children, he needed to step away. William hired Evelyn, who, at 42, had changed careers after a long and successful tenure in the military.

The day William announced Evelyn would be the next CEO, he talked extensively about the impact she had made on the business. Yet, several of the achievements weren't Evelyn's at all. While Evelyn had an effect on those areas, it was her focus on improving operational reporting that made these gains more visible.

"By the time I stepped into the job, everyone hated me. I heard that even some of our clients were joking about how William talked about what a good decision he made in putting me in charge." Within nine months of Evelyn taking over, and despite her best attempts to build relationships, both the COO and the sales VP left the organization. It took another two years for Evelyn to get the business back to where it was before the transition, though the new plan cut growth goals in half.

Predecessor Archetype #3: The Arsonist Firefighter

The Arsonist Firefighter sets the house ablaze, then rushes to the scene in the fire truck to play the hero. The crisis could be real or imagined, tangible or intangible. Regardless, to Arsonist Firefighters, the problem needs to be solved and can only be solved by him or her.

They need me to fix it.

Their Mantra: "They need me to fix it."

Typical Behaviors:

- ▶ Invents a crisis that only they can solve.
- ▶ Uses unpredictability as a tool to keep teams on their toes.
- ▶ Displays serious Jekyll-and-Hyde vibes.

Potential Drivers:

- ▶ Identity is tied to the organization or the job.
- ▶ Struggles to envision a positive post-transition life.
- ▶ Expresses insecurity about the success others might demonstrate when in control.

Transition Dangers:

- ▶ Successors don't know where they stand or what decisions can be made.
- ▶ Other organizational issues are not addressed.
- ▶ If the successor does well, the predecessor might counterintuitively act.

Approach to Succession: Varies widely. Can set the fire before, during, or even well after the transition, even if the succession plan was executed to perfection. Few succession patterns remain consistent with this archetype.

The Arsonist Firefighter in Action

Roger started a distribution company with nothing, growing it to revenues of more than $10 million annually. As a status-driven business owner, with his name on the building, he started to see others his age retiring early. Roger decided he'd build an executive team that could run the business so he could travel and pursue other passions.

Within the first six months of Roger stepping back, his executive team generated the most revenue in the company's history, but Roger felt compelled to stay active in the business. A short slowdown seemed to justify every accusation Roger threw at his executive team. The last three months of the year were so miserable that Roger decided he needed to come back full-time. He demoted his CEO, fired three of the other executives, and elevated young, inexperienced family members to the executive team.

Key customers and suppliers began to see him as unsteady and followed the fired executives to his competitors. While the business remains in operation, revenues are down between 25% and 50%, and the inexperience of the current executives forced Roger to return to his pre-retirement schedule. Roger had been days away from selling the business for a significant multiple before he decided to reinsert himself into the company.

Predecessor Archetype #4: The Puppeteer

The Puppeteer isn't physically present but remains the leader through governance (usually as a board president or significant shareholder) or manipulation. The successor ends up as a direct conduit of The Puppeteer.

They still need me to pull the strings.

Their Mantra: "They still need me to pull the strings."

Typical Behaviors:

▶ Continues to make decisions while using new leadership as the conduit.

▶ Leverages internal dynamics and conflicts to get results.

▶ Ensures they continue to have the final say.

Potential Drivers:

▶ Expresses concerns about the readiness of the successor.

▶ Shows a disconnect between timing and willingness to exit.

▶ Fears the organization operating without direct influence.

Transition Dangers:

▶ Successor cannot make any decisions without predecessor approval.

▶ Turns successor into a COO even if responsibility is as CEO/ president.

▶ Undermines successor's ability to learn; lack of preparedness if successor needs to step into the role in the future.

Approach to Succession: Usually praises the successor publicly but is a monster to the person privately. They will choose individuals who can be controlled during and after transition, usually confidants, family, or close friends.

The Puppeteer in Action

Jack, the founding entrepreneur who built an eight-figure enterprise from scratch, shocked customers at a business event, announcing that he'd be retiring at the end of the year, about nine months later, and that his daughter, Liz, would be CEO.

"It started almost day one," Liz confessed, after becoming CEO. Despite the very public handoff, Jack continued to play the CEO role, only this time as the Board Chair. Even decisions that he had delegated to Liz in the past became part of his influence, only this time hiding behind his "fiduciary responsibility to the shareholders." None of the changes Liz felt were essential to the business were on the table. It was Roger's way or the highway.

After a conflict about a client account that Liz felt was at risk, she launched into her father. "If you want to be CEO, then take the role back. But I'm not doing it anymore if you're just going to keep running the business and use me as the conduit." At a board meeting a week later, Jack announced he would be stepping down as chair, as he saw his approach being a distraction to the business and having a negative impact on his relationship with his daughter.

Predecessor Archetype #5: The Talking Head

If you've seen a retired athlete or politician on an analysis show, you've seen the talking heads. They're the people who lived the work every day, but now that they're out of it, they're sharing controversial opinions that can be disruptive to their target, sometimes intentionally. Unlike those who are "shouting from the cheap seats," Talking Heads can have a meaningful — and usually negative — impact on the organization they left.

They're doing it wrong and need to hear it from somebody.

Their Mantra: "They're doing it wrong and need to hear it from somebody."

Typical Behaviors:

▶ Becomes vocal critic of the new leadership team and its decisions.

▶ Issues sharp and personal critiques with a tone of expertise.

▶ Attempts to influence decisions using their bully pulpit.

▶ Often excuses commentary as "just sharing their thoughts," or "just spouting off."

▶ Not always aware of their impact.

Potential Drivers:

▶ Holds legitimate concerns about leadership's approach.

▶ Displays difficulty accepting a role as outsider.

▶ Struggles to focus in a direction that isn't related to the business or industry.

Transition Dangers:

▶ Successor can anchor decisions to the potential reactions of the predecessor.

▶ Predecessor retains a level of control that can undermine the successor's decisions.

▶ Can interrupt necessary organizational changes, especially tough 50-50 calls, where the external criticism tips the scales to the lesser choice.

Approach to Succession: The succession approach can vary widely as the Talking Head doesn't often emerge until the succession process is underway. Once the transition is in place, or in process, the Talking Head only then finds the opportunities to talk about new leadership's approach.

The Talking Head in Action

Peter was a well-known president in his industry, a tight-knit community in a region where there was little external competition. Before hitting retirement age, and growing frustrated with the owner of the business where Peter played successor-to-be his entire tenure there, he decided to resign and allow the owner to pick the next generation of leaders for the company.

While Peter had originally pledged to spend the beginning of his retirement on a Caribbean beach with his wife, the CEO of the regional trade association had abruptly resigned at a time where the organization was leading significant government relations efforts. Peter was the only one with the reputation to step immediately into the role. Just six weeks after retiring, he was back at the grind in this new job.

In the first few months at the new gig, Peter had tremendous success. He only considered himself a caretaker, yet he was able to ensure that a new state budget included crucial incentives for his industry. His "stock" was never higher.

At his previous organization, things were a mess. The owner had limited focus on the business, and those he elevated were unready (or unserious) about taking on executive-level roles. Peter's critiques about the company's decisions to friends and colleagues made their way to the new leadership group at the old company, complicating hiring and promotions decisions.

"I was blindsided to hear what Peter had to say about me, and some of the calls we made as a team," one of the executives said. "He's such an influential figure and I feel like he's making us look bad as a company and hurting our careers individually. It sucks."

Predecessor Archetype #6: The Legend

The Legend is one of the most influential people within the organization. Whether the leader or someone else who has made a dramatic impact, The Legend's words carry exceptional weight long after they have been first uttered. Status usually leads to a lack of clarity of the void The Legend will leave behind.

No one will exceed me.

Their Mantra: "No one will exceed me."

Typical Behaviors:

▶ Gravitates to members of the team who are willing to see the world similarly.
▶ Ensures staying "in the room" with key mantras that might limit decision-making.
▶ Can minimize others around them who might feel they could be a threat to their legend status.

Potential Drivers:

▶ Genuine desire to preserve legacy.
▶ Fear that succeeding leadership will stray from success drivers.
▶ Emotional need to feel irreplaceable.

Transition Dangers:

▶ The Legend can't be replaced, so the organization doesn't try; succession left to the team to "figure out."
▶ Overwhelming nature of The Legend's status makes knowledge transfer feel like an impossible problem.
▶ Inability to separate the brand of The Legend from the work contributions of The Legend leads to a succession process focused on the wrong outcomes.

Approach to Succession: The Legend is often unaware of the extent to which the successor needs to fill his or her shoes. With such a direct connection between The Legend's story and the company's story, there can be a kick-the-bird-out-of-the-nest-early vibe that sets the successor up for failure.

The Legend in Action

A large, well-respected regional nonprofit organization had been led by Rhonda, who had built a small empire that served as a national model and was known globally for her approach. Then, the bomb dropped — Rhonda announced her resignation, giving eight months' notice to the board of directors and six months to everyone else.

The day Tammy was announced as Rhonda's successor, phones pinged around the region. Was Tammy ready? Was she the right choice? Known as a dedicated professional who oozed competence, was that the skillset needed for an organization whose CEO had spent her time building the organization by glad-handing and raising lots of money?

Much to Tammy's credit, the organization has continued to thrive. Rebranding the organization and looking at it more broadly, she leveraged her approachable nature to advance the organization in her image. While not the consummate politician, she has built the right relationships to make the nonprofit even stronger.

It could be best summarized by a board member: "Tammy has been more than we could have expected and she has made the board look very smart. But, if we're honest, we didn't expect this level of continuity, and were ready to step in if needed. We're delighted that she made that a moot point."

Predecessor Archetype #7: The Ghoster

The Ghoster might have been described as one of the other archetypes before, but now has checked out and is nowhere to be found. Whether a shell of his or her former self, disengaged, or out of the office (temporarily or permanently), The Ghoster refuses to engage in any effort that would continue to support the business.

They'll figure it out (or not, I don't/ can't care).

Their Mantra: "They'll figure it out (or not, I don't/can't care)."

Typical Behaviors:

▶ Ignores asks from colleagues for support.
▶ Unable to offer essential support to successors.
▶ Withholds critical information or mentorship.

Potential Drivers:

▶ Health issues, family matters, or other personal distractions.
▶ Self-protection from the emotional experience of transition.
▶ Resentment for those who are stepping into decision-making.
▶ Burnout.

Transition Dangers:

▶ There is no transition; the successors must figure it out without context.
▶ Predecessor holds mission-critical information inaccessible to the succeeding team.
▶ Significant uphill climb to introduce successors to stakeholders like employees, suppliers, and customers.

Approach to Succession: For The Ghoster, the handoff date is the transition. No matter what might be outstanding, they're out of the picture. They've ghosted the succeeding team and, even if there are contracts involved, they've decided to make themselves completely unavailable. Successors must assess the situation and do their best to pick up the pieces.

The Ghoster in Action

Ronald started a boutique, museum-quality picture framing business. For 20 years, he built a company that made not only great moulding for frames but delivered museum-quality product to regional museums and big-ticket buyers. A decade prior, Ronald's son, Jake, joined the company as a framer, showing himself to be more of an artist than a businessperson. Unfortunately for Ronald, Jake routinely frustrated and offended customers.

Ronald had typically been able to keep his son away from customer interactions until abdominal pain became too difficult for him to ignore. The company's revenues, and fortunes, plummeted.

Despite the severe situation, Jake felt he was entitled to the pay he received regardless of the health of the business — and his father. Ronald saw it as an unbreakable covenant. After a couple of years of struggling, Ronald realized the stress and financial burden were too great to continue and decided to sell the business.

Jill, a recent MBA graduate, wanted to put her education to use at a business she cared about. After a series of negotiations, Ronald received $50,000 and a guarantee that Jake would be retained for at least five years in exchange for the business and a two-year commitment that Ronald would stay on as a consultant. The day after the transaction, Jill realized that she hadn't gotten keys to the facility. Jake was notoriously a late arriver, but Ronald wasn't answering his phone.

"That was when I knew something was wrong," Jill said. "I wanted to buy a business that needed help, not start a company with little flexibility and a senior director-level salary from jump." Jill closed the business three years later. "I paid $100,000 for my MBA and more than triple that to learn how business really works. I'm grateful for the experience, but still can't help to think if we wouldn't still be open, and Jake still employed, had Ronald done the bare minimum to help."

Predecessor Archetype #8: The Seagull

The Seagull steals from the popular idea of "seagull management," defined as a manager who "swoops in, craps on everything, and leaves the rest of the team to clean up the mess." As predecessors, Seagulls want the best of all worlds: the power to

If I don't jump in, they'll fail.

redirect organizational resources, the flexibility to check in whenever they want, and the confidence that this assessment — often with extremely limited or outdated information — is correct.

Their Mantra: "If I don't jump in, they'll fail."

Typical Behaviors:

- ▶ Swoops in to drive decisions inconsistently.
- ▶ Uses experience and authority to bypass agreed-upon processes.
- ▶ Strongly advocates for positions without full organizational context.
- ▶ Leaves the team to navigate rapidly changing priorities.

Potential Drivers:

- ▶ Boredom.
- ▶ A lingering sense of no longer being in the know or control.
- ▶ Distrust of the succeeding team.

Transition Dangers:

- ▶ Predecessor holds information that makes it more challenging to learn the thought process.
- ▶ The limited situations where The Seagull is additive justifies the many more situations that cost the organization stress and time.
- ▶ Successors struggle to distinguish when the predecessor can provide value vs. add organizational stress.

Approach to Succession: The Seagull might do everything right — or wrong — in the succession process, but it's when problems arise that the predecessor is likely to pull the rug out from the succeeding team. The result is a false succession process where the successor never has to know what it's like to make the decision without the predecessor around.

The Seagull in Action

Walt, the owner of a logistics company, hired a young general manager, Ike, to run a 40-person logistics operation. Walt was considering selling the business and looking at all options, from liquidation to employee ownership to selling to a strategic buyer, and he felt Ike could keep the engine running in the meantime.

As the owner of many businesses, Walt was approaching 70 and looking to cash out on his years of hard work, which were much less hard over the previous decade as he weaved leisure travel with managing his portfolio of companies. Since he saw the logistics company as his greatest "chip," he wanted to make sure Ike was in the best position to succeed.

Despite those intentions, there were many conflicts. Walt would go away for eight-week stretches, sometimes completely out of contact, leaving Ike to make tough calls that weren't his to make. When Walt would return, he assumed that the entire business was a mess, and would instruct Ike to follow directions that, in many cases, were the complete opposite approach that Ike had implemented. Once Walt was either tired or bored, he would head off to another adventure without anyone knowing when he would return.

The constant change was taking its toll on Ike. "This is terrible. I don't have access to Walt when I need him, so I do my best with limited information. When he does engage, he upends all of the work I've done to that point, and I have to start from scratch. I've lost two key people just in the last two months because of the chaos."

Ike left shortly thereafter. In discussions with Walt, he blamed poor leadership at the operational level for the failings and sold the business. "I knew I couldn't trust Ike. I just wish he would have leaned on me more as a resource."

Predecessor Archetype #9: The Immortal

The Immortal will never die — or so it is believed. Immortals choose to run the organization and build the leadership team in a way that relies on them as the unquestioned leader forever.

I'm not going anywhere.

Their Mantra: "I'm not going anywhere."

Typical Behaviors:

- ▶ Self-seen as the only leader of the business, now and forever.
- ▶ Rejects transition as unnecessary.
- ▶ Chases away talented teammates as the "immortal ceiling" cannot be shattered.
- ▶ Denies realities, such as declining faculties, awareness of trends, or other internal or external threats.

Potential Drivers:

▶ Fear of death or irrelevance.

▶ Total lack of trust in others.

▶ Extreme connection between the business and self-identity.

Transition Dangers:

▶ Predecessor is not transitioning anything.

▶ The Immortal might hint at potential future transition, but refuses to take meaningful action, using the "dangle" as a carrot that is never eaten.

▶ The succeeding team, if it ever takes over, does so by accident of (usually) biological inevitability.

Approach to Succession: The Immortal is opting out of succession. Any discussion of it is met with silence, resistance, or hostility.

The Immortal in Action

Starting with a single DIY car wash location on the outskirts of a central metropolitan area, Leslie expanded to nearly 50 locations across one half of the state. Leslie had a larger-than-life personality and was known and loved by almost everyone — even competitors.

Leslie and her husband of 40 years had two children, both of whom long decided they would get an education and work at the family business, taking over eventually. Everyone was on board with that plan except for Leslie. Several years prior, Leslie gifted 15% of the business to each child. The kids thought that was the start of the transition, whereas Leslie felt it was an appropriate acknowledgement of their contributions at that point.

Within a three-month stretch, Leslie's husband died, quickly followed by Leslie. The children were devastated — not only were they mourning the loss of their parents, but they also had an insurmountable tax burden. While elements of the core business were saved, many of the other parts of the company that both Leslie and her children valued were sold at a significant discount.

"For a woman who knew how to make decisions so well, this was the one she simply couldn't swallow," one of her children said. "I wish I could understand it better."

Predecessor Archetype #10: The Old Guard

The Old Guard has painstakingly built an organization over decades, and the proof is in the success. As a result of such a meticulously structured organization, transition is only about changing who sits in which seats. Everything else must. Stay. Exactly. The. Same.

They need to keep things the same or they'll break it.

Their Mantra: "They need to keep things the same or they'll break it."

Typical Behaviors:

- ▶ Shuts down discussion when changes are proposed.
- ▶ Filters information only through what has been seen as working in the past.
- ▶ Assumes that past contexts will apply in perpetuity.
- ▶ Acts as de facto "organizational historian," carefully explaining why decisions were made, even when those decisions no longer apply.

Potential Drivers:

- ▶ Protecting what the predecessor genuinely believes is crucial to business success.
- ▶ Fear that changes indicate prior decisions were poor.

- Worry that progress indicates growing irrelevance.
- Seeing the organizational structure and process as part of legacy.

Transition Dangers:

- Predecessor values successors who are committed to the status quo.
- Most transition and knowledge transfer efforts are dedicated to ensuring that little actually changes.
- High-potential employees with good ideas see insurmountable barriers and leave.

Approach to Succession: The Old Guard cares deeply about preserving the historical organization and sees that preservation as an enabler of, rather than a barrier to, organizational sustainability. With that as the decision framework, all transition efforts are dedicated to ensuring that successors are well-versed in exactly how things were done in the past. Most predecessors are keeping a keen eye out for a potential successor who wants to deviate from the formula.

The Old Guard in Action

"If you have good food and good people, you'll make money."

Marco took pride in his fine dining restaurant that sat on the top of the hill. Marco was also super proud that his daughter, Vivian, had decided to jump into the business after spending several years in waitressing and management at other fine dining spots in the city.

Post-pandemic, the restaurant was on the brink, and so was the father-daughter relationship. Vivian had tried for years to talk to her father about making updates — to the menu, to the interior, or even the types of beer that were in the cooler. No change was welcome. After the barrage of opposing views and slow nights, Vivian had it. She confronted her father with a plan to turn the business around. Marco balked.

She left her father behind to start her own restaurant, a more casual place that focused on craft cocktails and approachable menu items. Marco's longtime customers stopped in to say hello, and her place was named one of the best new restaurants in the local paper. Six months after Vivian left, Marco posted on Facebook a message to the 2,000 or so fans of the restaurant's page that he was retiring and that the previous Saturday was the last seating.

Vivian later recounted her father telling her, "If I was going to go out, I'm happy I went out my way."

Predecessor Archetype #11: The YOLO

The YOLO (You Only Live Once) has worked hard and now it's time to take advantage. YOLOs look to cash in on their legacy of success for the organization — and successors — to continue

They need to keep rewarding me for what I did.

to support an established lifestyle. The YOLO has no plans to really get out of the business, at least as long as it is supporting the real goals or objectives the YOLO is looking to achieve.

Their Mantra: "They need to keep rewarding me for what I did."

Typical Behaviors:

- ▶ Focuses chiefly on what the business is giving them; their value is supposedly "self-evident."
- ▶ Typically holds onto equity or other power to ensure control.
- ▶ Periodically reengages with the business, sometimes with vigor, but loses interest quickly.

Potential Drivers:

- ▶ As the name implies, a YOLO mentality.
- ▶ Interest in chasing thrills and victories.

▶ Leveraging the business and success for even greater opportunities, personal and professional.

Transition Dangers:

▶ Succession focus is on ensuring the business produces what is necessary for the predecessor's lifestyle.
▶ Typically lacks investment in the development of the business.
▶ Loses focus on leading or lagging business indicators; can lose track of the business quickly.

Approach to Succession: The YOLO is rarely looking for a successor — that would mean a loss of control —— but instead wants a succeeding team that can keep the ship afloat while pursuing other interests. When critical decisions need to be made, the YOLO either is nowhere to be found or swoops in the last minute to put his or her stamp on the decision. In almost all cases, the predecessor ignores any succession development, preferring an unhealthy dynamic that keeps the predecessor in the position of explicit or emotional power.

The YOLO in Action

Sandra went from unemployed to being named CEO of the Year by a local business publication. Seeing an opening in recruiting and placement that hadn't been filled, her company had become the go-to source for talent in medical operations like nursing and physician's assistants. But growing the business took a toll on her 30-year marriage, with Sandra and her husband separating shortly after winning her leadership award and divorcing within the year after that.

Sandra had built a leadership team of Susan, Dana, and Brandon, who were seen as generational successors. Each would get a 10% raise and an increase in responsibility. While she would continue to own the business, she believed her marriage had prevented her from "really living" and would be stepping back to a more part-time role.

A few weeks after an extended vacation, with the team needing many questions answered, Sandra lost patience. "Just make the decision," she said gruffly, "these kinds of conversations need to be below my pay grade," and left.

"We felt completely abandoned," Brandon admitted. In the rare situations where the team could capture Sandra's attention, she focused entirely on how they had made — in her mind — critical errors in judgment. Sandra felt the team was making too much and her too little. "If the financial performance doesn't improve, you might not be here long."

The company's performance didn't improve. Without Sandra handing off relationships to her operating leaders, clients felt the organizational disconnect and started to walk away. Within a year, the business had lost 33% of its revenue. Two years later, the company was half its original size. Sandra sold the business shortly thereafter, for about 10% of what it would have been worth at its height. Susan, Dana, and Brandon were told of the transaction, and their one-month severance, via email — sent from the Mexican Caribbean.

Predecessor Archetype #12: The Wrecker

The Wrecker is angry. Without necessarily knowing why, but this person knows he or she worked hard and whatever the transition may be providing — be it money, platitudes, a gold watch — it's just *not enough*. Not only that, the Wrecker is also convinced of his or her essential value within the organization — and believes this needs to be proven to everyone else.

I'll show them that they can't do it without me.

Their Mantra: "I'll show them that they can't do it without me."

Typical Behaviors:

- ▶ Sabotages the transition through active or passive means.
- ▶ Creates distractions designed to prove their value.
- ▶ Withholds critical information and relationships that could help move the business forward.
- ▶ Creates disharmony in the team.

Potential Drivers:

- ▶ Wants to continue to feel needed.
- ▶ Sees others' success as a threat to his or her unique value and legacy.
- ▶ Worried that no one will be around to keep the successors in check.

Transition Dangers:

- ▶ Passively or actively working to sabotage the successor.
- ▶ Lack of willingness to communicate crucial information increases succession difficulty.
- ▶ Might create a significant "poison pill" that could be unrecoverable.

Approach to Succession: Wreckers might not have begun the transition in that role, but eventually reach the point where they feel threatened. As a result, the relationship between predecessor and successor becomes fractured, usually beyond the ability to repair it. The Wrecker will use an informational advantage to create challenges and roadblocks for the successor. If the successor gets beyond those impediments, the Wrecker creates more. If the successor fails, the Wrecker celebrates with an I-told-you-so. If the successor leaves, the Wrecker sees it as validation since the successor didn't "have what it takes." Ultimately, it is tough to succeed the Wrecker.

The Wrecker in Action

Howard was a self-described serial entrepreneur in his early 70s who had a history of betting big on flagging businesses. Seeking one last opportunity to hit the jackpot, he met Andrea, a young innovator who had used her family home as collateral to fund commercialization of her invention. $500,000 spent with nothing to show for it, Howard welcomed the opportunity to make the next loan payment —and save her home — with him as the CEO.

At the start, Howard and Andrea meshed well. Howard provided the minimal resources to keep the business afloat until they raised an additional round of capital. Andrea was grateful for having a roof over her head. Eight months later, they had successfully attracted another $500,000 from outside investors led by Bill.

As soon as the check cleared, Howard and Andrea were in conflict. Within weeks of closing, Andrea accused Howard and the investors of "stealing" her business. Andrea was also found to have purchased personal items with cash she took out using a company debit card. Howard was fed up with Andrea's immaturity and lack of business acumen, and saw his "last chance" slipping through his fingers.

The fights escalated and the business tanked. Howard began telling investors he needed cash infusions for survival. After a few of those calls, Bill decided to pay a visit. An experienced executive, he wanted to understand the challenge with his own eyes. A week after he arrived, he fired Howard as CEO.

Bill stepped into the Chief Executive role and dug into the damage Howard left behind. The most shocking was a scheme Howard devised to bankrupt the firm so he and an international investor could buy the assets and relaunch the business, with email evidence showing that Howard believed only he could grow the company. After several domestic and international legal settlements, and additional cash infusions, Bill took Andrea under his wing and set the business on a course for success.

A decade later, the company is finally achieving the financial projections that sold Bill on investing in the first place, with a savvier Andrea at the helm.

Bill summarized the situation as follows, "I can't explain exactly what Howard's motivations were. On the one hand, I feel sad for him for being so insecure, but on the other, I remain shocked that he was willing to take down the whole ship just because he wasn't getting exactly what he wanted. I'm just proud that we have turned it around and built a company that all of us can be proud of."

Predecessor Archetype #13: The Desperate

The Desperate needs to exit the role or sell the business and is fighting between two incompatible ideas: exiting as quickly as possible and getting out on one's own terms. Given the significant conflict, the Desperate tends to make a rash decision that maximizes chaos instead of one that is more well-considered.

I need to get out of here, but it has to happen my way.

Their Mantra: "I need to get out of here, but it has to happen my way."

Typical Behaviors:

▶ Makes major swings in decisions; will often change drop-dead dates (retirement, closing, etc.).
▶ Threatens to "walk out" when feeling stressed or under pressure.
▶ Has little clarity about the right next move or decision.
▶ See-saws between heading toward the exits and defensively standing firm.
▶ Holds reasons for desperation close to the vest, including significant business risks.

Potential Drivers:

▶ External stressors or emergencies driving a need to move on before ready.

▶ Feelings of guilt related to unfinished projects.

▶ A sense of internal conflict due to pressures taking precedence over "doing it right."

Transition Dangers:

▶ Transition is limited to handing off responsibility; a tag/you're-it approach.

▶ There is no certainty of how the Desperate can serve as a resource after the transition.

▶ Chaos can destabilize the organization.

Approach to Succession: Whatever time has already been spent on succession is all the time that's going to be devoted to it. Now, responsibility needs to change, and it needs to change immediately. Despite the pressures, there's a give-then-take approach that might frustrate a prospective successor. From the successor's perspective, it's bad enough to have a challenge dropped in your lap — it's worse to have it dropped and taken back, over and over.

The Desperate in Action

Shannon and Terry had owned a sizable small-town hardware store together for the prior decade. Despite the appearances of relationship strength, Terry had grown increasingly resentful of Shannon. The slow burn of frustration broke out into a raging fire when Shannon was stopped by local police for driving under the influence. Several fights and hurtful words later, Shannon and Terry decided to end their nearly 20-year relationship, agreeing to sell the business, with Terry managing it full-time and Shannon moving away to live closer to family.

Without Shannon involved, Terry knew the business would decline quickly, as it was her eye for style and product mix that kept customers on their toes. To get the most out of the business, she needed to sell and sell fast.

A mutual friend, Dale, had the resources to make a fair offer after a career in tech startups. Terry thought to consider other offers, but felt that not only would Dale be the right fit, but speed would ensure she would get the most out of the sale while setting Dale up for maximum success.

As Terry began preparing the documents, she heard rumors of changes that Dale would be making to the hardware store, many of which were reversing or eliminating hard-fought decisions that Terry made. How could she sell to someone who thinks so little of her business acumen? Dale, seeing that the value of the business was decreasing by the day, came back to Terry with a lower offer, infuriating her further.

She called Dale, accepted his lower offer, and the transaction was closed within the week. Despite the transaction, no one was satisfied: Terry felt like she had been taken advantage of, Shannon felt that Terry lost her $50,000 (feeding Shannon's narrative of Terry's inflexibility), and Dale bought a business that had lost steam during its most important three-month stretch. Dale kept the business afloat, but it took another 18 months before it reached profitability again.

The Bottom Line on Chapter 3: Walking the Predecessor's Path

TL;DR:

Wildfires are the product of conditions (how the predecessor is feeling about the transition and out of your control; grief is the framework) and sparks (behaviors largely within your control) that can cause damage to the relationship and the organization. Minimizing the chances for sparks to fly, containing the damage when they do, and repairing the relationship is key. If you're struggling to understand why predecessors behave as they do, archetypes help provide context.

The Hits:

▶ **Preventing Wildfires:** Understand how unresolved conflicts can ignite and spread through the organization like wildfires. Learn to identify and extinguish sparks before they escalate into major issues.

▶ **Navigating the Conditions:** Recognize the emotional conditions that create a fertile ground for conflict. Acknowledge the grief and loss your predecessor might be experiencing, which affects their responses.

▶ **Managing the Sparks:** Be aware of common sources of conflict (the sparks) and how they can turn into wildfires. Develop strategies to minimize and manage these sparks effectively.

▶ **Be Aware of the Archetypes:** Get to know the typical behaviors of predecessors and learn to avoid their pitfalls.

Thought-Starter Questions:

▶ How can you gain a deeper understanding of your predecessor's journey and accomplishments?

▶ What strategies can you employ to empathize with the emotional challenges faced by your predecessor?

▶ What steps can you take to build a strong relationship with your predecessor based on trust and vulnerability?

▶ How can you effectively manage and mitigate potential conflicts during the transition?

Successor Strategies for Success:

▶ Write an alternate story of the predecessor that accounts for their emotional journey as they move onto a new chapter.

▶ Create a plan to connect with the predecessor regularly in a more personal way.

▶ Write a bank of personal and professional questions that help you to learn about the predecessor and their secrets to success.

▶ Develop a "mantra" to help you manage your emotions when conflicts arise.

▶ Create a process to filter predecessor behavior through your understanding of grief and mourning.

On Deck: Some transitions involve multiple successors, and a "horse race" determines the winner. You'll learn about a variety of approaches and how this can bring out the best, or worst, in you and others.

CHAPTER 4

The Ultimate Reality Show

You're the contestant. How you define success will determine who wins.

The Reality Showification of Succession

*I **hate** Shark Tank.*[viii]

With its attractive showcase of inventive ingenuity and the opportunity to achieve rags-to-riches success, *Shark Tank* presents an intoxicating and easy-to-replicate approach where most people understand the basic ground rules. It is a shorthand for "this is a fair (and fun) process."

Like those funding spaces, the reality show genre has influenced the way predecessors want to choose their successors, too. Despite a clear, obvious, productive, and drama-minimizing path — which we'll detail in the last part of this book — there is a gravitational pull to a more sensationalized approach.

It's not all their fault, either. Corporate and advisory boards, accountants, lawyers, and consultants have all been driving organizations to address succession issues. Everyone involved feels the need to create an unbiased approach. Why not one that feels like the winner does so on merit?

Digging Deeper: Why are leaders and owners, often the most sober-minded decision-makers out there, falling into this trap?

In situations where there are limited resources and relationships involved, decision-makers are looking to create a process that feels fair to all. Consider:

---

viii. I don't actually hate the show. I hate what the show has influenced in entrepreneurial culture.

▶ Predecessors want to ensure they are properly honored by choosing a replacement worthy of the job.

▶ Successors want to feel worthy and seen as having earned the opportunity.

▶ Advisors want to feel like they've helped the exiting owner or outgoing executive make the best decision possible (and justify their value).

▶ Other stakeholders want to feel like the process will maintain organizational stability.

Unfortunately, that emotional satisfaction of fairness comes at a cost. More on that a little later.

Bottom Line: Caught in the middle, of course, is you. You're subject to the Golden Rule.[ix] The good news is that you have a choice. The bad news is that none of the options are great. Your situation will dictate the right path.

Your Choices

You've reached a fork in the road, with three options:

1. **Opt out:** See the process for what it is and decide not to participate.
2. **Challenge the process:** See the process for what it is and directly push back on the approach.
3. **Play along:** See the process for what it is and leverage it for the victory.

The choices are challenging, but it helps to know what should influence the decision. Here is a not-comprehensive list of factors to consider:

▶ The quality and strength of the relationship with the predecessor.
▶ The Wildfire risk.
▶ The peer relationships involved.

ix. There it is, again. Missed it? Check out page 3.

- The "competitors," internal and external.
- Your comfort with being uncomfortable and in conflict with others, including people for whom you may care.
- Your personal and family situation.
- Your financial situation and goals.

Knowing what to consider, let's dig into each of these choices.

Option #1: Opting Out

The lowest-effort choice is to opt-out of the game. Opting out doesn't automatically mean you're not going to be the successor; it just means you're not going to play by the rules of engagement that you've been given. There are a few different approaches to opting out:

- **Ignore the game:** You know the game is being played and you're being judged by it, and you're putting blinders on to minimize its influence on your behavior.
- **Dodge the game:** You know the game is being played and you're being judged by it, and you're avoiding the game as much as you can.
- **Remove yourself from the game:** You know the game is being played and have decided you will not be participating, independent of anyone's judgment.

While opting out is an active decision on your part, those judging your succession fitness will likely see it as as a passive one. Regardless of your reasons or intentions, opting out cedes the decision control to others. Even if you have good reasons or intentions, opting out won't land well with your predecessor.

Option #2: Challenge the Process

You've stared down the barrel of the selection process and decided that not only is it not for you, it's a bad idea. By challenging the process, you're making a high-risk/high-reward decision prioritizing what you believe to be right over the potential outcome of the decision. Most people who choose this route do it because it aligns with their values and worldview.

When you challenge the process, one of following happens:

▶ **The challenge is rejected, and you are eliminated from contention:** The predecessor decides your disinterest or concerns about the process indicate something incompatible with the role.

▶ **The challenge is rejected, and you remain a viable candidate:** The predecessor makes it clear that the process is the process, and at that point you can choose to opt-out or play the game.

▶ **The challenge is heard, and the process amended:** The predecessor understands the flaws in the approach and alters it without removing it entirely. Again, the choice is yours on how to proceed.

▶ **The challenge is accepted on the surface, a new approach emerges with seeds of doubt:** The predecessor hears the case and sees the pushback as a negative reflection on you. The approach changes, but the predecessor now doubts your ability to step in.

▶ **The challenge is accepted, and a new approach emerges:** The predecessor hears your case and realizes that the process might do more harm than good and chooses an alternate approach.

▶ **The challenge is accepted, and your willingness to challenge it is seen as a reason to choose you as the successor:** The predecessor hears your case and perceives your pushback as a sign of a willingness to take leadership and engage in productive conflict, which is enough for the predecessor to put the process to an end and choose you.

In my coaching work, I tend to recommend that successors (respectfully) challenge the process. Bringing your concerns to the predecessor is an act of courage and, in many cases, uncovers crucial data that helps you. This data might include:

- ▶ The quality of the predecessor.
- ▶ The quality of the business.
- ▶ The Wildfire risk.
- ▶ Your developmental gaps.

Option #3: Play Along

So, you're looking at the situation and you decide that the best approach is to play along, for many good reasons. You may see the process as largely performative and going through the motions is better than trying to fight it. Or, maybe, it's the right call and there are multiple candidates who could fit the mold. Regardless of the reason, you're entering a brand-new game.

Buckle up. It's time to learn the rules.

The Rules of the Game

With all this high-stakes pressure, there must be some clear ground rules, right? Not a chance.

In 1964, U.S. Supreme Court Justice Potter Stewart said, regarding pornography, "Perhaps I could never succeed in intelligibly [defining it] . . . but I know it when I see it." That's the standard by which most successors are judged. In that same spirit, predecessors tend to ask themselves three questions:

1. Does the successor understand the business? Beyond the financials or business acumen, does the successor have a grasp of how the organization operates?
2. Does the successor understand the "people" context in which the organization operates?

3. Does the successor make me feel good about stepping out of the role?

What will make the grade?

More Context: "You're having an AM/FM problem."

A colleague was recounting a coaching session with a succession candidate for a billion-dollar private firm. The CEO was providing "advice" and "recommendations" that the successor heard as, well, advice and recommendations rather than directives. The result? Conflict and perceived insubordination.

The CEO thought he was being clear without micromanaging. The successor thought he was being given the latitude to make a different decision based on his own — rather than the CEO's — analysis. The issue? The band on which each was communicating. It's the difference between AM and FM radio.

Contributor communication happens on the AM band. It's a workhorse, travels for miles, and does its job. AM communication is perfect to deliver a can't-miss message to a broad group of people.

FM requires a different antenna for its richer, more complex sound, and for traveling shorter distances. Leaders and managers communicate at this band with bigger-picture, strategic messages to the right audience at the right time.

CEOs like the above communicate on the FM band. In this case, the CEO was signaling an approved approach while providing the latitude to figure out how to apply it. While not explicitly stated, the leader implied the solution in tone, culture, and historical leadership norms. On the flip side, the successor couldn't hear all of the nuance while listening amid the static of AM radio, so all that was left were the words of the message. Getting stuck on the AM band can get in the way of the succession opportunity. Predecessors want successors who "get it."

As referenced earlier regarding Effortless Expertise (page 63), predecessors don't even know what they know, let alone know how to tell it to you. They're relying on successors to pick up on trends, read between the lines, and move in the direction they're hoping you'd head.

Even More Context: I spoke with the same CEO about the problem from his perspective.

"Ya know, I am trying to give [the successor] the rope, but also see how the executives in the organization have to make decisions. If they can't see that they need to get advice, including from me, and help set that as an organizational standard, then I don't know what else to do. Maybe they're just not the right fit."

So What?: The rules aren't written, and not all predecessors employ the same rulebook. Yet, there are trends. Here are a few common rules that predecessors will say explicitly that they use to judge:

- ► **Commitment to retain relationships:** Most predecessors built their businesses on relationships, internal and external. Those relationships are founded on trust. Predecessors expect their successors to keep those promises.

- ► **Commitment to the leadership culture:** A surprising number of predecessors rose through the ranks, or started their own businesses, after a negative interaction with a boss. Their organization, then, stood in contrast to the poor leadership experience they endured.

- ► **Commitment to the predecessor:** There's a significant trust factor involved in handing over a role. Predecessors want to know that you have their back, not just before the transition, but after. They want to know there's a legacy that will be preserved or, at minimum, their reputation won't be trashed once they walk out the door.

The Shows

Not sure what's happening? Here's a handy guide to the succession-meets-reality-show genre:

Survivor

Premise: A set of potential successors are pitted against each other through a series of unrelated tasks to show their mettle, build alliances, and ultimately claim the prize of leader of the organization. In the process, successors show the worst  of themselves, often lying and backstabbing to achieve ultimate victory.

The Great British Baking Show

Premise: The kinder, gentler version of *Survivor*, each potential successor gets a combination of known and unknown challenges to tackle among a group of other well-meaning potential successors. There's less rivalry and more of a just-happy-to-be-asked flavor to the  interactions, but winners and losers emerge just the same.

The Bachelorette

Premise: Each potential successor showcases the attributes most likely to connect with the predecessor. The predecessor emotionally engages each succession candidate in a way that allows him or her to dream of  being the next leader, though the predecessor likely already has favorites. In the end, only one is selected and the whole exercise ends in tears.

Jeopardy!

Premise: The predecessor is more interested in what the successor knows than what the successor can do to carry the business forward. The test becomes a series of pop quizzes where the ability to answer the bell on the fly becomes the most valued skill. The binary nature of right/wrong creates an obvious winner, unless there's a significant Daily-Double-like opportunity that helps one potential successor overtake the opponents.

Wipeout

Premise: Several successors tackle obstacles nearly impossible to achieve, and likely to embarrass themselves trying. With judgmental-bordering-brutal commentary, most of the mistakes the potential successors make are revisited, repeatedly, in slow-motion for maximum damaging impact.

What Would You Do?

Premise: The predecessor holds cards close to the vest and watches the behaviors of potential successors closely. Through a series of tests, some staged and some serendipitous, the predecessor decides the worthiness of the successor based on the successor's actions in a given situation.

Family Feud

Premise: While there's a captain of the team — the eventual successor — two (or more) factions vie for control of the business. In this case, the predecessor doesn't just choose a successor, but an entire succeeding team, and one that might not all be qualified for their roles.

▶ **Commitment to the business over self:** Many successors are in the running because of their excellent individual performance or success in managing some headcount. Yet, in those roles, the successor is usually fighting for resources and inspiring a few teammates. They want to see you commit to the success of the organization itself rather than your own performance or reward.

▶ **Commitment to personal integrity:** The predecessor wants to see how you're going to behave when challenged in a different way. Regardless of whether the process is right or wrong, the intent matters. If it's clear that you, as a successor, aren't behaving in an ethically aligned way, you'll likely be unfit to be seen as a successor.

Bottom Line: All games have rules. Understanding the nuances and defining what you will — and won't — do provides a huge step to ensuring you stay in the running.

The Flaws

Gamifying succession is flawed. That doesn't mean the result is flawed — the process might get to the correct decision. Yet, that decision comes at a monster cost for existing leadership, the organization, and the candidates-turned-contestants who stand at the center of the show.

The "HiPo-potamus"

The high-potential employee (HiPo) of today is what used to be called a "rising star" in career cultures past. For earlier generations, being identified as a rising star was an achievement. While rarely having any meaning on its own, rising stars in organizations typically got access to leaders, assignments, leadership programs, and promotion pathways that accelerated their career growth.

Somewhere along the line, this process went from ad hoc to something more regimented. With greater discipline came the vocabulary, and now

there are a host of names for the same phenomenon: pre-suite, rising star, emerging
leader, next leader, high potential. That
discipline also creates expectations.

Predecessors — and those supporting
the predecessor's work — assume that
the designation means a higher level of
performance. As a result, there's more visibility
to their work output. That makes sense to predecessors as it aligns with
their own stories of success.

Successors, on the other hand, assume that being selected as a HiPo
means action: an opportunity for promotion, development, visibility to
executives, or special projects. This does not make sense to predecessors
— they see the designation as enough and asking for more as entitlement.

See the tension?

As a successor, you're initially energized by the fresh, exciting opportunities your new label provides. Then, the shine wears off. Maybe there's no
imminent promotion or learning opportunity. Or perhaps you're doing
the same (or more) work, just with more scrutiny. While the designation
is nice — and might even afford a short-term aura — everything you do is
now being watched.

What's worse, the goalposts have changed. Your victories? They're
expected — it validates your designation as a HiPo. You made a mistake?
Maybe you're not cut out for the big time. That's the HiPo-potamus.

If HiPos in general have it rough, succession candidates have it even
worse. Instead of just being judged on their performance, they're ana-
lyzed from every angle. While that's true for leadership in general, the
default assumption is that the successor can't cut it. It's guilty until
proven innocent.

Bottom Line: Don't get weighed down by the labels and expectations.

Win The Wrong Thing

The decision error that leads a predecessor to gamify succession is usually based on a belief that it reveals the successor's capability. The competition either elevates performance or the person wilts under pressure. That's a decision error for three reasons:

▶ **The competition is usually won by the person who likes to compete:** If you ask 100 predecessors if competitiveness is a good characteristic in a successor, 99 would say yes. However, it won't take long for most to qualify the statement, usually talking about making sure it's "healthy competition."

There's a difference between firm competitiveness (e.g. "we're going to win in the market") and individual competitiveness (e.g. "I'm going to get this role and you're not.") The first is a good thing for most organizational cultures, the latter, not so much.

▶ **The skill to win the competition might not align with the skill to lead the organization:** The Halo Effect[x] represents a decision bias stating that because someone is good at one thing, they're likely to be better than average at other things. When there's a competition for the top role, predecessors feel better that the winner "earned" it, even if the process showcased none of the skillset that the successor will need to do the job.

▶ **Winning might create a false sense of competence:** Winning the competition isn't the same thing as winning at doing the job. Your selection as the successor can feel like a false sense of security that you'll be successful in the role.[xi] That overconfidence can lead to all sorts of decision biases that will

---

x. A little more about the Halo Effect here: https://en.wikipedia.org/wiki/Halo_effect
xi. You'll see more about how that plays out in Chapter 5.

end up showing that, despite the use of a process, you were ill-equipped.

Bottom Line: The competition might put a salve on the worry that the successor isn't the right fit or didn't earn the role. While it might make the predecessor feel better, it's rarely the best approach to choosing a successor.

The Aftermath

The choice is made and, like the white smoke billowing from a chimney visible from St. Peter's Square, a new successor is chosen. While this should be a time for celebration and excitement in the organization, the process has created its own messes. Instead of catapulting the successor forward, this person needs to look backward, address whatever problems the gamification created, and, only then, be able to chart a future course for the organization credibly.

What types of messes get left behind?

Will the Real Slim Shady Please Stand Up?

You won the role. Congratulations. Which you shows up? Is it the you that won the succession process? Or is it the real you who wants to lead in a completely different way? Will the difference between the two be a natural progression or whiplash?

The nightmare scenario for a predecessor is picking the wrong successor. That might be you, especially if you approached the selection deceptively. It happens more than you think. Consider these cases:

▶ A CEO of a small bank hires a fast-talking former consultant COO who was inspired to lead massive change in the organization. The CEO, wanting to make good on his long-leash promise, lets the COO make significant decisions. Two years later, now unprofitable (for the first time in history) and carrying 40% more overhead, the CEO is left negotiating a severance and starting unprecedented layoffs instead of taking a retirement victory lap.

▶ The owner of a privately held professional services firm had doubled the business, and hired and groomed a VP of Operations who instituted changes seen as the antithesis of not just what made the company successful in the past, but what current customers expected. The VP was fired, and the owner restructured the entire organization with a new leadership team he's proud to field.

▶ The Chair and CEO of a large, closely held company had a three-horse race, but none finished the race. So, the predecessor picked the horse that got the farthest. A year later, the board fired the new CEO, the Chair stepped down to a board seat, and the company spent massive time, money, and energy finding a new CEO more comfortable with a turnaround than keeping things moving.

Sure, there's a chance that it's just a bad fit. More than likely, however, both parties were guilty of looking past concerns.

Teams

With multiple potential successors, people inevitably pick sides. Some prefer one leader's style versus the other and, in the structure of competition, the preferences become tribes that battle each other instead of other players in the marketplace. Once the dust settles, there's a winner. And one or more losers.

Succession is rarely a you'll-get-'em-next-year sport. The losers — and their tribes — are not at the top of the pecking order. It's exceptionally challenging to unwind this dynamic in the best of cases, even worse when there's family involved.

Play Like You Practice

There's a sports adage that you play like you practice. While most organizations would like their leaders to be aggressive, competitive, and work hard to win, those skills should be directed externally. Yet, the game has forced successors to spend their most crucial development time competing internally against colleagues and peers. This creates four challenges:

1. It's easy for the successor to assume that what made them the choice is the same as what is needed to lead the organization.
2. It prevents successors from learning and applying the leadership skills they need to be credible in the role.
3. Some of their weaknesses have been unhelpfully exposed in pursuit of the goal.
4. The successor is seen as self-driven.

Predecessors have taught successors the wrong lesson.

Can't Unring the Bell

The competition happened. While it requires everyone to move forward, forgive-and-forget is a pipe dream. Coming out of the competition, a few realities emerge:

1. Participants lick their wounds from a hard-fought victory instead of starting the new role with a full head of steam.
2. Anything that happened in pursuit of the role has been mentally filed among those who watched the situation happen.

No matter how savvy the successor is, there will be actions they must answer for, and those questions will linger for a long time.

The End is the Beginning

Congrats to you — you've put out the wildfires, weathered the storm, and are ready to step into the new role.

Smooth sailing now, right?

Hardly. Now we turn the focus on you — where you're likely to stumble, and how to improve.

The Bottom Line on Chapter 4: The Ultimate Reality Show

TL;DR:

The reality show format has infiltrated succession planning, turning a critical organizational process into a dramatic spectacle. At its worst, successors are pitted against each other in various "shows," each with its own set of rules and challenges. We explore the absurdities and pitfalls of treating succession like a reality show, highlighting the emotional and organizational costs. By understanding these dynamics, you can navigate the process more effectively and keep your integrity intact.

The Hits:

▶ **Recognize the Spectacle:** Understand how succession can be turned into a dramatic, competitive spectacle.

▶ **Emotional Rollercoaster:** Acknowledge the significant emotional toll the competitive nature of succession can take on participants.

▶ **Organizational Impact:** Be aware of how these reality show dynamics can disrupt team cohesion and create internal divisions.

▶ **Stick to Your Guns:** Learn the importance of keeping personal integrity amidst a process that may reward strategic gameplay over genuine leadership.

▶ **Prepare for the Unexpected:** Develop strategies to handle staged scenarios and unexpected challenges that test your capabilities in unforeseen ways.

Thought-Starter Questions:

▶ How can you navigate the competitive aspects of succession without compromising your values?

▶ How will you handle the emotional highs and lows that come with the process?

▶ What can you do to ensure you are evaluated on your true capabilities rather than just your ability to play the game?

▶ How can you prepare for and mitigate the impact of staged tests and unexpected challenges?

Successor Strategies for Success:

▶ Regularly engage with mentors and peers to gain insights and support during the succession process.

▶ Define your values and know when to speak truth to power.

▶ Create a personal plan to handle stress and support your mental well-being during the competition.

▶ Identify tools that help you to see the big picture when it would be easy to fall into a myopic focus on winning.

On Deck:

There are traps all around that can wreck you before, during, and after the transition. Learn about the eight types of quicksand that can slow you down or completely prevent you from reaching your goals.

CHAPTER 5

The Quicksand Survival Guide

You've got blind spots. Don't let them prevent you from winning.

Where's Quicksand?

Think back to your childhood. Do you remember how big of a threat quicksand was supposed to be?

It was a cinematic trope: Our overconfident hero wanders around a place with dirt or sand. At an inopportune moment, our protagonist unexpectedly — and unrealistically — sunk into the ground. And if they moved, heaven forbid, they sunk faster. Thankfully, our main character is saved in the nick of time, often aided by a friend and some nearby opportunistic lifeline.

Why It Matters: A speaker asked the audience, "What did it feel like to make a mistake?" The answers were what you might expect: "I felt stupid," "I was mad at myself," "I couldn't believe I had made such a bad decision." After a half-dozen or so answers, he stopped the group and challenged their responses. "That's how you felt once you knew the decision was wrong. When actually making the decision, it felt right."

Quicksand is a lot like that. While not the clear-and-present real-world danger we expected, the metaphorical hazard it presents to successors is significant.

Quicksand is deceptive — it looks like solid ground, so much so that you don't even think twice about stepping on it. Fortunately, unlike the one-and-done fatalities caused by landmines and pitfalls — two other common business buzzwords used to describe unseen dangers — quicksand is survivable. To make it through, you need to stay calm, be intentional with your movement, and rely on a helping hand.

Even More Context: We've been talking about sparks, now quicksand. What's the difference?

Sparks are the product of interactions between the successor and predecessor in the pursuit of transition. They're limited to your relationship and its impact on the business.

Quicksand is the product of your individual professional maturity and development gaps, and these traps exist independent of your succession opportunity. Regardless of whether the predecessor is bothered by them or not, they still pose a risk to your ability to be successful in your role.

Digging Deeper: To this point, we've aimed the cannons at Boomer and Xer predecessors. We've been explaining the emotional underpinnings for the thoughts and behaviors of these exiting owners and outgoing executives.

From here forward, we are digging into what you can do — and avoid — as you step into the predecessor's role.

Being a successor is a tough job. Yet only part of it is about managing the predecessor. The rest involves being competent in the role you're stepping into. That means more than just doing excellent work.

Years ago, Buddy Hobart, the founder of Solutions 21 (and writer of the Foreword), researched World-Class Performers, individuals who reached the pinnacle of their fields and stayed there. He discovered nine behaviors that drive their success:

1. They seek performance feedback or "game film."
2. They turn unconscious tendencies and habits into positive choices.
3. They manage their energy.
4. They realize that steps to improvement might be counterintuitive.
5. They develop a clear vision.
6. They seek coaching and mentorship.

7. They develop measurable action plans.
8. They move beyond losses and failures quickly.
9. They use positive self-talk effectively.

If you notice, none of those nine is "being good at what you do." That's a given — technical skill is the minimum requirement as the ticket to get in the door. The nine behaviors he uncovered are people skills, and they're mandatory if you want to take over from someone who had been there, did that, and did it well.

The Bottom Line: Whether you decide to step into someone else's shoes or start your own lemonade stand, quicksand can impact your ability to be successful if you don't dodge it. Let's look at eight examples of succession quicksand.

Quicksand #1: Pandas

Most research is about the winners. It focuses on the things that powered the subject's success. Sometimes the best insights come from those who didn't quite make the grade. That's where Pandas come into play.

Background: The metaphor comes from *The CEO Next Door*. The authors interviewed boards about the CEO candidates who were *almost* hired, but *something* about them fell short. Sometimes the gap was tangible, but usually it was "more of a feeling." Despite stellar track records and consistent performance, the candidates were . . . just not quite good enough.

Why choose "Pandas" as the metaphor? Because they're cute and cuddly, but their bite is ferocious — and deadly — much like the tendencies that can derail a career.

Going Deeper: When the chips fell, a vast majority (93%[xii]) of the reasons a candidate wasn't chosen was because of one (or more) of three things:

- ▶ Communication skills.
- ▶ Peer relationships.
- ▶ Executive presence.

The first two are intuitive. Most folks can grasp the need to be a better communicator or to build better relationships. What the heck is "executive presence?" It's the "Can I see this person leading our company?" test. And the reasons for "no" are plentiful, from how someone dresses to — as cited by the authors — body odor.

The worst part about Pandas? They're solvable, coachable problems. So, why don't they get solved? The first two reasons are leadership/management issues, which boil down to either:

1. Leaders and managers don't have the guts to address the issue directly, or
2. The organization over-values an individual's performance in the role they play, so much so that improvement and career progression might complicate leaders' lives.

The first is bad because it lacks courage, while the second is selfish.

The third reason?

3. You don't take feedback well.

You probably get defensive or dismiss it outright. Maybe you rationalize it away with, "That's the way I am," or "I made it this far, didn't I?"

That's the worst Panda of all. And it's in your control.

---

xii. For those who need to know the last 7% — excessive optimism and perfectionism. Not great, but small potatoes in comparison.

Pandas in Action

We were coaching a successor for a job that he considered to be the role of a lifetime and was sure he was going to get. His fifteen years at the company and unmatched technical skill made him a perfect follow-up to the executive who was planning to leave in the next few years. He carried himself with the confidence of someone who already had the job and was just waiting in the wings for the transition.

There was a barrier: His boss didn't think it was a good fit. Despite five-star performance reviews and max raises, the successor had significant professional maturity gaps. His boss laid this out to me in an update discussion about the candidate. I asked if he had provided this feedback to the employee. "I mean, I've joked about it enough with him that he should be picking up on the hint."

In other words, no. After confirming that he wanted the job, and thought he would get it, we challenged him with the following scenario.

"Let's fast-forward a few years. Your boss is gone but, instead of hiring you, they filled the role with an outside candidate. In addition to being disappointed about not getting a role you were sure was yours, you couldn't believe how bad your new boss is. The new leader shows up a little late and leaves a little early most days. Their office is disheveled, disorganized, and they struggle to find things. They get back to you at the last possible moment. They dress without consideration for professionalism. And they don't seem to hear feedback. How would you like to report to that person?"

The successor immediately jumped to what a horrible hire it would be and how much he would hate reporting to that boss. He said, "That hire would be the worst-case scenario." After letting him talk through his thoughts, we hit him with the punchline. "We were describing you."

Years later, we received an email from the successor with a link to the local online business newspaper announcing his promotion to the coveted role. "Thank you for having the courage to tell me the truth. You're the reason this happened." ▶

Going Even Deeper: The core self-deception that holds most rising executives back is their belief that they can achieve their goals on mostly their technical skills. To quote an individual I coached whose career stagnated, "I want to be so good at what I do that how I do it doesn't matter."

Good luck.

If you think more deeply about those three things — communication, peer relationships, and executive presence — each quality is ultimately about others rather than yourself.

One Last Thing: One executive presence killer? Relying on your relationships or reputation.

As the successor, you've got to prove your capability and show the predecessor, and the rest of the team, how you would behave in the role. Taking liberties just because you know the team will only serve to reduce their confidence in your ability to lead.

Bottom Line: Being good at what you do is the ticket to get in the door. It's not unusual or differentiating. What separates is the people stuff — communication skills, peer relationships, and executive presence. If you're not working hard on those three, you might get mauled.

Quicksand #2: Student Driver

I once knew a woman who liked to obey traffic laws to a degree that would drive her family and other drivers bananas. Tired of the hassle of her daily jaunts filled with irate drivers, loud horns, and inappropriate hand gestures, she devised a solution that made other motorists cut her some slack.

She put a "Student Driver" bumper sticker on her car. The result? Fewer honks, more kind waves, and a less stressful ride to the grocery store.

Why It Matters: As a student driver, people give you grace for your inexperience. As a successor, you're given a little runway. You hear it all the time from their colleagues: The successor is still "getting her feet wet," "learning the ropes," "making her own way," "getting used to the chair," and a hundred other ways of dismissing early missteps as inexperience. Those are all versions of the "Student Driver" bumper sticker.

The problem? The label makes it harder to distinguish inexperienced mistakes from true performance problems. Since it's a ready reason — and one out of everyone's control — it allows for all involved to look the other way even if the issue should be dealt with head-on.

Digging Deeper: There's nuance to the Student Driver. Instead of a binary, there are quadrants. It looks like this:

Figure 5.1
Using the "Student Driver" Label

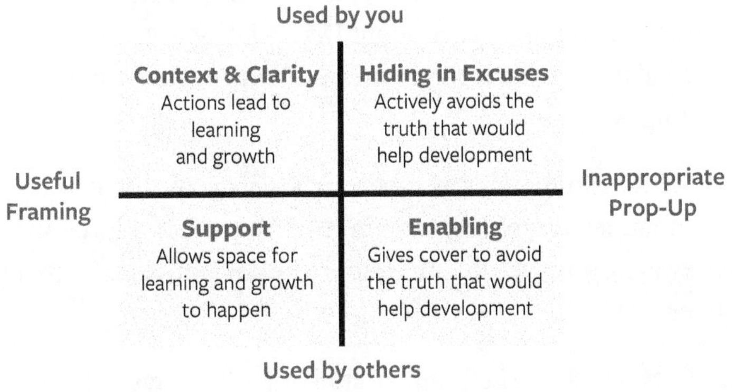

Used by you

	Context & Clarity Actions lead to learning and growth	**Hiding in Excuses** Actively avoids the truth that would help development	
Useful Framing			Inappropriate Prop-Up
	Support Allows space for learning and growth to happen	**Enabling** Gives cover to avoid the truth that would help development	

Used by others

Here's the breakdown:

1. **Context & clarity:** The Student Driver lets you ask questions that would otherwise be inappropriate or culturally dangerous. It allows you to leverage your need for more awareness to get more information and insight.

2. **Support:** The bumper sticker serves as a hint to your team that you could use additional information that your predecessor might have known through experience. It enables everyone to consider the ways they can help you to be a better leader.

3. **Hiding in excuses:** At its worst, the Student Driver becomes a crutch to explain poor performance. Instead of getting better, those who rely on the bumper sticker continue to blame their lack of experience even when asking better questions, learning more, or working harder could help.

4. **Enabling:** Teams that allow the successor to use the bumper sticker as a crutch enable you to do your worst. As a successor, it's easy to fall into a trap of allowing yourself to be enabled by those around you.

Sometimes it's good to have the bumper sticker. It helps people understand that you might need more context or clarity, or that you might not know the right answer. Being a Student Driver lets you exercise your judgment while having others around you who can provide crucial guidance for those things you can't see.

At its worst, the Student Driver becomes an excuse. Everyone in the organization agrees there's a problem, but instead of addressing it, it's explained away. Employees compliment the fashion sense of the stark naked leader.

A Little More Detail: The bumper sticker isn't always put on there by you. Sure, you might do it to avoid accountability or scrutiny. Others might do it, too. Here are the sources:

▶ **Your predecessor/other influential leaders:** They put it there as a form of bubble wrap to give you the flexibility to fail without significant consequence.

▶ **Peers:** Other executive leaders might put it there to protect you or to justify your mistakes in a kind and gracious way.

The Student Driver in Action

A large, family-owned distribution company had been working on its succession plan for the past five years. Handing off to the third generation, the middle son, Drew, had shown the most interest in stepping into the president's seat.

Drew, for his part, had earned the right to take on the role. He worked in the business for the past 10 years out of college, learning most of the roles across the enterprise. Five years before the transition, he started working more closely with his father, learning the ropes at the leadership level, and two years prior, he was put into a COO-like role as his dad progressively stepped away.

The first quarterly board meeting was a little uneven, which the group dismissed as first-time jitters — even if he had attended board meetings for years. His second was similarly badly received. After the third, which did not go well, his father and another board member met with Drew.

Drew felt he had just stepped into the job, while the board felt Drew had been given all the runway he needed. At the conclusion of the meeting, Drew's dad asked his board member, "Did we make a mistake with Drew?"

In hindsight, Drew said, "At the root of it, I was really scared. I had been so used to hiding behind my dad or our board, which is just a group of family friends, that I didn't know what to do when I was the one making the decisions."

Drew asked his father for authorization to hire an executive coach. "That was the turning point," Drew said. "The annual meeting went better than the prior three, and that gave me enough momentum to realize that I needed to step up in a different way." Since that first year, Drew's company has exceeded its growth targets. "I needed to take ownership for the results and realize I couldn't do it all on my own." ▶

- ▶ **The employees:** Employees of the organization might give you the sticker to insulate you while attempting to explain away challenges or frustrations they face as a result of your decisions.
- ▶ **Outside stakeholders:** For protection, sure, but these situations can be to signal to other stakeholders that the business is unstable due to your leadership.

Bottom Line: Careful with how, and how long, you embrace the Student Driver sticker. Once it's no longer useful, be sure to toss it aside.

Quicksand #3: Measuring the Drapes

In 1940, while Ohio Senator Robert Taft was pursuing the nomination for president of the United States, his wife, Martha, gave an interview expressing that her husband would be winning the White House and that she already had plans for the building's window decor. Given that Taft was never nominated by his party, let alone on the general election ballot, the idea of "measuring the drapes" became a sign of overconfidence or premature assumption of victory.

Sometimes, a predecessor assumes that the successor is measuring the drapes, creating sparks. At others? The successor has a tape measure in-hand.

Digging Deeper: The succession process is rarely smooth, and by the time the transition happens, everyone is sick of it. So much has gone into the handoff that regardless of how anyone feels about the transition itself, they're excited to see the process end.

Measuring the drapes assumes that you're aware of the measuring. So, why would you do it? A few reasons a successor might start:

- ▶ The predecessor has a reputation for being a roadblock to progress and the successor takes a the-sooner-the-better approach.

▶ The predecessor is not holding up his or her end of the bargain in the transition, and the successor is growing impatient.

▶ The successor believes it is "my time" and wants to get the predecessor out of the way.

▶ The successor believes the predecessor to be a danger to the organization.

Measuring the drapes is always a risk. The extent to which it is a risk is function of: 1) the Wildfire conditions, 2) the Golden Rule, and 3) the relationship between the successor and predecessor.

Why is it a risk? It's insulting. If you're doing it, you're a jerk. Measuring the drapes says more about you as a successor than it does about the predecessor.

Some Examples: Measuring the drapes is a metaphor. What are the ways you might be leaving this impression?

▶ Talking behind the predecessor's back and telling people of planned changes of which the predecessor would disapprove.

▶ Unnecessarily or prematurely changing the trajectory, or killing outright, a project that was near and dear to the predecessor.

▶ Stepping in to make key business decisions that would still be in the predecessor's sphere of influence, without consultation.

▶ Making changes to organizational symbols that the predecessor believes to be cornerstones to the culture.

Each of these examples is an overt attempt at showing up the predecessor and his or her wishes. It's a bad move and shows the successor to be petty and, in some cases, unworthy of the role about to be assumed.

Bottom Line: Measuring the drapes might feel good in the moment. It may feel like progress, or you want to send a message to the predecessor. Don't do it. It says more bad about you than about them.

Measuring the Drapes in Action

David had served as president of a name-brand university for the last two decades, greatly expanding the campus and its programs, and growing the school's endowment. His legacy at the school was iron-clad and well-earned after a nearly 35 years at the institution.

Seven years before he would retire, David identified Wendy as his likely heir apparent. He worked intensely with Wendy for the next five years, closely mentoring her as she took on greater forward-facing roles. She responded, following his direction throughout.

About a year before the transition, David started to catch wind that Wendy was unimpressed with a few of David's decisions and would be making changes on day one. "By the time I was a few months away, I couldn't wait to get out of there," he said. David and Wendy's relationship had soured, and while they were cordial, the days of mentor-mentee were gone. While David was hoping to enjoy closing out a career on his terms, Wendy was making it clear that she was just waiting for him to walk out the door.

Two weeks before David was to retire, during a meeting in his office with presidents from other local universities, two members of the campus facilities staff entered with ladders and tape measurers. David, annoyed, asked why. "Wendy asked us to measure the windows and the office for new furniture," the head of facilities responded, sheepishly. "I was mortified," David said painfully.

Wendy's tenure was complicated. While she had some wins, she made significant changes that angered alums. Looking back, David wasn't sure what he missed. "It pains me to know that I got it so wrong," David said, referring to Wendy's relatively short tenure at the university. "I thought she could temper her instincts to run over others, but I guess she felt I was in the way, too." ▶

Quicksand #4: Imposter vs. Incumbent

Much ink — and screen space — has been spent discussing imposter syndrome. A lot of people experience it. A study in the 1980s[44] showed that 70% of people experience it at some point in their lives. A few examples:

▶ The 41st US president, George H.W. Bush, fretted that history views his legacy as an "empty deck of cards."[45] The man had a long and impactful career in the CIA and in politics.

▶ Brahms, the legendary composer, wrote in a letter to a friend, "I shall never write a symphony! You can't have any idea what it's like to hear such a giant marching behind you." This giant was Beethoven, with his legendary shadow hovering over the composer, fueling his fear of not measuring up. It ultimately took 20 years for Brahms to write his first symphony and share it with the public in 1876.

▶ Maya Angelou, poet and Nobel laureate, said, "The exaggerated esteem in which my lifework is held makes me very ill at ease. I feel compelled to think of myself as an involuntary swindler. I have written 11 books, but each time I think, 'Uh-oh, they're going to find out now."

There are two problems with this.

1. It's not about being an "imposter," which is an intentional act to defraud others.
2. It's not a syndrome.[xiii]

---

xiii. Actual imposter syndrome, as defined by the American Psychiatry Association, is "a personality pattern characterized by pathological lying, which takes the form of fabricating an identity or a series of identities in an effort to gain recognition and status." If that's you, this book can't help.

Originally called "imposter phenomenon" and sometimes referred to as "imposter thoughts," we're talking about, as defined by the APA,[46] "the situation in which highly accomplished, successful individuals paradoxically believe they are frauds who ultimately will fail and be unmasked as incompetent." Pauline Clance, a researcher into the concept, identified six behaviors that can indicate imposterism:

▶ The impostor cycle (the loop of Fear > Work > Result > Praise).
▶ The need to be special or the best.
▶ Characteristics of superman/superwoman.
▶ Fear of failure.
▶ Denial of ability and discounting praise.
▶ Feeling fear and guilt about success.

Pick two of the above, and you are likely to fall into imposter thoughts. Additionally, imposter thoughts correlate with generalized anxiety, depression, and lowered self-esteem and self-confidence.

Here's a crazy question — Is being an "imposter whatever-you-want-to -call-it" a bad thing? Basima A. Tewfik, assistant professor at MIT Sloan,[47] dug into the idea and learned the following about imposter thoughts:

▶ They can be indistinguishable from being spooked about screwing up.
▶ They can make us more other-oriented.
▶ They have no measurable negative impact on performance and, in some cases, the higher emotional intelligence "spidey-senses" increase performance.

Her research also showed that people who are feeling imposter syndrome are often starting something new where they've been untested.

(Record screech)

Remember back when we talked about the spark of Effortless Expertise on page 63/64? In the four-phase learning model, Agonizing Awareness is the most challenging and stressful. It's the only stage where you are conscious of being incapable. It feels like crap.

Like predecessors, who have never handed off their life's work before, the same goes for successors. You're new to this. It's anxiety-producing. So, where's the quicksand?

Digging Deeper: There are two. First, there are mental health costs to imposterism. That can't be understated. Second, there tend to be three different counterproductive responses to the anxiety of imposterism:

- ▶ **Insecurity:** Insecurity tends to lead to behaviors that make leadership harder, like second-guessing and validation-seeking. Your leadership brand takes a major hit as people perceive you to be unprepared and outgunned.

- ▶ **Steel-jawed persistence:** Steadfastness means you're ignoring the signals that imposterism sends, and you're filtering out information that might be helpful to your approach. Your leadership brand is that you're a leader who's out of touch, lacking self-awareness, and unwilling to take feedback.

- ▶ **Overcompensation:** Instead of holding back or making yourself small, you're doing everything you can to make yourself big. Every idea is yours. You seek more power and control. Your leadership brand is that of a bully who wants to make everything about you.

The Twist: The interesting thing about imposterism is that, in one way, every successor is an imposter. To quote my colleague[xiv]: Everyone is an imposter until they're the incumbent.

Following the four-phase learning model, we start out clueless and work our way through the process until it becomes automatic. Part of the illusion of incumbency is that it's easy to believe the incumbent has always

---

xiv. Hat tip to Jason Davis.

Imposter vs. Incumbent in Action

"He's extremely anxious about taking this role and seems to be explaining reasons for his failure before getting started."

That was an assessment of Jeff, a candidate I coached who had been newly elevated into a supervisor role, running a $100 million job for a general contracting client. He had taken over for another supervisor who was very well regarded and, as a result, recently promoted to executive leadership. We had just started working together when he got the promotion, and he was terrified.

"I just know I'm going to miss something," Jeff said nervously in our first coaching session. "I'm so used to knowing every detail and now I have to rely on a team of people I don't even know. Everyone keeps telling me how Jerry did things and I keep thinking, 'There's no way I'm going to get there.'"

Six months later, Jeff had stabilized and, except for a few inevitable bumps in the road, had carefully led the team and the owner of the job through several challenges that required advanced skill. He had successfully commanded the room, built trust, and had the confidence of the executives of his company. There wasn't a rookie mistake to be found.

A year into us working together, and Jeff was on the doorstep of another promotion. When I asked about what he thought, he responded in a way that caught me off guard. "I'm not sure I can take on that role. I always knew I could make this one happen; I never had a doubt. That role? That seems way outside of my skillset."

I went back to my notes and shared my assessment from our very first meeting together. He was floored.

"Really? That was me? Gosh, maybe I am blowing this out of proportion."

He ended up taking that promotion. A year later, the CEO shared this assessment of Jeff: "He is the best addition to our leadership team in years." ▶

been competent. A conflict between predecessor and successor tends to be the approach to imposterism.

At some earlier point, the predecessor needed to overcome the discomfort of not knowing how to survive in the role. For the successor, overcoming it means achieving a high level of performance. The sense of urgency is as different as the top and bottom of Maslow's hierarchy.[xv]

> *Everyone is an imposter until they're the incumbent.*

Bottom Line: Whatever you want to call it, the anxiety of feeling like an underperformer can torpedo your succession efforts.

Quicksand #5: 1,000 Jumps

Skydiving is a rush. Even though it feels dangerous, it is incredibly safe and getting safer, with fewer than one in 100,000 jumps resulting in a fatality.[48] Deaths involving tandem skydivers,[xvi] the most common bucket-list version of skydiving, are basically non-existent.

So, who is most likely to die? The semi-experienced skydiver.

A vast majority of deaths involve jumpers with about 1,000 jumps. Why? The U.S. Parachute Association says, "Experience should be a real advantage in facing the challenges of skydiving, but overconfidence and complacency are killers."[49] How do you get to overconfidence and complacency? Two ways.

---

xv. We talk about Maslow's Hierarchy on page 60.
xvi. In this form of skydiving, you're strapped to a professional with thousands of jumps and hope like heck they know what they're doing.

1,000 Jumps in Action

Two partners started a high-end wealth management practice fifteen years after successful early careers in finance at some of the most impressive institutions in the country. Deciding they wanted to move home and have more control over their lives, they built a practice exclusively for high-net-worth individuals.

Within a few years, they realized that they needed help and hired a young gun from a name-brand firm. While they loved Jillian's tenacity, they saw her as a me-first person in an organization that was all about the client.

Over time the practice grew to a dozen, and two others — one in operations and an analyst — emerged as peers to Jillian. The three became the de facto administrators of the organization as the two founders started considering what to do with themselves — retire? a second act? — and the business.

Early coaching with Jillian proved fruitless. Despite an admitted gap in her leadership resume — she had only managed two people in her entire career, both within the previous two years — she was fully confident that her nearly two decades in the business were enough for her to take over as the leading executive. Any attempt to uncover a leadership or management weakness resulted in a counterproductive, defensive posture.

Things came to a head when Jillian demanded an equity arrangement with the founders. And if they didn't budge? She had two offers from high-paying organizations that would love her client management skill (and maybe even some of her book of business).

The gambit worked, at least for the short-term. Jillian got what she wanted, a phantom stock agreement, but it came with a caveat. Jillian was given twelve months to fully vest under two conditions: 1) she led the company to a couple of specific metrics; and 2) the two other peers would receive phantom stock. But only Jillian's was contingent on her convincing the other two that she could be CEO.

Jillian's overconfidence came back to bite her. It took only six months into the agreement for her to realize that she wasn't cut out to be the company's CEO. Not only did that close the door on her opportunity to grow within the business, but it forced the founders to eliminate a sale to internal buyers as a succession option.

"We realized that, as much as Jillian wanted to run the show, she couldn't," one of the founders said. "We're only sad that she and the rest of the team won't have the opportunities we had."

The business sold to a strategic buyer a year later. All three peers are now employed by that firm. ▶

- ▶ Mistaking Uninformed Ineptitude for Effortless Expertise (check out page 200 if it's not ringing a bell).
- ▶ Cognitive biases such as illusory superiority, also known as the Dunning-Kruger Effect, an oft-validated cognitive bias stating that[50]:
  - › Incompetent people overestimate their abilities.
  - › Incompetent people can't accurately estimate others' competence.
  - › High performers underestimate their skills.

Why It Matters: Most successors are metaphorically at around the 1,000-jump mark.

You've been working long enough to see the business through a few cycles. You know how things work and, if you're honest with yourself, it's coming pretty easily. You might even be looking at leaders around you thinking, "Has doing this really been that hard?"

Skydivers rarely die because the wind was smooth, the sky was clear, and everything went as expected. They perish because they either: a) encounter an unexpected emergency; or b) try something more complicated than their skill allows. They were less competent than they expected.

- ▶ Organizations encounter crises. A key member of the team leaves. The economic conditions change. A technology solution threatens the existing model. There's a global pandemic.

- ▶ New leaders can get hubristic. They make widespread changes. They overturn what's worked in the past. They make investments and take risks that might rub against a more conservative approach.

Bottom Line: The best successors — and leaders — remain vigilant against their assumptions and biases.

Quicksand #6: Brubeck vs. Bach

Dave Brubeck was one of the greatest jazz artists, combining unusual rhythms and time signatures to create some of the most influential jazz standards. (Google "Take Five" when you get a chance). It's hard to argue with his success. He appeared on the cover of Time in 1954 and released the album *Time Out* in 1959. Despite critics hating the album, it quickly went Gold and eventually was certified Double Platinum. Dave Brubeck couldn't write or read music.

In contrast stands Johann Sebastian Bach, the 18th-century German composer known for his technically sound orchestral music. His works are played by symphonies worldwide to this day, and several of his compositions, such as Toccata and Fugue in D Minor — the creepy intro to many a B-level horror flick — remain in the pop culture lexicon.

One musician, Brubeck, couldn't read music if he tried. The other, Bach, was as technically skilled as they come. Both were successful musicians who made a wide cultural impact. Their approaches were opposites.

Why It Matters: Most successful predecessors, especially founders, are jazz musicians. They don't write things down and they improvise on the fly. They create organized chaos around them, yet they're exceptionally good at what they do. Experience, street smarts, EQ, IQ, whatever it is — they leverage it for commercial success.

Other leaders are Juilliard-trained and technically perfect.[xvii] They create exact processes to ensure the organization runs smoothly every time. They are rigid, sure, but the quality is consistent and people know what to expect. The most common challenge? When the transition goes from a Brubeck to a Bach.

Digging Deeper: These transitions tend to happen in steps:

1. Predecessors want to step away and takes a successor under their wing. The outgoing executives attempt to teach everything they know.
2. Successors, while appreciating the perspective, see ample opportunities for improvement once the predecessor leaves. Successors believe improvisation exhausts the team and makes it harder to replicate success.
3. Once the predecessor leaves, the successor executes a strategy to "rationalize" and add process to what the predecessor built.
4. Chaos (most of the time).

Since the successor doesn't know — or fully grasp — what made the company successful, employees and customers alike start to feel a disconnect. They hear the music, but it no longer has soul.

Digging Even Deeper: Successors face a few dangers in transition that are a Brubeck-Bach problem. These are:

▶ **Culture gaps**: Successors don't completely understand or respect the culture driven by the predecessor.

---

xvii. The Juilliard School, one of the most famous music schools in the world, was founded in 1905. It's widely known as a classical music program, admitting 150 undergraduates annually. In 2001, Juilliard founded a jazz program that accepts between just seven and nine students each year. This comparison relies on Juilliard's historical reputation. Read it for yourself at https://www.juilliard.edu.

- ▶ **Misunderstanding the business:** Successors might not understand how the organization creates value, which happens three ways[xviii]:
  - › **Operational Excellence:** You make it so well, everyone buys from you.
  - › **Product Leadership:** You're the only one who makes it.
  - › **Customer Intimacy:** You know the client so well, you're hard to replace.
- ▶ **Silver hair bias:** Whether blamed on technology, or social change, or other modern movements, successors tend to assume the predecessor is out of touch.
- ▶ **Arrogance:** Said simply, some successors think they know better.

The Big Picture: In this model, there are two types of organizations:

Figure 5.2
Brubeck vs. Bach at a Glance

Situation	Brubeck	Bach
Success defined as	Sales and revenue	Operating at operations-defined capacity
What we do best to create value	Be flexible	Be predictable
Growth constraint	Revenue brought in	Comfortable operational boundaries
Sales success achieved by	Improvisation, relationships, and connection to specific client need	Being trusted to do the same thing every time
Rules are	Guiderails that might need to be rewritten	Sacrosanct
Stress is placed on	Operations to meet or exceed client expectations	Sales to achieve revenue targets to support operational comfort
Heroes are	Everybody: Sales celebrated for the deal and operations celebrated for stretching to make it happen	Operations for executing as expected

---

xviii. We'll discuss the Value Disciplines Model later on page 164.

Brubeck vs. Bach in Action

James, the founder of a successful business, was looking at retirement after 25 years. Coming from a flourishing sales background, he wanted to be super intentional with his transition. His hand-picked successor was a pedigreed operational maven, Candice, who he brought in specifically to hand over the reins.

The succession plan was a three-year effort, and James did everything he could to ensure the successor would be set up to do well. The 50-plus employees respected what Candice brought to the organization and saw the writing on the wall as she was elevated from VP to COO. The announcement of Candice as president was received warmly.

Despite all the groundwork and forethought, cracks formed within weeks of Candice's leadership of the organization. The first strike was her implementation of a time-tracking system for employees, who felt it represented a lack of trust. A narrative took hold that, as one employee put it, "We're not in Kansas anymore." The second strike was to elevate another process-minded executive to the leadership team. The shift away from sales-driven growth frustrated everyone and signaled a disappointing change in culture. Feedback from clients was strike three. They had started to feel like the relationships with the business felt more transactional, opposite of what had made the company successful.

In fewer than two quarters, Candice was losing clients and, by extension, the team. Longtime employees started talking on a grapevine that, prior to her taking over, didn't exist. The message was clear — she's wrecking the place and we're leaving. Six months into her tenure, she saw the mistake. To her enormous credit, she reversed course.

"In hindsight, I didn't understand just how much James knew and did for the business through sheer experience," Candice confessed. "I had to eat an entire humble pie and go back to our team for solutions."

The result? A humbler approach allowed Candice to add just enough structure while providing the freedom that most of the team craved. Two years later, the company is thriving under Candice's leadership. "I'll admit that I wanted to make my mark at the beginning," she said. "Now, I'm just happy to be leading this team to a more successful future." ▶

What It All Means: I'm presenting this as a false binary; the best music can be made when the Jazzers and the Juilliards join forces. It requires a masterful amount of leadership and focus on culture. How do you do it?

▶ **For the Jazzers:** Improvisation is great. It's even better — and easier — when you have a framework. While it might be uncomfortable creating constraints and writing down the notes, it allows the rest of the team to follow more effectively. Your superpower will be to learn to distinguish between the successes you've had because of your improvisation and the wins you've notched despite your willingness to play it by ear.

▶ **For the Juilliards:** Structure and standards can take an organization far. Calibrating those tools for what the business needs is even more important. While you might not appreciate lacking details, understand that the process might slow down the organization unnecessarily. Your superpower will be to find the areas of opportunity where improvisation creates potential for failure and work with the Jazzers to fill those gaps.

Bottom Line: Respect that the predecessor probably knew what they were doing and that relationships do matter. Technical competence is great, though sometimes you need to know how to get the audience's toes tapping.

Quicksand #7: New Sheriff in Town

In classic spaghetti Westerns, a familiar storyline unfolds as a brave new sheriff arrives to rid the town of outlaws, bringing hope to its beleaguered citizens. His unconventional methods, often pushing the boundaries, elevate him to a near-legendary status among the grateful townspeople.

Successors often see themselves as the sheriff.

Why It Matters: There are a few reasons successors do this:

- ▶ **Overconfidence:** Succession can breed arrogance, which can turn into poor decision-making.

- ▶ **Lack of feedback:** As it becomes more evident that someone is a successor, the political dynamics of an organization realign. Even in the healthiest of organizations, people naturally position themselves to be seen favorably by the new leader. That can reduce your access to valuable feedback.

- ▶ **Lack of information:** No matter how well a predecessor shares knowledge, there are blank spaces of data that you don't have, typically because of inexperience.

- ▶ **Reactivity:** Even in great predecessor/successor relationships, the successor can develop a gut instinct that reflexively goes against things the predecessor wanted, implemented, or valued.

Here are the ways successors fall prey to the quicksand:

- ▶ **Culturally ignorant decision-making:** You're not the predecessor, and that's okay! What's not okay is missing the positive drivers of culture that do everything from ensuring smooth operations to keeping people in their jobs. There's a reason Peter Drucker said, "Culture eats strategy for breakfast." It has way more to do with the success of your organization than you realize.

▶ **How you got there:** It's easy to deceive yourself that you deserve to be in the seat you're in, forgetting in that story all of the people who put you in the position to succeed. This can turn off the predecessor and teammates and lead to second-guessing of your selection.

▶ **Confusing complexity for rigor:** Successors are often eager to make their mark early in their tenure. Yet, without a full understanding of how the organization functions, they look for solutions that *feel* rigorous. This typically leads to complexity that the organization doesn't have the tools, habits, or needs to handle. This leads to the team wasting all sorts of time and energy on something that just *doesn't work*.

▶ **A bigger yacht:** Many succession stories start with a predecessor who was once the successor. Their story of success will be hard to beat. Yet, the successor is going to try, even if the added success or growth ends up being painful for the organization. As one interviewee said, "sometime the kid gets distracted by wanting a bigger yacht."

Digging Deeper: Avoiding this quicksand requires humility. Here's how to handle:

▶ **One business cycle:** Most successors walk in with an immediate game plan on how they're going to take control. This can lead to poor decision-making and a fundamental change in the organizational trajectory for the worse. One of the best ways to avoid those decisions? Wait a year (or whatever your business cycle looks like). Unless the organization is in dire straits, you can likely run the business on existing processes for longer than you think. In that year, the organization will naturally reveal what needs to be changed and in what priority.

The New Sheriff in Action

A pair of brothers who successfully grew their business over 30 years were working to hand off the business to a new generation of leaders. Investing in leadership development enabled them to identify several candidates who were worthy to step into decision-making roles.

While there was an executive leadership team in place, two successors elevated themselves above the pack. While the brothers retained the CEO/COO titles, the two successors — each with more than 15 years at the firm — were acting in those roles at the encouragement of the owners.

The succession process was going to near perfection until they looked to evaluate their core operating process. Despite a decades-long history of success leveraging a simple model that drove goalsetting, the successors — with some support of an advisory board — suggested exploring new models that would be more effective.

While committed to allowing the successors to begin to make decisions, the two brothers saw danger ahead. "I don't think they know how much work we did in the background to influence decisions," one of the brothers said. "It's not their fault that they don't have that context, but it's dangerous that they're looking to upend something that worked — and will likely continue to work — so well for so long."

Despite a couple of nudges to change directions, the successors pushed forward.

The result? Confusion. The organization had no context for the new process, and thousands of man hours were wasted trying to communicate about and implement a much more complex system of establishing and tracking goals and tactics, distracting from what the organization truly needed to impact.

Eighteen months later, the new process was finally abandoned. Chastened, the successors asked the CEO for advice. "You should have learned how we work first, rather than just what we do," the CEO said. "You would have saved us a whole lot of heartache had you been a little more curious and patient." ▶

▶ **Know your value:** Few organizations know how they deliver value. Fortunately, there's a model to help us. Known as the Value Disciplines model,[51] it boils down to three approaches:

> › Operational excellence — We're so good at what we do, it doesn't make sense to go anywhere else.
> › Product leadership — We do things so differently/innovatively, no one else can match our results.
> › Customer intimacy — We know you so well, it will hurt too much to get rid of us.

Most organizations need to be proficient in all three, though it's best to identify one as a strategic focus.

▶ **Sell it:** The fastest way to understand the business is to sell what you do. Whether that's creating new customer relationships in a company or raising money in a nonprofit setting, driving revenue is one of the quickest ways to learn the strengths and challenges of the organization. Even more, you can credibly speak to what the market is saying, using that experience to drive strategic decisions.

Bottom Line: It's too easy to believe you've got all the answers. The implication that the predecessor made significant mistakes can further drive a wedge in your relationships. Be humble and open to learning, and do the work.

Quicksand #8: Indicators

There are two types of indicators: leading and lagging.

Lagging indicators measure the stuff that happened in the past, allowing you to dig through that historical data to understand potential causation or correlation between variables. This gives you insight into what might happen next under similar circumstances.

Leading indicators measure things that give insight of what is to come, using current information to help predict the future. This allows you to "see around corners" and preemptively make decisions about things that are likely to happen next.

It's easy to confuse the two. Successful predecessors are rarely *only* known for their career success. They tend also to have other notches under their belt, to include:

- ▶ **Material wealth:** Memberships to exclusive clubs, expensive hobbies, costly homes, luxury cars, and oversized toys.
- ▶ **Community leadership:** Board seats and a visible presence that is well-recognized.
- ▶ **Philanthropy:** Lots of deference from powerful people, names on buildings, and swanky fundraisers that appear in the social pages.
- ▶ **Awards:** Under-decade awards, C-somethings of the year, halls of fame, governmental proclamations, and honorary (or actual) street namings.
- ▶ **Symbols of success:** The parking spot in front of the building, or the biggest corner office.
- ▶ **Wine:** I know I already listed "expensive hobbies," but this one gets a special call out. Are you a good predecessor if you don't have a wine cellar?

The challenge comes when lagging indicators get confused for leading indicators. Successors see the things that predecessors have achieved — in and out of the organization — and think, "I want that, too." The "stuff" becomes an end in and of itself.

Consider a predecessor CEO who had won a CEO of the Year award. I sent him a congratulations, and with part humility, part grumpiness, he responded, "Just another situation where I have to put on a black tie and shell out two grand for a table."

On the flip side, one of his key employees is anxious to win an under-decade award. "I think it will boost my presence in the organization and community," she told me. She's not wrong — those awards can be a huge boost personally and professionally — but she hadn't quite done the work she would need to be seriously considered. Yet, she was pursuing it because she saw it as a milestone to her eventually landing in the corner office.

Why It Matters: I've always considered the word trappings—of the "trappings of success" phrase—to be a double entendre. Sure, they're visible signs of success, but they're a trap (quicksand?).

There's a thin line between having a goal — buying something expensive for you or your family, achieving financial freedom, winning an award — and the distraction that lagging indicators can bring. Let's break it down.

Goals are, as the pithy quote puts it, "dreams with a deadline." They're the things you've chosen as motivators for your life and work. Most importantly, they tend to involve others. Perhaps you want to achieve a specific goal for you and your friends or family. Or maybe it's an organizational goal. Or, perhaps you want to achieve a level of financial independence that enables you to give in a way that aligns with your values.

A process-focused approach drastically impacts motivation, and attaches the sense of achievement to the incremental steps rather than the final result.[52]

Lagging indicators are, by definition, the results. A results-focused approach is self-driven and allows you off the hook for the day-to-day. It's a binary result: Either you have achieved the lagging indicator, or you have not. Here's the rub:

- ▶ **You can't always control the result or the timeline:** You can't win an under-decade award if you're older than the cutoff. CEO of the Year is a subjective decision (that might, *shh*, have something to do with ad revenue). There might not be a lake house for sale where you want it.

- ▶ **Hedonistic adaptation:** We get used to what we've got. No matter what our goal is, we are primed to see that lagging indicator as old news and crave something new. While there are plenty

Indicators in Action

Tim, an aging executive, was a barrier to progress when at his best but had become a significant obstruction as the leader of the company's most revenue-producing division. Despite Tim's resistance, the company had a robust succession plan. David, a 10-year employee who joined the organization out of college, had worked his way up from selling small projects to leading the company's largest strategic client relationships. Tim respected David and vice versa, though there were significant tensions as David's ideas were consistently put on ice to cater to Tim's never-change approach. As Tim continued to freeze out David's contributions, David grew increasingly agitated at the speed, or lack thereof, of change.

Despite the considerable tension — and thanks to hours of coaching — David's patience paid off. With Tim's permission, the company announced the transition of David into Tim's role, and Tim's new job in the organization. After months of collaboration leading up to the transition, Tim had a blowup with the managing partners of the business just a week before the transition would commence. He wouldn't give up his office.

All parties — except Tim — assumed that David would move into Tim's office when he stepped into Tim's role. Tim had other ideas. As a shareholder and key decision-maker, not to mention a 30-year occupier of the window-filled office, he wasn't budging.

While David was looking forward to moving into the new digs, he saw that the fight wasn't worth the reward. Tim saw the office as part of his identity, and David knew that taking Tim's office would create an even greater rift when they had to work together. "I'll work out of a closet if I have to," David said publicly, and there was never talk about moving offices again.

"Not going to lie, it it upset me," David said. "I did a visualization years ago where I saw myself sitting in that office. I realized that I'd get it someday, and it was more important to show leadership by standing down. Even if it still tweaks me, I know I made the right call." ▶

of philosophies that remind us to be grateful for what we've got, it's too easy — and human — to take it all for granted.

▶ **They don't matter:** Lagging indicators often have little to do with the person's success, even if we've tied them together in our minds. Maybe that predecessor *hates* the country club, but the in-laws insist they stay members. Perhaps, like our CEO above, the award is more of a shakedown than an honor.

A Story: One candidate I coached talked about a future vision, and a big part of that was having the money to join one of the most exclusive country clubs where he lived. While he loosely saw it as an opportunity to grow his business, he talked about joining the young executives club and going to the exclusive events he had heard about from others. Looking back at my notes, I wrote down his exact words: "That is how I'll know that I made it." I challenged him on whether that was a goal or an indicator. "It's a goal."

About three years later, and the best sales year of his career, he had the money to join the club, which he did. He gleefully wrote the check and was excited to tell me about it. I was truly happy for him. Eighteen months after that, we connected. Of course, the first thing I asked about was the club. His tone completely changed.

Within that time, he and his wife had a baby who needed more intentional care. He was working more to both support the newborn and make up for the family's lost income as they agreed that she should stay home for a little while. At the time, the country club was a stretch, but with the change in family situation, it became an albatross.

"Honestly, I wish I'd never done it." The hardest part about confused indicators is that they rarely live up to the hype. You can only drink so much wine. You only have so much time to spend on a boat. You can only leave the country so often. At some point, you get tired of the constant asks for money.

Bottom Line: Mistaking lagging indicators for leading ones is a shallow orientation to the world that will make you distracted, less happy, and unproductive.

The Bottom Line on Chapter 5:
The Quicksand Survival Guide

TL;DR:

Succession is full of traps that can undermine your success if you're not careful. Much like quicksand, these obstacles can seem harmless but can pull you down quickly if you're not prepared. We explore the common "quicksand traps" successors face, such as falling short in critical areas like communication and peer relationships, becoming overconfident, making premature decisions, dealing with imposter syndrome, and becoming complacent due to experience. Knowing the quicksand is there lets you develop strategies to avoid it.

The Hits:

▶ **The Most Common Traps:** Successors fall short in common ways, like communication, peer relationships, and executive presence, which are crucial for effective leadership.

▶ **Avoiding Overconfidence:** Overconfidence can lead to reckless decision-making. It's essential to stay aware of your limitations and seek continuous feedback.

▶ **Making Informed Decisions:** Premature decisions and changes can be detrimental. Fully understand the existing dynamics and culture before making changes (even small ones).

▶ **Overcoming Imposterism:** Successors often struggle with feeling incompetent. It's normal and there are ways to make you feel more confident and capable.

▶ **Staying Vigilant:** Experience can sometimes lead to complacency. Successors rarely see the whole business at the start. Avoid overconfidence.

Thought-Starter Questions:

▶ What steps can you take to ensure you receive valuable feedback throughout the succession process?

▶ How will you approach making decisions to avoid premature changes while respecting the existing culture?

▶ What strategies and resources can you use to overcome the inevitable moments of imposterism?

▶ How can you avoid overconfidence and ensure continuous learning and growth?

Successor Strategies for Success:

▶ Actively ask for feedback from peers and mentors to identify areas for improvement.

▶ Take time to thoroughly understand the organization's culture and dynamics before implementing changes.

▶ Identify and use outside support systems that can provide context and guidance when you feel inadequate.

▶ Focus on building strong relationships with key stakeholders to gain their trust and support.

▶ Stay committed to continuous learning and personal development to avoid complacency.

On Deck:

Strong leadership skills have a predictable positive impact on the successor's ability to move into the next role. We narrow the big, nebulous idea of leadership down into the concepts and skills that successors who do well most consistently employ.

The Bottom Line

Install a Leadership Upgrade

Upgrade your leadership toolbox in preparation
for the career challenge of a lifetime.

Putting the Pieces Together

That's when you need to put yourself to the test and show us a passage of time.

You're watching a movie about an underpowered underdog preparing to take on their nemesis. Improvement must happen fast to beat the enemy (and hold the audience's attention).

The solution? The montage.

Scenes flash, one after another, showing the protagonist getting better and better until they're ready for the confrontation. What makes the the technique believable?

1. The hero demonstrates the willingness to do the work.
2. The hero is learning the crucial skills needed to win.

In that sense, this chapter is your montage. What we're about to discuss are the foundational skills we help next leaders to understand as they look to advance their careers. While extremely helpful for success at almost any leadership level, the ability to incorporate these skills and ideas is what differentiates successful successors from those who fail.

They all have a few things in common:

- ▶ They're ideas that prioritize people over process.
- ▶ They're crucial to successfully driving organizational change.
- ▶ They're mental frameworks that create clarity in the fog of transition.

Let's go, Karate Kid. You've got a fight to win.

Role Mindsets

Running the stairs is about more than just doing cardio.

A succession candidate was complaining about the challenges of a recent promotion. At the core of the frustration was a team of subordinates who were consistently taking the wrong actions, forcing this successor into the details of solving problems below her pay grade.

"It's driving me nuts. I'm working 60 hours a week and still not getting everything done. Yet, my team is making it to happy hour any chance they get."

What's worse, her inability to get out of the weeds was reflected in the work she was to be delivering to her peers for the executive team. The word on the street was that she was too disorganized and overwhelmed to take the next career step. At it's core, it wasn't true. She was simply locked into an outdated model.

Background: Much of our modern approach to work is rooted in the post-war boom of the 1950s, led by Greatest-Generation managers and leaders influenced by the victories of the Allies' military-oriented hierarchy.

The "career ladder" metaphor is even older, first used in 1835.[53] Baby Boomers — the live-to-work generation — embraced the idea whole-hog because, as stated in an article in Harvard Business Review titled *Why Hierarchies Thrive,*[54] "Hierarchies fulfill our deep needs for order and security." Later, an even more on-point statement: "Hierarchies show us how fast we are climbing the ladder of success; they give us identity."

With that model came a key feature: When you achieved a new rung on the ladder, you abandoned the previous rung. Climbing was the goal. "Up or out" was a mantra of many organizations. And a lateral move? Much like an actual ladder, it was career suicide.

Then . . .

You've Got Mail: There's a legend about a high-end, mahogany-walled business club—the kind of place where old-school politicians and titans of industry smoke cigars and sip scotch as they decide the fates of millions. The club had a "nap room," where members—largely working executives—could lay their head and snooze during the day, usually after their two-martini lunch at the luxury hotel across the street.

Then, sometime in the mid-to-late 1990s, they turned the nap room into a fitness facility. Apparently, everyone stopped using the nap room.

Why? Email. The rise of email forced executives to answer questions at an unheard-of speed. There was no more time to take a nap.

Fast-Forward: Today, there isn't a CEO that we work with who isn't expected to deliver some type of Contributor-level work. Similarly, there isn't a front-line worker we hear about who avoids the expectation to provide a level of leadership.

In other words, even in the most specialized jobs, workers are expected to be a jack of all trades — doing the work here, looking over someone's shoulder there, picking and choosing what resources get applied in this corner, and then seeing into the future to anticipate what's to come.

The ladder doesn't work anymore.

Digging Deeper: Instead of doing "a job," we're looking to perform at our best by applying a variety of approaches — we call them Role Mindsets — that, when used at the right time, maximize our success hit rate.

There are four mindsets to master:

- ▶ **Contributor mindset:** The contributor mindset is focused on the task at hand, getting the work done. If you spend most of your time in this Role Mindset, you're likely thought of as an individual contributor.

▶ **Supervisor mindset:** The supervisor mindset is overseeing the tactical work of others, making sure they're doing the right thing at the right time. If you spend most of your time in this Role Mindset, you're likely seen as a team lead, supervisor, or similar job.

▶ **Manager mindset:** The manager mindset is assigning resources and monitoring progress toward larger goals and objectives. If you spend a lot of time in this Role Mindset, you're likely thought of as a manager or director.

▶ **Leader mindset:** The leader mindset is creating an environment to maximize the organization's capabilities by establishing and reinforcing the culture while looking to the horizon to determine opportunities, roadblocks, and risks. If you're dedicating a majority of time in this mindset, you're likely a senior leader with a title to match (senior director, vice president, C-suite).

Quick Stories: What do we mean? Here are a couple of vignettes.

▶ A COO of a $50 million firm is annoyed that the company is spending so much on office supplies, with the spike happening as back-to-school season approaches. The COO leads a task team with procurement, human resources, and site leaders to spend hundreds of hours instituting policies for employees to only take the supplies they need — a $10,000 problem, at best. As a key leader of the organization, he's investing his and others' time in the Contributor mindset.

▶ A production worker sees his team leads get more and more agitated about flagging productivity, reduced morale, and, subsequently, even worse productivity. As a pick-me-up, the worker brings in cupcakes for everyone, then suggests that the production team should rotate who brings in cupcakes every week, which turns into an ad hoc competition about who makes the best cupcakes. The camaraderie built by this now-established tradition helped the production team communicate its needs to supervisors, tipping off operations leaders to make changes that improved productivity. Despite their job as the ultimate Contributor, that worker established culture using a Leader mindset.

Digging Even Deeper: The way to visualize these Role Mindsets is as a staircase, like this:

Figure 6.1
Role Mindset Theory

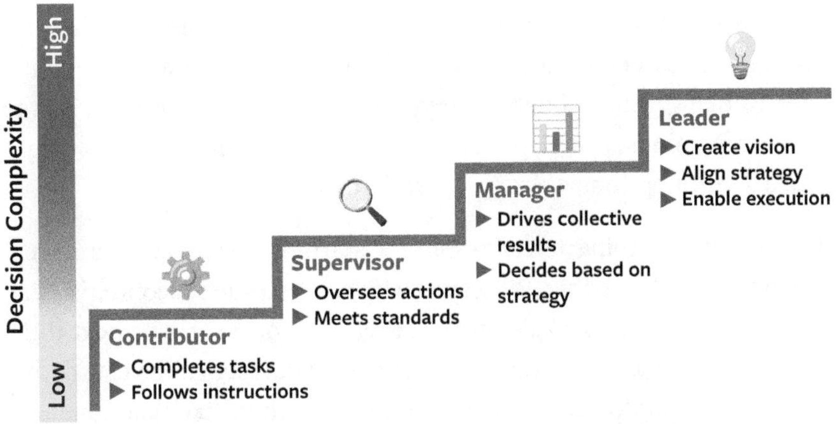

It's not about "achieving" a level, but having the Role Mindset Agility to "run up and down the stairs" to apply the right mindset at the right time. While it sounds easy, it's like any other staircase — we're subject to the law of gravity. We're prone to falling down and tripping up.

Falling Down

Falling down is a universal challenge of anyone from the team lead to the C-suite. It's too easy to let gravity pull you to the ground level. There's a reason people are more likely to tumble down ten flights of stairs than run up them.

While there are lots of reasons why those in power fall to the Contributor mindset, it's almost universally rooted in an emotional battle: As you spend more time at higher levels, you win less often.

When you're an individual contributor — and most of your time is in the Contributor mindset — winning is easy. It typically takes having just a little more luck, work ethic, or street smarts to catapult over your peers. You typically win — promotions, bonuses, raises, recognition — and win a lot. Not that it's easy, per se, but the road to winning — doing what you're told, going the extra mile, and following the pre-defined path — reduces complexity. Winning becomes part of your identity.

As you take on more responsibilities, and reach new job heights, the path to winning becomes harder. Your decisions aren't so black-and-white, you're thinking more about strategy than the tactical thinking of the Contributor mindset, and you're faced with judgment calls that might include a set of options where none of them are objectively "good."

When you start seeing fewer results, it starts to feel a lot like losing. Winning less feels terrible. When you win less, you start second-guessing yourself. You start to seek comfort in what got you here. The next thing you know, it's 10 p.m. and you're working on some tactical-level task that isn't your job, but doesn't it *feel good* to get something like that done?

This is at the heart of why delegation is so challenging. You'll hear people say that Delegation is an "act of trust." I agree, and I'd take it one step further. Delegation is a mini succession problem. Only now, you're the predecessor.

Tripping Up

Humans have a low tolerance for the changes in the height of stair risers — the distance between the previous step and the next. A difference of more than 3/8 inch (9 millimeters), and people tend to take a tumble.

Legend has it that this used to be intentional. As the tale goes, most multi-story houses have the bedrooms upstairs. To prevent a burglar from going undetected, builders would insert an uneven riser into the staircase, which would be invisible to the naked eye and to which the residents would get accustomed. A charging intruder, however, would misstep and fall, alerting the home to the unwelcome visitor.

In the staircase of Role Mindset Theory, the uneven riser is between the Supervisor and Manager mindsets. This spot is known as the "tripping point."

Figure 6.2
Role Mindset Theory and the Tripping Point

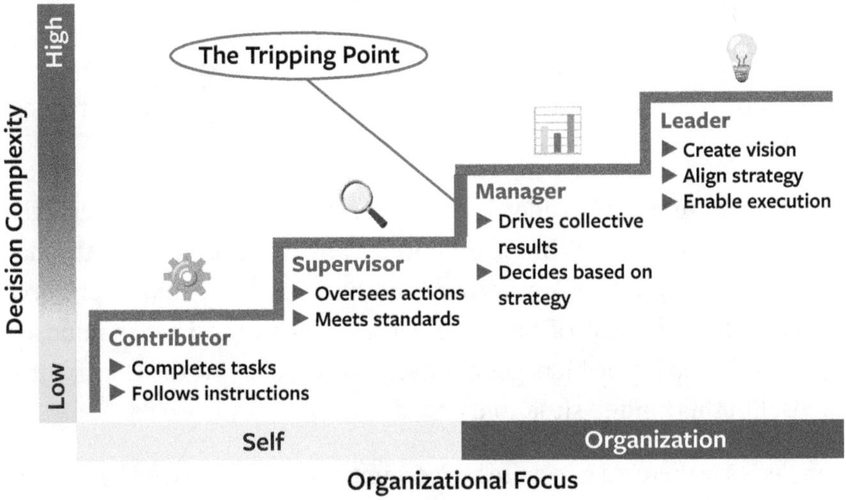

While falling down is a challenge for someone already in leadership, tripping up is almost exclusively a problem for those who are developing their careers. What makes that spot so special? It's where the center of focus shifts.

In the Contributor and Supervisor mindsets, you're worried about yourself. By and large, your focus is internal and on whether you are praised or punished for your performance. Even if you're overseeing others' work, you're most concerned about how their efforts reflect on you.

The Manager mindset is where the center of focus shifts outward. No longer is it about how you are personally impacted, but how the organization performs collectively. Regardless of your job, this mindset is the beginning of you thinking about things through a wider lens.

When we have seen next leaders fail to rise above their current job, it is almost always because of tunnel-vision pointed toward individual wants and interests. The next leader is unable to see anything beyond what has a direct impact. This person just can't get beyond the tripping point.

Running the Stairs

If the killer skill is Role Mindset Agility, how do you know when you're falling down versus appropriately stepping in to help solve a tactical problem?

Here's an example. Consider a senior executive who rose through the ranks as a salesperson. While she's now occupying the C-suite, to this day she manages a couple of key accounts both to stay sharp and to preserve revenue. Despite most of her time being spent in the Leader mindset, closely followed by the Manager mindset, she's employing the Contributor mindset in this limited situation.

Now, let's say there's a not-quite key account currently managed by an inexperienced, high-potential salesperson that's at risk. The executive could:

- ▶ Swoop in and take over to solve the problem.
- ▶ Review, revise, and approve all communications between the salesperson and the key account before it's sent.
- ▶ Provide tools, processes, and training for the salesperson to follow to minimize the risk of losing the account.
- ▶ Ask questions and coach the salesperson on the approach and let the situation play out.

What's the right answer? Who knows? We need more info. The executive would have to consider the following:

- How important is the revenue?
- What's the impact — business and reputational — of losing the account or other accounts?
- If I solve this problem, will the client skip the salesperson and come to me?
- If I solve the problem, will the salesperson need me to solve the problem the next time?
- How will other salespeople react? Will they want the same help? Will they feel abandoned for not having a leader who stepped in sooner when they struggled?

Considering those strategic questions is necessary for the executive to make the right decision. When there's Role Mindset misalignment, there's risk: to the organization, to the culture, to your brand, and to employees. Here's a visual of how misalignment can impact how others perceive you:

Figure 6.3
Role Mindset Interactions

What the individual or team needs

How you choose to approach it		Contributor	Supervisor	Manager	Leader
	Contributor	"Great work!"	"They can't let go."	"They're a control freak."	"They want it only to be done their way."
	Supervisor	"They're not a team player."	"Thanks for showing me!"	"They hyperfocus on details."	"They're overbearing."
	Manager	"They're riding us too hard."	"They're hands-off."	"I appreciate the help with solving it!"	"They're a micromanager."
	Leader	"They're asleep at the wheel."	"They ignore our struggle."	"They're unwilling to address it."	"Thanks for the insight that led to a solution!"

Putting it Into Practice

Now that you're convinced that you're subject to the same forces as even the greatest leaders, it's time to think about how best to apply Role Mindset Theory to your work. Assuming that you're in a job where you should be spending most of your time in the Manager or Leader mindsets, there are a few go-to questions worth asking:

- ▶ Am I letting the law of gravity win?
- ▶ Am I doing something to make myself feel good, or am I putting the organization in a better position?

A Side Note About Asking: It's great to ask yourself these questions. It's unfair to ask the predecessor. In particular, there are two questions that set leaders and predecessors up for failure:

- ▶ After describing a scenario: "What do you think I should do?"
- ▶ After proposing an action: "Do you think that will work?"

You're setting a trap for the predecessor, and you might not even know it.

The predecessor's Effortless Expertise says you've provided all the information needed to offer you good counsel. In both cases, the predecessor ends up falling down the stairs and sharing advice with you. He or she might even ask a question to appear as if consulting you, wording it like, "Have you considered [fill-in-the-blank solution]?" The reality is, he or she can't truly judge, because the problem can only be seen through your lens.

For predecessors and leaders, saying "I don't know" takes conscious effort. It's not, well, effortless. To reduce discomfort — and save time — an answer is given and everyone moves on. It's not the predecessor's fault.

Sure, exceptional leaders — with time on their hands — will ask questions rather than answer yours, and they're likely to align with several of what we just discussed. Do your best to avoid putting them in that position.

The Scout Team

In 2007, Tyler Palko graduated from the University of Pittsburgh, where he served as the starting quarterback from 2004-2006. Despite an impressive collegiate career throwing to the likes of surefire Hall of Famer Larry Fitzgerald, and being the first visiting quarterback to throw five touchdowns at Notre Dame, Tyler went undrafted in his class.

Undeterred, Tyler signed with the NFL's New Orleans Saints as an undrafted free agent, meaning he would be very unlikely to make the team, and if he did, he would most likely run the scout team — a collection of players who mimic the offense of the upcoming opponent to help the defense prepare. The expectation of the scout team quarterback is to do the work with the ultimate Contributor mindset.

Not Tyler.

Understanding that the scout team players would benefit from getting to used to the Saints' ways of calling the plays, Tyler made a request to the coordinator: could he call the play in the huddle as if it were a Saints play, giving everyone experience with the language and lingo of the offense in which they hoped to play someday? Think about what it took to make that request:

▶ Tyler had to recognize that he and his teammates would benefit from getting more experience with the team's way of calling plays.
▶ Tyler had to have the backbone to ask the coordinator to change a well-established practice.
▶ Tyler needed to know the lingo well enough to call the play correctly in the huddle.

That's a Leader mindset. There's a reason Tyler remained in the league for nearly six years, with several starts under his belt. His leadership ability, with his unstoppable work ethic, made him both an excellent quarterback and teammate. ▶

▶ Is applying this Role Mindset solving a short-term issue but creating or reinforcing a longer-term problem?

▶ If I do this now, what task that *only I can do* isn't getting done?

▶ How much time will it *really* take to guide someone else to find and execute a solution?

▶ Is there a bad cultural habit that I'm teaching by taking this action?

In the end, your decision of which Role Mindset to apply is based on both the short- and long-term implications of the decision. Ask yourself the right questions, choose wisely, and be diligent in the knowledge that our bias is to let gravity win.

Bottom Line: Build your agility so that gravity doesn't win (as often).

Figure 6.4
Role Mindsets at a Glance

	Contributor	Supervisor	Manager	Leader
To-do	Task completion	Action oversight	Achieving results	Organizational progress
Complexity	Low	Low	Medium	High
Uncertainty	Low	Low	Medium	High
Independence	Low	Low	Medium	High
Impactful skill	Mastery	Measurement	Self-correction	Emotional intelligence
Greatest Challenge	Context	Hyper-focus	Competition	Distance
Orientation to others	Listen and follow	Show and tell	Question and update	Guide and recommend

Profitable Intelligence

Brad needs more than a big brain.

What color is your parachute? Your hat? Your Real Color or True Color? Your Performance Index, DISC, Myers-Briggs? Top five strengths? These are modern versions of a question that philosophers, psychologists, and social scientists have been asking for millennia.

Followers of Hippocrates[55] — yes, the guy whose oath each doctor takes — were the first to put people's personalities into four "Temperaments" that corresponded to certain body fluids, like blood and bile, around 120 BCE.

Since then, we've developed diverse tools to measure human behavior and our personality. Whatever system you prefer — from the binary Type A/Type B to the more academic Five-Factor Personality Theory, we're able to apply advanced analytics to the idea that's been intuitive for more than two millennia: We all think and behave differently.

This insight, backed by a lot more data and research, serves as the foundation for what is the most profitable intelligence.

The Big Picture: Our expectations of what executives bring to the table have changed drastically in a short period of time. A team from Russell Reynolds studied nearly 5,000 job descriptions for CEO and other C-suite roles from 2000 to 2017.[56] Specifically, they were looking to understand how hiring organizations prioritized the technical parts at the executive level — like resource and financial management — compared to people-focused social skills.

To quote the authors' definition of "social skills": "We mean certain specific capabilities, including a high level of self-awareness, the ability to listen and communicate well, a facility for working with different types of people and groups, and what psychologists call 'theory of mind'—the capacity to infer how others are thinking and feeling."

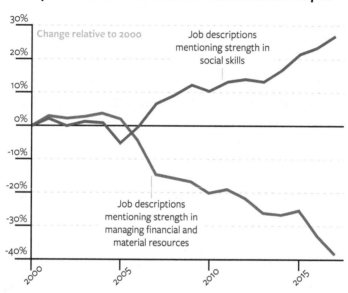

Figure 6.5
Help Wanted: CEOs Who Are Good with People

From 2000 to 2006, the proportion of each stayed about the same compared to the start of the study. Then, in 2007, there came a breaking point.

Today? Executives need people skills and technical skills.

Digging Deeper: You've probably heard of Emotional Intelligence (sometimes shortened to 'EQ' or 'EI'). For the rest, you already know the thesis, backed by a significant amount of research, that the modern work world rewards EQ more than IQ.

Travis Bradberry, author of *Emotional Intelligence 2.0*, looked at the data[57] and found:

► 90% of top performers also score highly in emotional intelligence.
► High EQ individuals outearn their low EQ counterparts by $29,000 annually, and $1,300 per additional point (using his proprietary self-assessment).

So, what *is* emotional intelligence, exactly?

Digging Even Deeper: There are a lot of models of EQ out there. Daniel Goleman wrote one of the first books on EQ in 1995, with other writers and researchers contributing to the field over time. The landscape is still unsettled, mainly because it's easier to measure IQ than EQ.[xix]

Let's focus on the model Goleman originally proposed, which was also used by Travis Bradberry in his bestseller. The model looks like this:

Figure 6.6
Model of Emotional Intelligence

	Personal Competence	Social Competence
Awareness	**Self-Awareness** Emotional awareness Accurate self-assesment Self-confidence	**Social Awareness** Empathy Service orientation Organzational awareness
Regulation	**Self Management** Self-control Transparency Adaptability Achievement drive Initiative	**Relationship Management** Developing others Influence Communication Conflict management Leadership Change catalyst Building bonds Teamwork & collaboration

- ▶ **Self-awareness:** the ability to understand your own emotions and your impact on others.
- ▶ **Self-management:** the ability to separate how you feel from how you behave.

---

xix. Most assessments rely on self-assessing, yet high EQ requires self-awareness. Not everyone is self-aware enough to get a valid result. The most valid tools include others' assessments of you.

▶ **Social awareness:** understanding the emotional context others are experiencing.

▶ **Social management:** adapting your behavior based on your ability to manage your own emotions and behavior and respond appropriately to others.

While the skills are discrete, they impact each other in the following ways:

1. Self-awareness allows you to separate your emotion from your action, leading to productive self-management.
2. Your awareness of your own emotion gives you the empathetic capacity to understand others' emotions in situations, making it easier for you to relate to that person.
3. Leveraging your ability to change your behavior and understand others, you can manage your interaction with others in a productive way.
4. By managing that relationship publicly, you achieve the results you hoped.

This only works if:

1. You have an in-depth understanding of what you feel and how it connects to your behaviors and priorities.
2. You have adequate perspective on others' (potentially different) priorities and the impact that might have both on their behavior and your interpretation of it.
3. You can adapt your approach by giving them more of what they want and need in the way they can understand it.

The approach is tougher than it seems. According to Bradberry, only 36% of people can accurately name the emotion they are feeling in the moment.[xx] Fortunately, if you're not already part of the minority, you can develop the skill. According to almost all EQ research, it can be developed, in contrast to IQ.

---

xx. We first mentioned this stat back on page 68.

Why It Matters: As a successor, you're facing what will likely be the greatest emotional intelligence challenge of your life.

Here's why:

> ▶ **Self-awareness:** The better you know: 1) your behavioral tendencies overall; and 2) your emotions in the moment, the better you tee yourself up for successful self-management.

> ▶ **Self-management:** Knowing yourself, you can choose to make a different decision about how to behave.

> ▶ **Social awareness:** You have many audiences: the predecessor, peers, employees, your family and friends — they're all a part of your social consideration. Understanding each and how your approach interacts will make a difference in how smoothly the succession process happens.

> ▶ **Relationship management:** Equipped with your ability to manage yourself and understand others, you can adapt your approach to each audience.

With so much at stake, you must maximize your chances for success. EQ will be the difference-maker as you work to build confidence with all your stakeholders.

If you want a model, DISC (each letter in the word DISC corresponds to one of its four primary behavioral styles) is an excellent tool to achieve self-awareness and for insight to understand others. The styles (using the Wiley model as reference) are:

> ▶ **Dominance (D):** Focused on results and the bottom line, individuals with this style are assertive, competitive, and direct.
> ▶ **Influence (I):** These individuals are enthusiastic, persuasive, and enjoy social interactions, often inspiring and motivating others.
> ▶ **Steadiness (S):** Calm, reliable, and supportive, people with this style prioritize cooperation, consistency, and dependability.

▶ **Conscientiousness (C):** Detail-oriented, analytical, and systematic, individuals with this style value accuracy, quality, and expertise.

Two books about DISC can help you better understand the model and adaptation:

▶ *The Platinum Rule*, by Dr. Tony Alessandra, posits that the Golden Rule (the *real one* that states that you should do unto others as you would have done unto you) is insufficient for our interactions, and that we should treat others as how *they* want to be treated.

▶ *Surrounded by Idiots*, by Thomas Erikson, also leveraging the model, takes a different tack that helps individuals understand why they feel so crazy in their communication efforts.

Interested in something more in-depth and personalized to you? Let me know.[xxi]

Why It Matters: We've hinted at adaptability and EQ throughout this book, though we've largely talked about it in terms of the relationship with the predecessor. Now that you're sitting in the "big chair," your EQ needs to be at its best for all of your stakeholders.

Bottom Line: Don't rely on your gut instinct; use a proven model to add context and habit to what you might already know.

---

xxi. We're happy to introduce you to the tools we use in our consulting work. Feel free to reach out to me, my contact information is on page 280.

The Helicopter

Adrian started a structural lumber business fifteen years prior with just a few employees, growing the business to more than 200 when he sold it to private equity seven years later. After just three years, the company was in shambles and the PE firm paid Adrian to take the business back. Five years after retaking control, the company had more than 250 employees and was running at peak efficiency. The expanded headquarters, complete with employee amenities like a new cafeteria, gym, and locker rooms, were a sign of success.

When Adrian was away, which was more frequent as he was looking to move away from day-to-day management, the culture fell apart. The result? Higher-than-average turnover that was still half of what competitors experienced despite the labor-intensive, low-paying jobs that had to be done outdoors in the Sun Belt. His next-tier managers were to blame.

Hired to assess the organization and its culture, I walked the grounds to see the business in action while waiting for Adrian to arrive. Arrive he did — among the sea of early-model cars and motorcycles, there was a concrete pad sitting about 40 yards from the edge of the parking lot. That was Adrian's parking spot, and where he landed his helicopter.

Given the disparity between early-'90s Buicks and Adrian's aircraft, I assumed that employees might resent Adrian and his wealth.

After hours of interviews, and working two days on-site with his employees, I was dead wrong. They loved him and were fiercely loyal. I heard stories of him caring about them and their families and offering financial support in crisis. To most, Adrian was like family.

Then, I received his DISC results. His style? DC, a style that tends to be relentlessly driven and detail-oriented, and typically not naturally a people-focused leader.

Sitting down with Adrian, I admitted that I was completely baffled by his success and his team's reaction to him. "I wouldn't expect any of this would come naturally to you, but it obviously does!"

"I assure you, it doesn't," Adrian admitted. He then told me that he knew early on that his business' success would be based on whether he could get his team to follow. "This would only work if they were committed, and I realized I had to put my ego aside and get to know each one of them as people," Adrian said. "It has been some of the most rewarding work of my life."

Adrian finished with a lamentation. "I just wish the rest of my management team could get out of their own way and see how much better we would be if they just cared about their employees as people." ▶

Decision-Making

Sometimes the right call can be inconceivable in the moment.

In 1971, two researchers published a paper titled *Belief in Small Numbers*, which asserted that people (and particularly other researchers) are susceptible to applying conclusions from a small group (say 20) to the population overall.[58] It was one of the first pieces of research that directly challenged a world that saw itself as completely rational — backed by measures of validity — with the assertion that their results were anything but.

And so began the prolific — and groundbreaking — partnership between Daniel Kahneman and Amos Tversky, who changed the world of economics and first introduced the idea that instead of rational actors, people are greatly impacted by their cognitive biases and decision heuristics. "Behavioral economics" was born.

Their core conclusion? Humans are predictably irrational. Yes, that means you.

Our culture associates all sorts of bad things with being irrational, so that statement might sting. Yet, as tough as that is to hear, our biases and heuristics are still essential to our ability to function as humans. Our brains cannot process all the information. We have no choice but to take mental shortcuts, or we'd never be able to get out of bed in the morning.

Exactly how heavy is the load? The human body processes 11 million bits of information per second, or something on the order of one of those old 3.5 inch floppy disks. Yet, our conscious mind only makes us aware of about 50 bits.[59] I can prove it to you.

Until you read this sentence, you weren't consciously aware of sensation coming from the bottom of your foot, whether in a shoe, under a sheet, or feeling the breeze barefoot.

Why It Matters: The world is complicated, and we can only process so much information. As a result, we need to use every tool at our disposal to cut down the amount of data, decide, and learn from that lesson so we can apply it in our next situation.

In other words, if we had infinite time and energy, we probably wouldn't need these shortcuts. But we don't, so we must make things easier on ourselves.

It's in this process where we make mistakes. Perhaps we filtered out good information that could have helped us make a better decision. Or maybe we applied the wrong decision tool to the problem. Or, perhaps we simply didn't see the level of urgency the decision needed.

Digging Deeper: There are more than 200 cognitive biases that have been found through research. Instead of trying to learn them all, Buster Benson made this easy on us.

The author of *Why Are We Yelling?: The Art of Productive Disagreement*, with an impressive career that includes working with Amazon and Twitter, Buster is nearly obsessed with biases. After hours and hours of work, he developed a super simple model that helps us understand the blessings and curses of biases. We face three conundrums that make it incredibly hard to make truly rational decisions:

- ▶ **Too much information:** There's too much information to process, and we have limited attention to give, so we filter lots of things out. **Information and noise become signal.**
- ▶ **Not enough meaning:** Lack of meaning is confusing, and we have limited capacity to understand how things fit together, so we create stories to make sense of everything. **Signal becomes a story.**
- ▶ **Limited time:** We never have enough time, resources, or attention at our disposal to do everything that needs doing, so we jump to conclusions with what we have and move ahead. **Stories become decisions.**

Connecting the dots — the noise becomes signal, we turn that signal into a story that makes sense to us, we use that story to decide, and the outcome of that decision itself becomes a mental model, which in turn becomes signal. It's a feedback loop.

Figure 6.7
The Decision Process

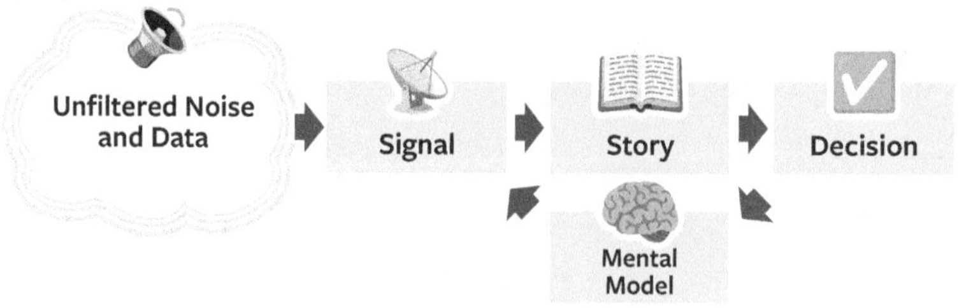

| Unfiltered Noise and Data | Signal | Story | Decision |

Mental Model

Fortunately, all hope is not lost. We're predictably irrational! Therefore, we can guess that, depending on the situation, we'll do one or more of the following:

- ▶ **Filtering information**: We'll look at information in its context and notice anything that is strange, novel, or out of whack.
- ▶ **Confabulate stories**: We'll confidently write a story to fill in the gap, lean on what we already know, and simplify the world around us.
- ▶ **Jump to conclusions**: We'll tend to stick to our guns in action and in thought, and do the thing that feels safest.

So, with all this getting in our way of making decisions, what do we do?

Get There Faster: We all want to make better decisions and be more wise. Typically, wisdom comes from experience because we didn't have another way to accrue it. Yet, if wisdom is about making good decisions, we can be wiser by learning how we make decisions and to make them better.

One way to outsmart our biases? Use an algorithm.

In 250 studies of professional decision-making, an algorithm beats the human half the time. The other half? They tie.[60] Maybe humans have a good reason to fear the robots.

Sometimes, there's no good way to build an algorithm. What then? How do leaders minimize noise and bias to maximize opportunity to make better decisions? The authors of *A User's Guide to Debiasing* have us covered[61]:

- ▶ **Thinking about the future:** We think too narrowly about potential outcomes and our estimates are typically way off. Since so much of leadership is about seeing around corners, biased thinking about the future can be a huge liability. Here are some strategies:

> **Make three estimates:** Not sure of future results? Instead of a guess or a two-number range, make three estimates (low, middle, and high). The low and high cases should be unlikely yet still possible. It's more likely the middle estimate is correct.

> **Think twice and take the average:** Create a single estimate then assume that estimate is wrong. Rethink the problem and devise a new estimate. Then average the two. That average is more likely to be accurate than relying on any one of the original estimates.

> **Use premortems:** Plan for future failure by imagining that the approach you took was disastrous. Start with a simple question, like, "Imagine five years from now and we've lost half of our business, why?" There are a few benefits:

  - It tempers expectations.
  - It lets you prepare backup plans.
  - It can highlight success or failure points.
  - If done with others, it provides a forum for dissent.

> **Take an outside view:** You're likely looking at the world from an inside-the-organization view. What about the outside world? Has someone else tried this, and what are their results? It helps to analyze odds more accurately and assess the worthiness of the approach.

> **Thinking about objectives:** People tend to narrow to just a few goals, which means they miss the larger goal. Mapping out all conceivable objectives allows you to prioritize what you want to do and see connections you might have missed.

> **Seek advice:** Sometimes you just need to see things from someone else's lens, so look for outside counsel. Avoid taking that perspective as truth by ensuring that you've already set

a clear picture of what you see, and don't tip the scales by sharing your perspective first. When making joint decisions, have each person make a list and combine them.

> **Cycle through your goals:** Instead of trying to check all the boxes, take the goals one-by-one and devise solutions based on those individual goals. Not only will you find more solutions, you'll find solutions that fit the maximum number of goals.[xxii]

▶ **Thinking about options:** There is rarely only one solution to a problem; devising one or more strong[xxiii] contenders helps to achieve a better result. This helps us avoid yes/no binary thinking and allows better ideas and solutions to float to the surface.

> **Use joint evaluation:** We tend to make decisions in a vacuum. A great way to avoid that is by considering an alternate hypothesis by asking the question, "What would I be missing if I make this choice?"

> **Try the "vanishing options" test:** Many leaders like to decide and move on once they have a workable choice, avoiding exploring superior alternatives. A mental trick to solve this? Assume you can't choose any of the options available to you and ask, "What else could I do?"

▶ **Fighting motivated bias:** What if we're not looking for the *best* choice, but instead the one that satisfies some sort of need we have? It's easy to distort the cost/risk/benefit equation in that frame of mind. The solution? Set "trip wires," that force us to redirect our efforts if we've not achieved our goals within a certain set of conditions.

---

xxii. It's like the old "pick two of: speed, cost, and quality." If you can't do all three, you can probably do two really well and even the third serviceable.
xxiii. Strong is the operative word. Too often, we structure a choice among other alternatives where the choice is too obvious. It creates an impression of rigorous decision-making through a biased process.

Bottom Line: Biases are our brain's way of ensuring survival. Balance the good with the bad by staying aware and using a few simple techniques to make your decisions as good as they can be.

The Learning Model

You oughta know, but it takes experience and reps to get there.

Remember that fourth spark we talked about, The End of Effortless Expertise? That's not just the predecessor. That's you. That's the team. That's everyone affected by the transition. Let's flash back to page 63/64:

Figure 6.8
The Learning Model

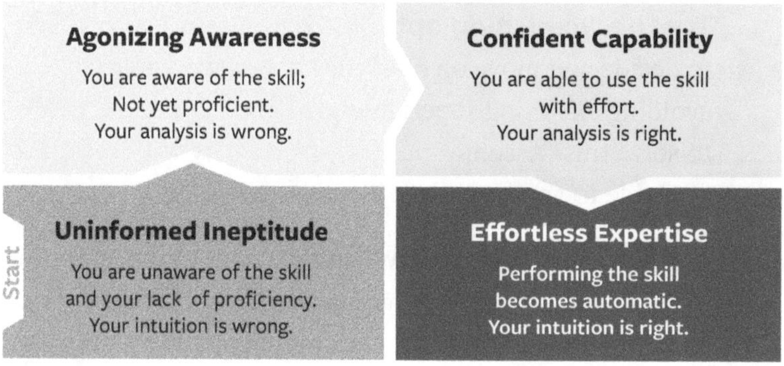

Agonizing Awareness	Confident Capability
You are aware of the skill; Not yet proficient. Your analysis is wrong.	You are able to use the skill with effort. Your analysis is right.
Uninformed Ineptitude	**Effortless Expertise**
You are unaware of the skill and your lack of proficiency. Your intuition is wrong.	Performing the skill becomes automatic. Your intuition is right.

▶ **Uninformed Ineptitude:** Summarized as "You don't know what you don't know," these are situations where you don't understand how easy — or hard — something is.

► **Agonizing Awareness:** You've given something a try and have become fully aware that you don't know what you're doing. This is the stressful moment when you understand that you either have to work harder to get better or give up.

► **Confident Capability:** The training wheels are off and you're confident that you can do the thing. While you might have to give it a little thought, you know that you can accomplish the task because you have practiced enough.

► **Effortless Expertise:** Not only are you confident in your ability to do the thing, you're not even aware of the steps that you take to achieve the results you do. The skill is second-nature and you can do it in your sleep.

Why It Matters: All involved have been running the organization in Effortless Expertise. Things just worked as-is, regardless of the processes and systems used to achieve results.

Succession changes things. No matter whether you're a spitting image of the predecessor or you're committed to putting your own spin on things, the change itself creates uncertainty.

We've already called out that people are painfully bad at naming why they're feeling what they feel in the moment.

Digging Deeper: The learning model gives us a framework to consider the struggle we and others are facing as they take on new roles and challenges.

The biggest issue we face as we drive organizational change?

Small changes are bigger than they seem. And many small changes compound on each other. Instead of adding incremental difficulty to the day-to-day, each change multiplies that challenge. We tend to make our most significant organizational mistakes when we underestimate the impact of even small changes, especially in the backdrop of a leadership transition.

The result? Organizational stress and frustration as people feel trapped in Agonizing Awareness.

Some best practices:

- ▶ **Change is still change:** No matter how small the changes might seem, they have an impact. Be patient.
- ▶ **Consider the context:** Know that organizational transitions create organizational stress at baseline. Each additional change has a disproportionate cost; decide accordingly.
- ▶ **Bundle changes:** If you have to make several changes at once, connect them to one reason or decision (example: "Because we've decided to pursue this new line of business, we're instituting the following: a new organization chart, implementing a new ERP system, and adding a new location.").
- ▶ **Communicate with clarity:** Keep your messaging tight and repeat it often.
- ▶ **Give space for feedback:** It's easy to push back and challenge others' feedback in change. To maximize people's buy-in, allow for feedback (and, where possible, incorporate it.)
- ▶ **Inspire:** The fastest way to get people to overcome their discomfort with change? Excite people to the point that they don't care much about the danger.

Bottom Line: *Everyone* in the organization is learning, which introduces organizational stress (and reduces the available energy to serve your customers). Stay in tune with where the team is on the learning model.

Prioritize What Matters

Most of us have our priorities out of whack. It takes an open mind for a different view.

A little more time, more effort, or more efficiency will do the trick, right? When we work with next leaders and successors, we hear one word over, and over, and over again: "Busy." Beyond a descriptor, "busy" has become an aspirational symbol on par with a trendy vacation spot, an exclusive country club membership, or luxury watch or handbag.

"Wait," you might be saying to yourself, "I'm not so shallow as to pursue busyness for the sake of status." okay, but what if being busy makes you feel like a *good person*?

In another study, across three continents (North America, Asia, and Europe), the findings showed that the culture considers it to be "morally admirable" to exert high effort.[63] In our time, being busy is the modern equivalent of being an upstanding citizen AND fashionable.

> *. . . a busy and overworked lifestyle, rather than a leisurely lifestyle, has become an aspirational status symbol.*[62]

The killer in all of this? All of this busyness is being lauded despite not getting anything done. In other words, we're stressing ourselves out by filling our time with tasks and worry that don't actually accomplish anything. Busy is an illusion of productivity.

The Big Picture: You're a "winner," or you wouldn't be a successor. At the same time, you can't fit 10 pounds of your favorite material in a five-pound bucket. Yet, our experience tells us a little more time, effort, or efficiency will get us there.

What if, instead, you just — and hear me out — didn't do it anymore? In coaching, this suggestion typically inspires an audible gasp and a litany of reasons why the candidate can't let go of the task. As a successor, your job is about to change significantly. To quote Semisonic and their '90s smash hit *Closing Time*, "Every new beginning comes from some other beginning's end."[xxiv]

As you transition to leading the organization, you have no choice but to abandon tasks that once seemed to be essential to your success. In this way, you are the predecessor (plot twist!) and subject to all of those challenges we discussed in Chapter 3. This requires you to acknowledge the following:

► What got you here — your operational problem solving — won't get you where you want to go. There's a whole book about it, called *What Got You Here Won't Get You There*. Almost everything you need to know about the book is in the title.[xxv]

► Your time is better spent creating the conditions for others in the organization to make things happen. The more you're in the Contributor Role Mindset, the less you're able to elevate into the strategic leader the organization needs.

► You will need to define winning differently, taking joy in others' individual victories and the collective organizational success over your own.

► What you know today isn't what you knew when you started (back to that Effortless Expertise idea), and that others will need to experience the learning model the same way you did.

► We sometimes trick ourselves into believing that being busy is being effective.

---

xxiv. It's low-key about having a kid. No, seriously. https://s21.us/closingtime
xxv. I just saved you $29. This book has now paid for itself.

▶ Others who step into doing what you did will do it differently and, perhaps, better than you did.

With those acknowledgements in hand, let's find a tool that will help you quickly judge how to analyze your tasks and decide where to put your focus.

The History: Dwight D. Eisenhower, 34th president and former military general who had served in both World Wars during his career, is a 20th-century giant in the history of both the United States and the world. Quoting J. Roscoe Miller, the 12th president of Northwestern University, at a speech to the Second Assembly of the World Council of Churches, Eisenhower said, "The urgent are not important, and the important are never urgent."[64] And thus The Eisenhower Decision Matrix was born.

The Model: The Eisenhower Decision Matrix is a simple four-quadrant decision tool that helps us decide how to prioritize our time. It works like this:

Figure 6.9
The Eisenhower Decision Matrix

- **Urgent/Important = *Do*:** These tasks are what you — and only you — can do, and their importance and priority make them worthy of your immediate attention.
- **Not Urgent/Important = *Decide*:** These tasks matter a whole lot, but will tend to get left behind by the tyranny of the now. Block time in your calendar to ensure you have the adequate time and space to get it done.
- **Urgent/Not Important = *Delegate*:** These tasks might matter, but they're not important for you to do. These are tremendous opportunities to hand off or outsource tasks.
- **Not Urgent/Not Important = *Delete*:** These tasks aren't going to move the needle, and there's no timeline for them to get done. They're worth getting rid of entirely.

This intuitive approach is only as effective as how we define "urgency" and "importance":

- **Urgency:** Eisenhower's instinct was backed by later research, which showed that people will complete a low-value task about 2.5 times more often when it is presented as urgent.[65] Successors will often fall into the "everything is urgent" trap as they continue to want to show their ability to perform.

- **Importance:** Successors struggle between "important to do" and "important *for me* to do." Handing off tasks — delegating — feels counter-intuitive for those who have proven their value by being reliable doers.

Why It Matters: Few successors start their tenure in leadership saying, "I hope the organization stagnates under my tenure." Yet, the need to stay intimately involved with lower-level decisions — falling down the stairs — limits the organization's growth to where you can invest your focus.

Bottom Line: You're beyond the point in your career where you can win by just working harder. Work smarter with expert prioritization.

Know It All

The specter of the exited CEO-turned-board-chairperson (Miguel) hovered over the new CEO, Evelyn, now in her 13th month in the role. Their close relationship strained, she was at her wits end after dealing with his constant second-guessing and questions from out of nowhere.

Despite strong financial performance, she inherited a mess. The predecessor, Miguel, believed in a flat organizational structure, using his cult-like leadership status to keep loyalty and push people to their limits. When he stepped out of the CEO spot, he had 13 executive-level direct reports and would often comment, "I really have 500 — anyone in this organization can come to me at any time."

His approach stifled growth and innovation by forcing his leaders to spend their time understanding every detail of their function, down to operational deadlines. "If you don't know when things are happening and how your department works, how can I trust in your decisions?" he'd ask mockingly as a corrective action, often in front of peers and executives. In Miguel's view, the fact that the company grew from $50 million to more than $1 billion shouldn't change how the organization functioned.

Evelyn had other ideas. Believing she could make CEO-like decisions, she proposed a new organizational structure to the board of directors. In this adjusted approach, the CEO would have four direct reports and delegate most of the operational decision-making to the next layer. This would give the CEO the opportunity to meet with customers and explore strategic acquisitions.

Miguel was livid. "You can't be CEO of this company if you don't know what's going on. You're the head firefighter. I don't care if they're our largest or smallest client, if there's something wrong, they want to hear from the CEO. I'm embarrassed that you would have considered this approach."

The result? Evelyn is still in the role, now with 16 direct reports. Her first year was marred by the lowest profitability in the company's history. As chief problem-solver, she is working at the operational level to address issues. She no longer has proactive meetings with any of her direct reports and has instructed them to reach out to her on only an as-needed basis.

"I don't think this makes any sense, and I'm miserable and exhausted," Evelyn admitted, "but Miguel has done this longer than I have, and I guess I just have to take his lead." ▶

Do the Leadership Work

Don't get bogged down by the overwhelming amount of leadership advice.

Frustrated by the thousands of leadership books that gave vague and contradictory guidance, the authors of *The Work of Leaders* spent six years to answer a basic question.

What do leaders *actually do*?

The result of their work is a practical model that demystifies leadership and sheds light on its best practices.

Digging Deeper: In each section, you'll learn about the best practice (listed first) in contrast to the more challenging tendency. Note that the

Shameless Plug

At Solutions 21, we use a behavioral assessment that includes *The Work of Leaders* feedback in our work with executives and next leaders. It's an exceptional tool and I have seen it change the direction of organizational decision-making if you're interested in learning more.

challenging tendency isn't bad overall, but it might not be helpful in doing that kind of leadership work.

It All Starts with Vision

Creating a compelling vision for the future is the first step in effective leadership. Why? Research shows it works (more on that when we talk about implementing an operational model on page 227). This involves:

1. **Exploration**: Leaders must remain open to new ideas and prioritize the big picture. This means resisting the urge to settle on the first solution and instead explore multiple possibilities.
   > **Remaining open vs. seeking closure**: Keeping an open mind versus quickly deciding on a course of action.
   > **Prioritizing the big picture vs. prioritizing details**: Focusing on overall goals versus concentrating on specific elements.

2. **Boldness**: Developing a bold vision requires leaders to take risks and speak out about their ideas. Boldness inspires others and sets the stage for innovative thinking.
   > **Being adventurous vs. being cautious**: Willingness to take risks versus preferring safe and tested paths.
   > **Speaking out vs. holding back**: Advocating for your ideas versus keeping them to yourself.

3. **Testing Assumptions**: Validating your vision through seeking counsel and exploring implications ensures that the vision is grounded and realistic.
   > **Seeking counsel vs. deciding independently**: Asking for advice versus relying solely on your judgment.
   > **Exploring implications vs. pushing forward**: Carefully considering the impact of decisions versus moving ahead quickly.

Building Alignment Throughout the Organization

Alignment involves gaining buy-in from those who will help turn the vision into reality. Based on data from hundreds of leadership teams I've worked with, this is where leaders most often stumble. This requires clear communication and engagement to get the team excited about the work ahead:

1. **Clarity**: Communicating the vision clearly by explaining the rationale and structuring messages effectively.
   > **Explaining rationale vs. offering intuition**: Providing logical reasons versus relying on gut feelings.
   > **Structuring messages vs. impromptu messaging**: Delivering organized communication versus off-the-cuff remarks.
2. **Dialogue**: Engaging in meaningful dialogue by exchanging perspectives and being receptive to input ensures that everyone feels included and heard.
   > **Exchanging perspectives vs. presenting information**: Inviting feedback versus simply sharing information.
   > **Being receptive vs. challenging**: Welcoming others' ideas versus questioning or opposing them.

3. **Inspiration**: Inspiring others by being expressive and encouraging helps build enthusiasm and commitment to the vision.
   > **Being expressive vs. being reserved**: Openly sharing emotions versus maintaining a reserved demeanor.
   > **Being encouraging vs. being matter-of-fact**: Motivating others with positive reinforcement versus a neutral approach.

Championing Execution

Execution is a danger point for successors; they're used to getting the work done.

Championing execution is about creating the conditions for the team to execute.

In the most black-and-white sense, you pull the levers, the team makes it happen. That works through:

1. **Momentum**: Leaders drive execution by maintaining momentum and proactively initiating action.
   > **Being driven vs. being low-key**: Setting a brisk pace versus a more relaxed approach.
   > **Initiating action vs. being reactive**: Starting projects proactively versus responding to situations as they arise.

2. **Structure**: Providing the necessary structure through planning and in-depth analysis ensures that everyone knows what is expected and can work efficiently.
   > **Planning vs. improvising**: Creating detailed plans versus adapting on the fly.
   > **Analyzing in-depth vs. following first impressions**: Thorough analysis versus relying on initial thoughts.

3. **Feedback**: Ensuring continuous feedback by addressing problems and offering praise helps keep the team aligned and motivated.
   > **Addressing problems vs. maintaining harmony**: Confronting issues directly versus avoiding conflict.
   > **Offering more praise vs. offering less praise**: Frequently recognizing achievements versus minimal acknowledgment.

Why It Matters: Few people always do the best practice (or the challenging tendency). Most of us fall somewhere in between. You probably guessed that a few are strong, a few are weak, and many fall somewhere within those poles.

Your goal? Identify the best-practice behaviors that you struggle to implement and actively plan the time and energy to do them effectively.

The Restructuring

Art, a CEO client, reached out for help with a challenging communication problem: He was about to start a significant organizational restructuring. Inheriting a mess — and saddled with a board that provided no useful support — Art worked with his executive team to create a new organizational structure better aligned with the current business.

Executives came to two conclusions: 1) the organization would be laying off about 20% of its staff; and 2) the company needed $1 million to keep or replace employees that are likely to see danger and run for the hills in the first six months after the announcement.

With board approval, Art laid out a communication plan to me. He would send a personal email to all employees, then travel the country over six weeks to visit the company's five locations. "I want to own the decision and make sure people knew I cared."

We talked Art out of that plan. Known for his shoot-from-the-hip style, we convinced him that there was zero chance employees at the fifth location would hear the same message as the first.

When the day came to announce the transition, each employee received an email from the CEO that he wrote, which was about two paragraphs. Attached to the email was a three-page memo outlining the changes and a slide deck that featured talking points and a visual of the new organizational structure. He allowed his executives to take the lead, and each site had a town-hall meeting with a VP or C-suite leader before the end of that week.

"You saved us $1 million," Art told me later. Not only did the company retain all if its employees, the overwhelming message to leadership was that the employees who were left were energized by the new approach. ▶

Leadership is not about rigidly adhering to a single style but about being adaptable and responsive to different situations.

Bottom Line: Leadership doesn't have to be overwhelming. Stick to a simple model and focus your energy on adapting to the things that make an impact but don't come naturally.

Know the Problem

Whether you've got one problem or 99, know the complexity to improve your solution.

Consider two different people. One sees any problem as something that requires blowing up the status quo and rebuilding it. Another sees every problem as something that, with a cautious, regimented approach, can use best practices to achieve the best outcome.

Both are right. And wrong. It depends on the problem's complexity. Instead of asking the solution to the problem, perhaps the first question should be, "What kind of problem is it?" Enter the Cynefin framework.

The History: In 1999, Dave Snowden, a consultant working for IBM, developed the Cynefin framework. Pronounced *kun-NEV-in* and a Welsh name meaning "place of multiple belongings,"[66] the process has been adopted across many industries as a tool to make sense of the situation in front of you.

Why It Matters: Our biases lead us toward preferred ways of solving problems, which isn't always the right approach. The Cynefin framework gives us a way to sort through the variables and find the best way to get a positive result.

The Model: The framework names five decision-making frameworks, or domains, that help us narrow down what our approach should be. These are (from simplest to most complex):

Figure 6.10

The Cynefin Framework

- ▶ **Clear:** Situations where cause and effect are well understood, allowing for straightforward solutions using established best practices.
- ▶ **Complicated:** Scenarios requiring expert analysis where cause and effect are knowable but not immediately obvious, relying on good practices.
- ▶ **Complex:** Environments characterized by unpredictability where cause and effect can only be deduced in retrospect and solutions evolve through experimentation.

▶ **Chaotic:** Contexts with high turbulence and no clear cause-and-effect relationships, requiring immediate action to restore order.

▶ **Confused:** Previously known as "disordered," this domain is a state of conflict where it is not obvious which of the other four domains apply.

Digging Deeper: The mistake leaders make? Underestimating or overestimating problem complexity.

Two examples:

▶ **Underestimation:** A successor finds that a group of employees are unhappy and there's turnover in a specific department. The successor knows the leader of that department to be a "good person" and assumes the employees are to blame. To the successor, the problem is clear (employees are being a pain) or complicated (there are other factors, but the manager is probably not one of them and the employees just need to get over it). In reality, poor management and resource allocation, combined with a few bad apples and badly needed upgrades to systems, have created a complex problem. The successor's solution: A half-day seminar on communication — is not up to the task of addressing the issue.

▶ **Overestimation:** A newly minted leader steps into the CEO role and, within a few months, the company loses two sizable clients. While not catastrophic, the losses hit the business hard enough to be noticed. The CEO decided to direct all resources to client retention, while pausing other operational efficiency initiatives that would affect client satisfaction. The issue? The lost clients were a result of acquisitions by larger firms that had a preexisting replacement partner. There's nothing the company could have done to keep those two clients. The CEO's missed mark set its operational efficiency efforts back by a year while having no meaningful change on already-high client satisfaction.

How to Apply It: Most of the other tools you've learned in this part help you to uncover the right approach.

- ▶ **Hit the pause button:** The more anxious we are, the more complex the problem looks and vice-versa. Assess the problem from as neutral a mindset as possible. It's easy to get caught up in the emotion created by a problem. Ask the questions on page 75.
- ▶ **Assess complexity:** From a neutral frame of mind, assign a level of complexity and prioritize accordingly.
- ▶ **Find whose problem it is to solve:** Is this one you need to solve, or are you falling down stairs? Can naming and implementing the solution be a development opportunity for someone else?
- ▶ **Seek outside counsel:** If you lack clarity, get a third-party perspective.
- ▶ **Watch for biases:** As we said in Decision-Making on page 194/196, we're not great at making decisions. Use the techniques there to avoid trouble.

Bottom Line: Size up your problems the right way, and right size the solutions to match. Missing the mark can have huge direct and indirect costs.

Leadership Upgrade Complete

You have been upgraded successfully.
There are a few more steps to follow,
and then the real work starts.
Congratulations.

Turn the page to continue

The Bottom Line on Chapter 6: Install a Leadership Upgrade

TL;DR:

Succession isn't just about inheriting a title; it's about upgrading your leadership capabilities to meet the demands of the role. You don't have another decade to sit on the bench. We delve into the essential leadership skills, mindset shifts, and practical strategies to help you transition smoothly and thrive in your new role. By focusing on strategic oversight, operational excellence, culture building, community engagement, and continuous improvement, you can ensure a successful leadership upgrade that aligns with both personal and organizational goals.

The Hits:

- **Role Mindsets:** It's too easy to fall into old habits when we step up into leadership. Your secret weapon is agility, running up and down the "stairs" to apply the right mindset at the right time.
- **Culture Building:** Creating and maintaining a strong organizational culture is essential for long-term success. Leaders must build, standardize, and communicate effectively.
- **Emotional Intelligence and Biases:** Our decisions are based on what we see and how we feel. Learn to use that data more effectively to consistently make better decisions.
- **Know Where You're Learning:** The learning model is a tool to help put your current level of comfort into context.
- **Solve the Right Problem:** The mistake leaders make is usually at the beginning — defining the problem. Accurately assessing both what the problem is and its complexity helps you dedicate the right resources in the right direction.

Thought-Starter Questions:

- ▶ How can you shift your mindset — and action — from doing to leading?
- ▶ Which of the leadership skills outlined do you feel most comfortable employing? Least comfortable?
- ▶ What is in your toolbox that you can implement tomorrow to be a more effective leader? What will take some time to develop?
- ▶ How can you get helpful feedback about your approach to emotional intelligence skills?
- ▶ Who can you rely on to challenge your biases?

Successor Strategies for Success:

- ▶ Have a bias toward delegation over doing day-to-day tasks.
- ▶ Use the pause button to think differently about potential challenges and solutions.
- ▶ Always assume good intent. People rarely wake up thinking, "How can I mess this up today?"
- ▶ Keep laser-focused on priorities and focus your energy on what is important.

On Deck:

Making the transition involves a few variables: you as the individual, the organization, and your relationship with the predecessor. You'll learn a simple, practical approach to implement in your organization to keep those three aligned.

The Bottom Line

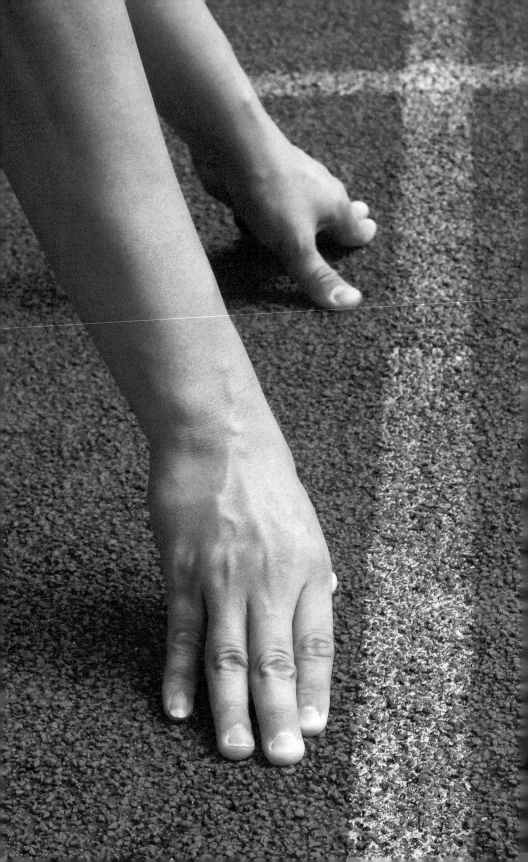

CHAPTER 7

It's Go Time

It's time to take charge. Here's the playbook.

Whether you're standing at the precipice or have already stepped into the succession role, you need tools to be the best you can be.

Three things need to align for you to win.

- You.
- The organization.
- The predecessor relationship.

Having developed leaders and aligned teams for three-plus decades, we at Solutions 21 know a thing or two about how to do this well. Our approach follows these principles:

> *Progress over perfection.*
>
> *~ An Inspirational LinkedIn Post*

- **Simple:** Complicated tools and systems are hard to learn and follow. Using simple, well-studied frameworks makes it easier to implement new ideas.
- **Forward-looking:** We minimize looking backward, and only as far as it's useful data, to make sure we're making progress.
- **Momentum-building:** So much progress is building repeatable habits that eventually become momentum.
- **Celebration-worthy:** One of the more pervasive mistakes leaders make is their inability to celebrate victories.
- **People-centered:** No matter your culture, operational maturity, or experience level, your organization is made up of people. All of the tools we use acknowledge that we're all fallible and need to build that "humanness" into everything we do.

Let's look at the toolbox.

You

Leadership is hard. Prepare yourself to take charge.

There comes a point in our core program, Next Leader Now, when individuals in the cohort want a clear, clean solution to their challenge when none exists.

What do we tell them?

"Leadership is hard."

Unfortunately, somewhere along the line, "hard" came to mean "bad."

What follows is hard — you are going to make tough decisions, solve challenging conflicts, and overcome obstacles you couldn't have anticipated.

Doing what's hard is what makes you better. Let's get to it.

Successor(s)?

Teamwork makes the dream work?

The entire book is about you, the successor, in the singular. In many transitions, there's more than one successor.

Here's why:

- ▶ The predecessor role has grown to be too big for one person to be effective.
- ▶ The work the predecessor did now spans multiple specialized skills and disciplines.
- ▶ The successors are uninterested in the live-to-work lifestyle of the predecessor.

▶ There are business reasons (family transition, management buyout) for there to be multiple successors.

Quick story: Two parents started a professional services firm, growing it significantly over their careers while raising six children. Many aunts and uncles enabled the couple to work up to 70 hours a week in the business. While the kids appreciated never wanting anything, they hated how little time they spent with their parents and vowed never to duplicate it. As their parents approached retirement age, and with five of the six working for the company (plus three cousins), the overall organization was handed over to the eight family members, with each owning an equal percentage and running a specialized division within the practice. The second generation created a flexible work environment that allowed every employee to spend more time with their family.

Digging Deeper: I've already said we won't dig too far into the five transition factors (Ownership, Governance, Management, Leadership, and Brand) beyond making you aware that they exist.

Yet, there are best practices you will want to consider as you think about having multiple people with decision authority.

▶ **There's someone in charge:** While there is fantastic research on organizational structures — and we'll delve more into that on page 239 — there is one inescapable reality: Someone needs to be in charge.[xxvi]

▶ **Define the decision process:** Clearly define and communicate how you will make decisions about the business (and, ideally, get it in writing).

▶ **Everyone contributes:** Everyone in a controlling leadership role must contribute, even if the contributions aren't equal among members. Agreeing to that ahead of time is paramount.

---

xxvi. That doesn't mean that having multiple equal leaders *can't* work, but the conditions are rarely right for it to be the best solution.

Three Angry Brothers

"The day Dad died was the worst thing that ever happened to our family, we just didn't know it yet."

Dave, the oldest brother of five siblings, was lamenting how his family fell apart after the patriarch and founder of the family business passed away. The father had handed the successful distribution business to his kids in equal parts, even though two of them had never worked for the company. That decision served as the start of a series of family squabbles.

"Mark and Grant both worked for the company and wanted more leadership responsibility. They both resented that I was always in the leadership role because I had been in the business longer."

While the three brothers were able to buy out their two sisters, the transaction wasn't smooth. Each insisted on owning more than the other, with a stalemate leaving each with 33% of the company.

To preserve relationships, Dave wouldn't make decisions about the business unless both Mark and Grant agreed. Growth ground to a halt as any potential choice led to second-guessing and, ultimately, stagnation.

Things came to a head as the brothers began discussing transition. Each brother was within a decade of retirement age but spoke about his role in the business as if he were just getting started. The idea that any of them would give up control after such a long wait was unfathomable.

The company lost ground and key talent to competitors as the brothers squabbled about everything from IT investments to whether to develop their high-potential leaders. Dave mentioned a quote from an exit interview of a high-potential employee they hoped to retain. "I don't want to die before I get a promotion," Dave shared. That employee left for a VP role and a 60% pay increase. "I just know we can't keep managing the business like this."

Despite urging from outside advisors, the brothers haven't been able to come to agreement on the best approach forward, though they've been able to spend time together again.

"At this point, we might lose the business, but at least we can spend time together at the holidays again." ▶

- ▶ **Eliminate stalemates:** Running a business with multiple leaders inevitably leads to conflict. Make it impossible for a single decision-maker to hold up the process.
- ▶ **Establish common principles:** Define the principles on which everyone will make decisions. These are the no-compromise, bottom-line behaviors and goals that provide the foundation of trust.

Bottom Line: The transaction is a symbol, but that symbol has consequences. Make sure that you have set up the ground rules if more than one of you is running the organization.

Your Vision for You

Before you start, you've got to get right with you.

That means knowing who you are and where you want to go. For successors, this isn't easy. There's typically a strong connection between their succession opportunity and identity (sound familiar?).

Your objective should be to define what you want in your own terms and make clear how the new role will fit into that story. That story you're telling? That's your vision.

How It Works: You'll see a lot about vision in the coming pages — it's one of the most impactful tools you have in your arsenal.

Why?

Visions work. Research shows[67]:

▶ They put us in a positive frame of mind.
▶ That frame of mind makes us feel good about pursuing our goals.
▶ Feeling positive about our goals means we're more likely to be committed to achieving them.
▶ Increased commitment leads to progress and, ultimately, the likelihood of achievement.

Short version? When you feel good, you do good.[xxvii]

What makes a good vision, and differentiates it from a goal?

Mental contrasting — vividly imagining a better future than what you are experiencing today — offers the key to success.[68] Not only does this activate our conscious efforts, but it gets in our subconscious, too, enabling us to take action to get to where we want to go.[69] By creating a compelling future vision, we're able to be more resilient through obstacles.

Put It In Action: Since most next leaders are so *tactical*, we've developed two simple exercises to help them define this compelling vision.

▶ **Step 1:** Think about five years from now. Everything went exactly as you planned. You've not encountered one single roadblock on the way to achieving all that you hoped for, personally and professionally. What does that look like? What signs and symbols are around you that represent markers of that success?

▶ **Step 2:** Imagine you're telling the story to a good friend, someone who will be genuinely excited for you to share this amazing progress. How does it feel to tell the story? What feelings would you describe to this friend?

---

xxvii. Please, Mr. Editor, leave this grammatical error for effect.

Assuming you made this something so exciting you can almost taste it, you've just laid the groundwork for your conscious and subconscious mind to take meaningful steps toward making it happen.

One Caveat: One common thread across all successful (or, at least emotionally healthy) transitions?

The successor has options.

The change caused by transitions means there's excessive focus on the organization and the process. Especially if there's another component — family, close relationship — pressure can build on the transition that isn't helpful or healthy. The successor accepts the challenge but rejects the pressure.

If you don't feel like you have options, create them. How?

Get support. (More on that next.)

Bottom Line: Vision creates an "imagined future" that — once others buy into it — empowers your team to take actions that capitalize on strengths and mitigate weaknesses; it is a psychological secret weapon. Use it.

Coaching & Mentorship

You can't make much happen if the emperor (you) is walking around naked.

Confession time — whether this book is amazing or terrible, you're going to need more than just what's in the pages to be successful. This book can't know your exact context.

That's where mentorship and coaching come in.

While you'll see those terms used interchangeably (and the definition of "coaching" stretched further and further), there's an important distinction between the two:

▶ Mentorship is "an informal association focused on building a two-way, mutually beneficial relationship for long-term career movement."[70]

▶ Coaching is a more formal relationship designed to help the person unlock new levels of performance in themselves through good questions, accountability, and feedback.

Here's the challenge: Mentorship alone isn't enough.

The Limits: Adam Grant, the well-known researcher and podcaster, published *Hidden Potential*, where he dug into research on mentorship and found a few surprising results.

If you're taking an introductory course, is it better to learn from an experienced lecturer or a non-expert? Overwhelmingly, students learn more from the latter. The result was true across disciplines for data of more than 15,000 students. It's not close.

> *. . . if you're taking a new road, the best experts are often the worst guides.*

The reason?

To quote Grant,[71] ". . . if you're taking a new road, the best experts are often the worst guides." He cites two reasons:

1. Experts don't know how far they've travelled and don't clearly remember what being a beginner was like.
2. The curse of Effortless Expertise—they don't even know how to explain it to someone who doesn't already know it.

Adam also found some great research about lawyers aspiring to become a partner in their firms and had access to mentorship. The results?

► Lawyers with a single mentor were more satisfied and committed to the firm but saw no difference in the speed of their promotion than someone without one.

► Lawyers with as few as two or three mentors were more likely to make partner.

The difference came down to the approach. A single mentor can give you a map from point to point, which might be outdated or lead you astray. Multiple mentors can give you tidbits of information that act as a compass so that you can find the destination on your own.

Where Coaching Comes In: Full disclosure — we do *a lot* of coaching.

We're not alone. Between 2019 and 2022, the number of coaching practitioners jumped 54%.[72]

The reason? It's effective. Executive coaching enhances goal attainment, resilience, and workplace well-being.[73]

Even more so for successors.

In our experience, the most effective coaching approach involves asking questions, addressing gaps, and helping to make invisible gaps visible so the successor can address them. This uncovers core issues and allows successors to address them as quickly as possible. Most importantly, having a third party — unconnected to the day-to-day of the organization — serves as a hugely impactful resource.

Interestingly, it's not just the scheduled, one-on-one interactions that make a difference. When a coaching candidate gets feedback and recommendations just in time, development magic happens.

Here's an example. A succession candidate felt he had been strung along by leadership for a few years. The successor felt he had come to a decision point — either the transition begins, or he looks for another job. A quick call to his coach (me) changed his career trajectory. Expecting a supportive voice who would storm the castle with him, he instead got significant pushback that connected to his personal vision. The candidate realized he was about to make a near-catastrophic career mistake. Today? He's been the Chief Operating Officer for the last 18 months and will be the CEO in the next year.

Bottom Line: You need help and the more the merrier. Strong coaching support with excellent mentorship is the recipe for your personal success. Take advantage of both.

Leadership Brand

You're not a leader if there's no one there to follow. Why are they there?

Earlier in the book, we talked about transitioning the organization's brand.

That exiting leader has a brand. You do, too. What's yours?

Some Context: Past generations prized a company's "good name," preferring for their kids to stick with name-brand companies that they could brag about to their friends. The pedigreed talent would gravitate to those organizations, with smaller businesses left to find diamonds in the rough.

That's no longer true.

Organizations differentiate themselves not by the brand on the side of the building, but the leadership brands of individual leaders.

Though Tom Peters sparked the idea of applying branding principles to the person,[xxviii] the idea of managing brands in a variety of areas, including "employer brand" is all relatively new. That's the reason awards like Inc.'s "Best Workplaces" are only four decades old.

---

xxviii. I mentioned this back on page 37.

Digging Deeper: Allowing your leadership brand to happen on its own isn't a risk worth taking.

Fortunately, outlining a leadership brand is pretty simple:

> *. . . talent wants to hook their career wagon to a strong leadership horse.*
>
> *~ "The Leadership Decade"*

- ▶ **Step 1: Identify what you think makes a good leader:** Consider the best (and worst) leaders you've had. What did they do that worked well? What didn't land with you? Write those ideas down.

- ▶ **Step 2: Consider the current and future state:** There are many well-known historical leaders whose methods would fail in a modern context. What do followers expect from their leaders today? (Hint: the section on Profitable Intelligence on page 187 is a good start.) How are those expectations likely to change? Write those down.

- ▶ **Step 3: Define the values that drive your decisions:** Are you tough, but fair? Do you like to be inspirational and people-focused? Do you want to be known as someone who gets things done? Name three to five values that you lean on when you work with others. Jot down those values and a short definition for each.

- ▶ **Step 4: Write a leadership brand statement:** Like a vision or mission statement, a leadership brand statement is a short, easy-to-remember phrase that epitomizes your leadership approach and philosophy. A few examples:
  - > I am committed to achieving our goals while ensuring my team can stretch to further heights.

> > I support my direct reports through providing resources, development opportunities, and feedback that allows them to maximize their potential.

> > I inspire my team to achieve their goals and reward their successes along the way, ensuring that they believe in themselves.

> > I commit to providing clear and direct guidance in a way that ensures every member of the team has the tools and resources for them to do what they need to for themselves and the organization.

Outlining the brand isn't enough; you then have to put it into practice. Here are a few steps to make sure you're living up to your brand:

▶ **Seek direct feedback:** Share your brand with others and get their thoughts. Does the brand work for you? Does it explain your leadership priorities well?

▶ **Explore a 360:** Getting feedback from all directions, ideally through a formal process, is a great way to understand how well-aligned your leadership brand truly is. This information can confirm your brand or give you crucial information to revise it.

▶ **Share your brand when it's ready:** Once you've settled on a validated brand that works for you, don't be shy in sharing it.

▶ **Ask for accountability:** When sharing your brand, be explicit about asking for feedback to ensure you're behaving in alignment with that brand. More importantly, don't hesitate to absorb feedback when you're off track. Living your leadership brand 100% of the time is impossible; do what you need to do to stick to it as closely as you can.

Bottom Line: A leadership brand is only words unless you behave in ways that align with it. Define it, seek feedback, and be accountable to become the kind of leader your organization needs.

Leadership Development

It's tough getting comfortable hanging out at the top of the Role Mindset stairs; don't let the fear of heights stop you from success.

Two data points get cited by anyone in the leadership development space:

▶ Globally, companies spend more than $80 billion on leadership development annually.[74]

▶ Managers are in people-leading roles for an average of ten years before getting any formal training or development.[75]

Some More Context: Yet, if you look around, it doesn't seem like we're spending nearly the entire federal transportation budget on developing leaders, does it?

Despite the big top-line number, it makes more sense when looking at the per-employee spending. The average? About $175,[76] or roughly the amount the average American family spends on their mobile phone bill in a month.[77]

If you can't get reliable cell service for $175, how are you going to develop exceptional leaders with that annual per-person budget?

Digging Deeper: A lot of different approaches exist. These components work when employed together:

▶ **Performance feedback:** Much of what we consider performance feedback, often through a traditional performance review process, is broken and often does not produce the hoped-for results.[78] In its place, we recommend a more specific, personalized series of feedback tools that offer actionable insights based on data rather than opinion.

▶ **Cohort-based learning:** Despite the explosion of self-paced e-learning, (nearly $7 billion in 2023[79]), learning as a cohort is better for organizations looking to build a strong leadership culture. The structure, collaboration, and accountability make the learning more impactful overall, and easier to implement when leadership conversations occur in the context of what is happening in the organization.

▶ **Individual coaching:** It's next to impossible to take in so much information and learning, and apply it well quickly (hence The Learning Model on page 200). Coaching helps to take all of that "stuff" and prioritize what matters to you in your individual and organizational context. Connecting the content to your context greatly improves your ability to incorporate those new approaches into your daily work habits.

▶ **Peer interaction:** Within the cohort-based learning model, people in the cohort can interact and learn from each other based on their varied perspectives within the organization. Not only does this give everyone in the cohort a wider view, but it helps entrench the leadership lessons more widely.

▶ **Consistent reinforcement:** The forgetting curve says that you forget about 80% of what you learned just 30 days prior.[80] That is, of course, if there's no reinforcement in between. Introducing additional learning opportunities, ideally self-paced, that restate the concepts in an engaging way ensures the concepts take a stronger hold.

▶ **Personal planning:** Making the content matter to you is the key difference-maker when getting people aligned to develop their leadership skills. Creating a plan that helps individuals define a future vision, identify skills and gaps, set goals, and outline tactics and timelines ensures that the process leads to tangible, highly rewarding progress.

Does that sound like $175 to you?

High-quality leadership development isn't cheap, and the per-person investment is typically $8,000 to $12,000.

(Deep breath.)

It's worth it, to the tune of around 7x each dollar invested, according to one study.[81] And that's just the tangible benefits; strong leadership has shown to deliver an additional 2-4x EBITA at sale.[82]

Why it delivers such high returns:

- ▶ Improved business performance.
- ▶ Better decision-making.
- ▶ Lower turnover.
- ▶ Increased business stability (crucial for business valuation).

Why It Matters: Few organizations have done the hard work of developing their leaders before they stepped into key roles. As you develop your own leadership skills, you'll need a team of people who can serve as peer leaders. You can't achieve that by happenstance.

Bottom Line: Growing your leaders is an investment that acts as an insurance policy against many of the greatest risks a transitioning business can face.

A Case for Community

Want to maximize your value as a leader? Get your hands dirty.

Let's talk about Ed Satell.

Ed Satell founded and served as CEO and Chairman of a multi-division media ecommerce provider headquartered in the Philadelphia region. In 2016 at the age of 80, he founded the Satell Institute, what he refers to as a "Think and Do Tank," to advance Corporate Social Responsibility at the CEO level.

He believes free enterprise should support the quality of life for people in their communities.

His model is one-of-a-kind. He's endowed the organization 100%, and no one can join the network by contributing to the institute itself. Instead, the corporation makes a *minimum* $25,000 annual commitment for four years to a nonprofit of their choosing. With that commitment, the CEO joins, as does the nonprofit.

His impact? Nearly $80 million has been committed to nonprofits by members of the Satell Institute since 2016.

Be like Ed.

Why It Works: Nonprofit work provides the most effective leadership training ground. Here's why:

- ▶ **It's free:** Working in your community is a no-cost leadership lab.
- ▶ **It's lower-risk:** You're focused on an organizational mission that is likely less urgent than your day-to-day.
- ▶ **It's hard:** Leading people volunteering their time takes more savvy than using positional leadership.
- ▶ **New lenses:** Nonprofits open your mind to problems and solutions you might not have known before.
- ▶ **Expand your network:** Many nonprofits have other successful professionals on their board.
- ▶ **Becomes part of your brand:** The reputational benefits of service are far-reaching.

The danger?

Don't make it about you.

> **Don't make it about you.**

My Opinion: I get it — you've got a lot going on. Family. Kids. The transition. Work-life balance. Faith. Fitness. Laundry.

I'm not sitting in judgment if you're not a do-gooder, or if there's not a cause that moves you, or if you don't have the flexibility.

Yet, one consistent thread that connects the best leaders I've met at all ages and levels is that they serve. They fill the vacuum and make an impact. It's in their bones.

Maybe it isn't today because you've got too much going on. I'd ask you to consider making space for making an impact.

Thanks for coming to my TED Talk.

Bottom Line: Practice makes perfect. Serving your community is a great training ground.

The Organization

It's not (just) about you anymore.

As we talked about in The Montage, you've grown beyond focusing on your personal goals and objectives. It's now about the organization.

What does that really mean?

Your organization has stakeholders. Who they are is unique to you, but tend to fall into the following categories:

▶ Stockholders
▶ Fiduciary and advisory board members
▶ Executives
▶ Organizational leaders and managers
▶ Staff
▶ Clients

- ▶ Prospects
- ▶ Vendors and partners
- ▶ Industry trade groups
- ▶ The community

That's a lot of people who care a whole lot about your transition. They all need to feel as confident as possible about your leadership.

Fortunately, some simple approaches that, when executed well, maximize your chances at a smooth(er) leadership change. It involves three efforts:

1. Strategic planning.
2. Repeatable operational model.
3. Succession culture.

Let's tackle these one by one.

Strategic Planning

Every successful leadership transition in my research involved a well-developed strategic plan.

Organizations without them? Few were as successful as hoped due to emotional flareups, changing priorities, and unanswered questions. The lack of structure and accountability made it almost impossible to know where the team was on the journey or what to do next.

Why do strategic plans work?

The plan creates a separation between the long-term objective and short-term performance. It de-personalizes the transition, turning the focus toward performance rather than the emotions of those involved. It serves as a type of North Star that the team follows when times get tough.

The stakeholders benefit, too.

For the predecessor, the plan:

- ▶ Creates tools to validate that the organization understands its goals and objectives.
- ▶ Serves as a set of meaningful metrics and milestones that help everyone understand the state of progress.
- ▶ Defines triggers and handoff points that make it easier for the predecessor to have confidence.

The plan gives the successor:

- ▶ Certainty about when the successor will have opportunities to take on elements of the next role.
- ▶ Pressure points if the predecessor "moves the goalposts."
- ▶ A scoreboard that makes it easier to know what the predecessor is measuring.

For the team, communicating the plan gives:

- ▶ Clarity that a plan exists to make a smooth transition.
- ▶ Comfort that the details have been thought through.
- ▶ Context about the future direction of the organization.

For everyone else, knowing a plan exists allows for:

- ▶ Confidence in the new leadership team.
- ▶ Trust that interactions will continue to be positive, or even improve.
- ▶ Willingness to continue to invest in the relationship.

Digging Deeper: In some circles, strategic planning has a mystic quality.

It's not magic.

In our work in developing strategic plans for companies ranging from ten to 10,000 employees, we've used the same basic approach.

General Guidelines

These general practices help ensure a successful plan:

- ▶ **Location:** Get offsite, ideally somewhere relaxing but productive for the team. The office tends to be a distraction, and strategic planning goes best when the participants are focused.

- ▶ **Attendance:** The people attending should have: a) an understanding of the business and its future positioning; b) the authority to have a meaningful impact; and c) sufficient commitment to be willing to work through the process.

- ▶ **Time:** A full day to two and a half days is common. We've found one and a half days to be a sweet spot to get good work done without burning out.

Pre-Work

Focusing the team on the right things before the event speeds up the process. You'll want to ask questions that help the group identify the situation in which the organization is operating. Here are a few that tend to work well:

- ▶ What about the organization makes it great to be a part of or to lead?
- ▶ What in the organization is getting in the way of making it even more successful?
- ▶ If you could change one thing unilaterally, what would it be and what impact would it have?

You can ask these questions of the planning team or organization-wide, depending on how much information you're looking to have prior to the meeting. This pre-work can be as easy as these thought-starter questions, or as complicated as an organization-wide survey. Regardless, you want the planning team focused on solving its issues when they walk in the door.

Retreat

The planning event is where the team will "roll up their sleeves." There's a simple agenda that works in the vast majority of situations:

1. Create shared understanding by providing the team "game film," or data about how the team is likely to work together and make decisions. Assessments of team performance are a great tool to provide feedback to the team before getting started.
2. Establish a story that captures the long(ish)-term accomplishments of what the organization can become. Between three and five years tends to work best.
3. Complete a "pre-mortem" exercise[xxix] to allow for teammates to poke holes in the plan and unearth potential challenges. This is the "sacred cow" killer.
4. Explore the environment. SWOT (Strengths, Weaknesses, Opportunities, and Threats) is a well-known thought exercise.[xxx] Other frameworks, like PEST (and its many, many variants) pair well with SWOT if you think you need to dig deeper.[xxxi]
5. Identify trends and themes from all the information you've collected.
6. Prioritize which of those themes require the most attention.
7. Define your areas of effort — typically referred to as objectives or pillars.
8. Choose meaningful goals that, when achieved collectively, get you to your overall objectives.
9. Create a tactical plan that breaks the big goal into bite-sized chunks.

I recommend this simple agenda (only nine steps!) to allow the space for the complexity of your organizational variables to shine through.

xxix. Harvard Business Review has a great article about this: https://hbr.org/2007/09/performing -a-project-premortem
xxx. Mind Tools is a good resource if you're unfamiliar: https://www.investopedia.com/terms/s/ swot.asp
xxxi. Wikipedia comes through with PEST and its variants: https://en.wikipedia.org/wiki/PEST _analysis

You know you've been successful if:

- ▶ Everyone participated.
- ▶ The team is confident in the results.
- ▶ The strategies, goals, and tactics align with the vision outlined at the beginning.
- ▶ The outcome feels accomplishable.

Best Practices

It's not just about the agenda — there is art to the process. Here are the best practices to follow for you and the planning team:

- ▶ **Get it facilitated:** It's nearly impossible not to bias the result if you, or someone on your team, leads the process. Having a third party do the work gives you the ability to maximize your role as participant and minimizes the chances that the outcome will be doubted due to your excessive influence.

- ▶ **Embrace the discomfort:** The process is uncomfortable. Most participants will feel like a fish out of water made worse by the sometimes challenging conversations the planning team will engage. Acknowledge from the beginning that discomfort will eventually lead to shared understanding.

- ▶ **Take advantage of the separation:** If you do choose to have it facilitated, allow the facilitator to take the pressure of keeping the process on track. Once the process is done, lean on the third-party facilitation as a validator that the outcome is correct.

- ▶ **Minimize biases and anchors:** Especially in successful enterprises, it's easy to anchor to all that has been done prior. Maintain a critical eye on your own biases and anchors to ensure that you get the best outcome possible.

▶ **Maximize the definition of "what could be":** Many strategic plans aren't bold enough. Challenge yourself, and your planning team, to think as big as possible.

▶ **Align the tactics:** Planning teams get tripped up when goals and tactics connect and overlap. This is inevitable. Make connections and determine the order of operations without overthinking it.

▶ **Close is enough:** The famous Mike Tyson[xxxii] quote aside, the plan should be adjusted when it hits the buzzsaw of reality. Don't obsess about making it perfect.

▶ **Spread the wealth:** As you home in on tactics, make sure to spread ownership of those tactics throughout the organization, at least one or two levels down from the planning team (if your team is big enough). Planning teams tend to hoard the work, which creates a huge missed opportunity to use tactics as a talent development opportunity.

▶ **Be realistic about timelines:** Every strategic plan front-loads the due dates. In every one of those plans, the due dates move. Be realistic about what you can do — *on top of your existing full-time jobs.*

▶ **Define the celebration:** All of this is hard work. Celebrate and celebrate often. Celebrate completing the plan, making progress on tactics, and achieving goals.

Communicate the Plan

The organization needs to know the plan.

How you communicate the plan, and to what audiences, is up to you. Yet, there are commonalities in what the best organizations do:

---

xxxii. "Everyone has a plan until they get punched in the mouth."

▶ **Bias toward transparency:** Even the best organizations struggle to communicate the vision and objectives across the enterprise. The more transparency about the plan — and what you want to achieve — the more employees will be engaged and aligned.

▶ **Simplify the message:** Too many strategic plans are wordy and complicated. Keep it short, simple, and memorable.

▶ **Communicate often:** Talk about the strategic plan, and how actions align to it, at every opportunity. Few employees are going to have the same understanding of the organization as you do, and that means you might not realize what they *don't* know. Communicate the message until you get eye rolls.

▶ **Connect the dots:** You're moving fast and making a lot of changes. When you're making decisions, you're doing them in alignment with the strategic plan. Your team might not know that! When making changes, decisions, or communicating company strategies, connect the message to the strategic plan.

It's so easy to connect decisions to your plan. All you need to do is start your sentences with, "In alignment with our strategy to [fill in the blank]," or "Since we are pursuing the goal of [fill in the blank]." This helps people see the link between the strategy and the actions, and lowers the anxiety of change.

A Little More Context: Strategic plans are used for a range of reasons that typically have two extremes.

On one end is operational — the strategic plan is designed to help the organization make things happen.

Figure 7.1

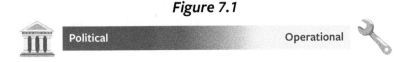

The other end is political — you're creating the plan to influence others.

Before you finalize the plan, know where you fall on that axis.

Bottom Line: The plan is just one step to ensure excellent operational performance. Next, you need a model to make your vision a reality.

The Right Operational Model

85% of companies lack the ability to implement strategy they've developed.[83]

Seemingly unrelatedly, researchers estimate that 84% of adults experience back pain at some point in their lives.[84]

The reasons are parallel.

In both cases, there are two systems at play: the skeletal, which provides structure, and the muscular, which supports the structure and provides power and movement.

Working in tandem, people can move mountains.

When something is out of whack, there's pain. You've probably felt it before.

The Big Picture: Every organization has an operating model.

The model is how organizations decide priorities, make decisions, set goals, and ensure that efforts at all levels align to those objectives.

Most operating models develop organically over time and in response to individual and collective successes and failures. Since "how things always worked" has worked, leaders have seen little need to change it.

When there's a succession handoff, many organizations take the opportunity to rethink the way they do business. You'll know it's happening when people say, "We want to preserve our culture, but we want to spend our time doing things that are more productive," or in the (over?)used, "We need to spend more time working on the business than in the business."

The response? Quicksand in the form of (most) formal operating models.

The Blue Screen of Death: There are a whole lot of operating models and systems out there, some of which are so complex that you need to learn an entirely new language to implement them.

Our experience? Most of them don't work. Quicksand is mostly to blame. Here's just a few examples:

1. **Quicksand #6 (Brubeck vs. Bach):** The pendulum swings from jazz to Juilliard, and organizations struggle to adopt the habits necessary to implement the process well. At its worst, the organization experiences lots of organizational stress implementing the model instead of enabling the organization to serve its clients and employees faster.

2. **Quicksand #7 (The New Sheriff):** Implementing a rigid operating model often gets branded to the successor — with all of the wins (and more likely) losses to go along with it. It's especially bad when the successor chooses a tool for its complexity, mistaking it for rigor.

3. **Quicksand #8 (Indicators):** Successors often see implementing a well-known operating model as an indicator of organizational success. The efficiencies and alignment promised is intoxicating, and they mistake those stories, which are lagging indicators, as leading indicators.

Do you notice the common thread?

The gap is people. People are imperfect. It's hard to change their habits. An operational model that doesn't consider the inevitability of human error is a manifesto.

Yet, there's an even bigger danger.

The Second Problem: A friend and mentor[xxxiii] once said there are two problems in business: sales and everything else.

Every company that has hired a consultant to implement [redacted] is a mess. It just doesn't work for the vast majority of businesses.

~ A Fractional CFO with hundreds of small business clients

Implementing most operating models solves the second problem while distracting from the first.

So What Now?: Doing nothing isn't an option — you know that the organization needs to be more disciplined — but you don't want to drown in quicksand.

Three principles of a good operating model include:

- ▶ Simple to follow, such that there are clear efficiencies gained.
- ▶ Trackable enough to celebrate wins or to clearly see and prioritize gaps.
- ▶ Flexible enough to account for inevitable human variables.

---

xxxiii. Greg Coticchia has had multiple significant exits in his career and is one of the most giving leaders I've ever met. You can read a collection of his insights at https://www.amazon.com/Start-Your-Startup-Right-Entrepreneur/dp/0692950648/

That's why we[xxxiv] designed the Organizational Fitness Principles (OFP). This model incorporates the best practices of most operational models while enabling leaders to create the conditions for their organizations to implement them well.

There are two parts to OFP.

The Backbone

Figure 7.2

Organizational Fitness Principles

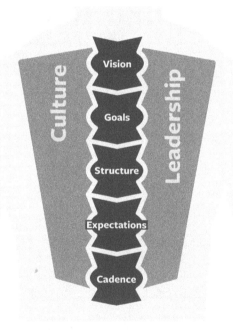

As in human fitness, you can't achieve organizational fitness if you don't have healthy bones in alignment. The bones are the key actions that

xxxiv. "We" is doing some heavy lifting. Solutions 21's own Rob Salome developed the model, which has helped dozens of our clients overcome structural dysfunction to be more effective organizations. Most of this section is an outright theft of his ideas.

organizations take to ensure alignment. What you'll see below isn't rocket science and most operating models have variations on these themes.

Create Vision

At its simplest, vision is where you want the organization to go in the long term.

The idea is deceptively simple — when employees know where the organization is going, it's easier for everyone to make decisions and take actions that head in that direction.

The deception comes in when you try to write down something that might be "more of a feeling."

At its best, a well-defined vision[85]:

▶ Articulates the organization's core values and purpose.
▶ Vividly describes a compelling BHAG.[xxxv]

Need a few examples?

▶ **Southwest:** To be the world's most loved, most efficient, and most profitable airline.[86]
▶ **Solutions 21:** Be the partner of choice for forging elite leaders.
▶ **IKEA:** To create a better everyday life for many people.[87]

Despite their differences, each vision helps the organization focus its energy. One has a metric (most = be #1), another has an effect (be a partner of choice), and the third is highly aspirational (create a better everyday life).

It's harder to get to a good vision than you might think. Here's why:

▶ It's difficult putting future-focused ideas into words.
▶ "What could be" can be hard to pin down.

---

xxxv. BHAG = Big Hairy Audacious Goal, a term from Jim Collins' *Built to Last*, one of the most Boomery of Boomer business bestsellers.

- ▶ It's scary to state where you want to go if you're not sure you can get there.
- ▶ It can ruffle feathers if the updated vision leaves people or longstanding approaches behind.
- ▶ Some leaders struggle to see too much further than what's right in front of their faces.
- ▶ In an attempt to be complete, the vision can get too wordy, complicated, esoteric, or disconnected from the front lines.

You'll know you've developed a good vision when:

- ▶ It's short and memorable.
- ▶ It's compelling, exciting, and maybe even a little scary.
- ▶ You can connect the vision to the work every employee in your company does.
- ▶ Applying it avoids work that wastes time and energy spent on other efforts.

Set Goals

Goals define what the organization wants to get done on its way to carrying out the vision. Goals articulate priorities and help everyone in the organization minimize wasted time and energy.

Typically, you're looking at three levels of goals:

- ▶ **Organizational:** What the organization needs to achieve; executives are responsible for achieving these goals.
- ▶ **Team:** What the departments or divisions need to achieve within the overall organization; managers at various levels own these goals.
- ▶ **Individual:** What employees must achieve individually to contribute to sub-organizational and overall organizational goals; the individual owns these goals with the support of their managers and leaders.

The best goals are set using the SMART(ER) framework. These goals are:

- **Specific:** Clearly define what needs to be achieved.
- **Measurable:** Establish criteria for measuring progress and success.
- **Achievable:** Set realistic goals that can be accomplished with available resources.
- **Relevant:** Ensure goals are pertinent to the organization's direction.
- **Time-bound:** Set deadlines to create urgency and accountability.
- **Energy-aware:** Acknowledge the time and energy required to make the goal happen.
- **Resource-specific:** Spell out what resources will be needed to achieve this goal.

Ideally, goals then flow to individual tactics, defined as:

- The steps you must take to achieve the goal.
- The "scoreboard" for progress.

When defining goals and tactics, someone needs to be responsible. The easiest method to define who does what? RACI, a process that started in software development. It works like this:

- **Responsible:** The responsible party is on the hook for doing the work.
- **Accountable:** This is the person who ensures the work gets done and keeps the effort on track.
- **Consulted:** These people are spoken with prior to a decision or action to understand the best approach.
- **Informed:** These people are intentionally notified after a decision or action to maximize understanding and alignment.

With those best practices, here are a few traps to avoid when you're trying to set goals:

▶ **Don't frontload deadlines:** Be realistic about when things can get done and don't assume the current excitement will continue.

▶ **Remember your day job:** Most of the tasks you're taking on are *in addition to* your (and others') day-to-day work and responsibilities.

▶ **Research can be a goal:** Sometimes we know we need to do *something*, but don't know *what*. In this case, it's okay to "plan to plan," and name a goal where you will research a set of solutions before acting.

▶ **Stop-keep-start:** When you're adding new things, you'll have to take a few things off your list. Creating a "stop doing" or "anti-goal" list is just as useful as creating goals.

Define Structure

In 1962, Alfred Chandler Jr., Harvard and Johns Hopkins professor, wrote a line that has served as a foundational approach to organizational design ever since.

Structure follows strategy.

The concept? That the organizational structure should be decided by what the organization wants to achieve and not the other way around.

When most of us think of organizational structure, we think of the "org chart," where the executive leader sits at the top and everyone else lands in different functional areas.

Is that the right approach for your organization?

Digging Deeper: PwC published "10 principles of organizational design,"[88] a framework that makes it much easier to think through how best to align people and teams. Those are:

1. **Declare amnesty for the past:** Focus on the future and let go of past organizational designs. Start with a clean slate, emphasizing a forward-looking strategy.

2. **Design with "DNA":** Use a framework of eight building blocks divided into four pairs: decisions and norms, motivators and commitments, information and mind sets, structure and networks. These elements should guide your design process.

3. **Fix the structure last, not first:** Focus on aligning the organizational design with the strategy and capabilities before altering the structure. This ensures the changes are meaningful and sustainable.

4. **Make the most of top talent:** Ensure that leadership roles and structures match the capabilities needed for the strategy. Balance technical skills with leadership qualities.

5. **Focus on what you can control:** Address scarcities and constraints that limit organizational performance. Prioritize changes that can realistically be executed.

6. **Promote accountability:** Establish clear decision rights and rapid information flows. This enhances execution and fosters a culture of ownership and responsibility.

7. **Benchmark sparingly, if at all:** Avoid over-reliance on best practices from other companies. Focus instead on your unique capabilities and the specific needs of your strategy.

8. **Let the "lines and boxes" fit your company's purpose:** Design spans of control and layers in the org chart to reflect the strategy and support critical capabilities, ensuring the structure aligns with the company's goals.

9. **Accentuate the informal:** Leverage informal networks and relationships within the organization to support formal structures. Informal elements can significantly impact the effectiveness of organizational changes.

10. **Build on your strengths:** Identify and build upon the existing strengths of your organization. Ensure that new designs enhance these strengths rather than undermining them.

The takeaway? The ideal approach takes the best of the Jazzers and the Juilliards.[xxxvi]

Why It Matters: Organizations fail to execute on their strategy because of their ill-fitting structure, not because of a bad strategic approach. Most often, the structure is a barrier because the organization is too tied to the past or worried about offending certain members of the team. New leadership gives you an opportunity to do things differently.

Bottom Line: Structure follows strategy. Don't let the past prevent you from making the future happen.

Establish Expectations

You've created a vision, set up goals, and built an organizational structure.

After all this work, doesn't it feel like your team should *just know* what to do next?

If only. Which is why nearly half of employees don't know what's expected of them at work.[89]

Some Context: As leaders, we need to be able to answer the question, "What do you want me to do?"

Years ago, you might have gotten away with answering, "Your job," though you would have been a bad leader.

It's that type of approach that led Mark Sanborn to uncover[90] the five reasons employees don't do what you want them to do (from most to least likely):

- ▶ **They don't know *what* to do:** You've not set expectations.
- ▶ **They don't know *how* to do it:** You've not trained them properly.

---

xxxvi. If you need to refresh, see page 160.

- **They don't know *why* they're doing it:** You've not explained the context.
- **They *can't* do it:** You put them in a position to fail.
- **They *won't* do it:** They're unmotivated or you've created a demotivating environment.

If you didn't notice, four of the five are on you, and the fifth one might be, too.

Digging Deeper: According to Sadie Banks, assistant general counsel and human resources consultant at Engage PEO,[91] there are many workplace factors in setting expectations, including:

- Industry expectations.
- Internal and external company image.
- Client, customer, and vendor relationships.
- Employee knowledge of products or services.
- Company policies and performance.
- Social media use.

From there, we must look at expectations in two directions:

- What leaders expect of:
  > The individual
  > The team
- What employees can expect from leadership.

Let's break it down.

For the individual, leaders need to define:

- **Roles and responsibilities:** Beyond a job description, roles and responsibilities define the work each individual does and the priorities they should be placing on certain activities.
- **How the work connects to vision, goals, and structure:** Expectations *must* connect to the aims of the overall organization.

For the team, leaders must define:

▶ **Behaviors that the organization incentivizes:** How work gets done is just as important as what gets done. Alignment with culture can make or break an individual's ability to perform within a team and a team's ability to deliver collective results.

▶ **Expected results:** Leaders need to clearly define and explain what "good looks like." Quality of work, deadlines, attitude, and approach all fall into this bucket.

Leaders need to set expectations for themselves, too. Employees need to know that leaders will:

▶ **Provide training, support, and leadership:** No one wants to feel like they're being set up for failure. It's your job (see the five things above) to ensure that doesn't happen.

▶ **Full disclosure and explanation of the job responsibilities, company policies, and procedures:** Be clear about the factors that leaders will use to judge how the employee functions within the organization.

▶ **Regular feedback on performance from supervisors or managers:** More on this in cadence; clear, productive, and development-focused feedback is non-negotiable.

Bottom Line: Set expectations to ensure that your team is in the best possible position to succeed. Ambiguity is your enemy.

Communication through cadence

Your organizational communication needs work.

▶ 86% percent of employees blame lack of collaboration or ineffective communication for workplace failures.[92]

▶ 92% of those employees believe that a company's tendency to hit or miss a deadline will impact bottom-line results.[93]

The payoff? About a 25% increase in productivity for organizations that are well-connected.[94]

One other barrier to connectedness? Size. The general cutoff seems to be 150 employees; larger than that, and "knowledge sharing reduces due largely to increased complexity in the formal structure, weaker interpersonal relationships and lower trust, decreased connective efficacy, and less effective communication."[95]

Digging Deeper: Communication happens with a well-designed cadence.[xxxvii]

> *"The first thing I would do when I would take a new command is cancel every meeting on the calendar and then see which ones people really needed."*
> *~Former special operations commander*

Here's how to get started:

Figure 7.3
Cadence Development Process

| Step 1: Explore & Identify | Step 2: Determine Audiences | Step 3: Choose Format | Step 4: Create Calendar | Step 5: Monitor & Revise |

This only works if your meetings are effective.

Quick Story: A client struggled with meeting overload, and several of their executives spent 30 hours a week or more in meetings related to running the business, leaving little time for client interaction or business growth. In one particularly egregious example, a weekly meeting attended

---

xxxvii. Cadence, in business-speak, is how often a regularly scheduled thing happens. More here: https://www.merriam-webster.com/wordplay/words-were-watching-cadence

by all managers, which the organization acknowledged was a waste of time, cost the business nearly seven figures in staff time over the year.

Meeting Hygiene: People hate meetings. Why? Because they feel like they're wasting time.

To analyze whether or not you need a meeting, ensure it serves one of three purposes:

- ► Make decisions.
- ► Refine priorities.
- ► Allocate resources.

If you're not doing one of these three things, or if the meeting isn't crucial to establishing or reinforcing culture, it can probably be an email.

Mano a Mano: Part of the cadence should be regular one-on-one meetings. This leadership tool, when used well, gets the most out of your team and provides clarity for those who aren't stacking up.

A bad structure can make these meetings feel like a chore and wasted time. Avoid that by sticking to these principles:

- ► **Maintain a useful cadence:** Hold them quarterly at a minimum (ideally 8-12 times annually) and with every direct report. Your goal is to have them often enough that each employee feels like they are progressing and getting what they need from you.
- ► **Avoid the day-to-day:** One-on-ones should be a strategic discussion about progress and performance, rather than a status update on projects (which could be an email). The aim is to provide bigger-picture feedback that can improve performance.
- ► **Choose the right venue:** If things are going well, an informal setting works well. If not, you might want to choose a more formal venue.
- ► **Talk specifics about performance:** You want to share feedback, positive and negative, to help the employee progress. Ensure there's agreement on both.

- ▶ **Ask questions:** Your job is to ask open-ended questions and listen as much as possible.
- ▶ **Capture quotes:** Don't just listen to what the employee says, capture what they say in notes in *their words*.
- ▶ **Celebrate success:** Avoid the trap of harping on the negative and set aside specific time to talk about wins.
- ▶ **Follow-up note:** After the meeting, send a follow-up summary with captured quotes. The trick is to write the note within the frame of what they said or what you agreed. "You said that you would accomplish X by Y," and "We agreed that you would deliver this project by Z," are best practices to follow. Let the employee provide feedback if you captured something incorrectly. Most importantly, avoid putting things you *didn't* talk about in the note.
- ▶ **Use the last note:** The agenda should follow the last note you wrote. This approach minimizes the burden of the process.
- ▶ **Call out repeat misses:** One miss is recoverable, two is a concern, and three is a performance issue. Capturing these instances creates a "red flag mechanism."[xxxviii]

Bottom Line: Whether the entire organization or a single employee, communication is a leadership and accountability tool. Make it intentional.

The Muscles

A skeleton can't stand on its own. It needs the connective tissue to provide added stability while enabling movement and power.

This is where almost all operational models fall flat. Unless there's leadership showing the way and a culture to reinforce it when leaders aren't in the room, a well-intentioned operational model will waste time, cause friction, and fail.

---

xxxviii. A "red flag mechanism" is a way of drawing attention to problems, first introduced in *Good to Great* by Jim Collins.

Figure 7.4
Organizational Fitness Principles

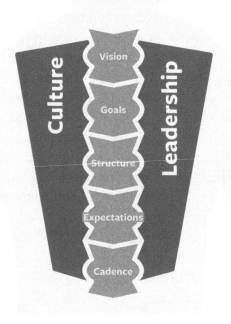

Culture

The highest-performing organizations develop and protect a culture that continues when they're not in the room. The culture is the context in which everyone functions.

Executive leaders can only drive so much; the rest of the team has to follow suit and show leadership themselves.

What does that mean?

It's like a farmer tilling and fertilizing the field. While the farmer can't force a seed to grow, he can provide the right environment and nutrients to maximize the chances growth will happen.

Those conditions are your culture.

Ten Square Miles

"I know governments are known for inefficiency and ineffectiveness. I can't change all of government, but I wanted to show that it can be done."

Winnie is a career public servant who had been selected to lead her small town of 8,000 residents. Hired to replace an old-school, back-slapping leader, Winnie knew she had a tough task ahead of her when she inspected the budget. Overtime and paid leave were out of control, yet the town had problems addressing even the basics of governmental services regularly.

She started by interviewing every member of the staff, more than 50 employees across administration, finance, and public works. She was horrified to find out that these were the first conversations many had with municipal leadership since they were hired, and for a few of them, that covered a multi-decade tenure.

Her next step? Hard conversations through a rigorous one-on-one process. She was understanding but firm; she knew it wasn't their fault that they were elevated into senior roles without development, but she knew the municipality couldn't continue as-is. She was clear: Get on board or find a new job.

"My lieutenants were delighted by the challenge, and I'm shocked they responded so well," Winnie shared. "It shows how much people will respond to having something more exciting to shoot for."

Over the next two years, about 40% of the staff left. Most decided to retire in a higher-demand environment, though a few were let go for performance reasons. In each case, she had her area leaders provide a plan to replace the role. The result? Only half of the jobs were backfilled.

"Once we were able to help all of the employees understand that they were there to serve the members of the community, we got a different level of engagement. We're employing about 20% fewer hours but getting much more done than when I started."

Her mantra stuck with her team. "We can't change the world, but we can change our ten square miles, and that will mean the world to someone." ▶

How It Works: Leaders get there in three ways:

- ▶ **Building the team:** When done intentionally, recruiting, hiring, onboarding, and development become a company's biggest asset as new teammates seamlessly integrate into the already-moving organization. For companies in construction, manufacturing, and similar fields, safety plays a part here, too.
- ▶ **Standardizing the approach:** From systems and processes to standardized operating procedures, leaders ensure energy isn't wasted. They accept that the organization might need to slow down and retool to set itself up for faster future growth.
- ▶ **Communicate the context:** A cadence isn't enough — great organizational communication ensures that messages travel top to bottom and bottom to top while creating cohesion through storytelling and transparency.

Bottom Line: Leaders who ensure these outcomes are putting their money where their mouths are and showing they're about more than just platitudes. They walk the walk, which drives culture from top to bottom.

Leadership

Leadership looks a little different in the context of an operational model.

While we've spilled a lot of ink talking about leadership through the book, when thinking about it in terms of running the organization, it's about making the collective achieve its goals.

The best part? Your leadership style can make it happen. Whether you're a charismatic leader who attracts people with your charm, or a relentlessly detail-oriented leader who makes sure people are driving to the right results, the same principles apply.

A Note About Accountability

To avoid saying "corrective action" or "punishment," many business leaders have chosen "accountability" as their more palatable euphemism.

It misses the mark.

Accountability isn't just the downside risk of faltering. Being accountable is also the positive — celebrating well-earned victories. Don't allow the negative connotation to take root; it loses its impact.

How It Works: Using the OFP points to three things:

- ▶ **Drive to results:** Leaders are looking externally for trends that can affect strategy, create an environment of accountability, and ensure the organization is growing.
- ▶ **Clarify actions:** With a relentless focus on priorities, leaders reinforce what matters by sharing their intent[xxxix] for a specific effort, creating alignment behind that effort while building trust.
- ▶ **Coach development and performance:** Leaders use the two types of coaching (performance for specific skill improvement, and development for overall professional development) to ensure the team stays on track to achieve long-term goals.

Bottom Line: Leadership at this level is about your IQ and EQ.

Final Thoughts

As James Clear wrote in *Atomic Habits*, a bestseller that argues that our ability to build habits is the difference-maker[96]:

---

xxxix. Intent-driven leadership is an approach where a leader will describe an objective, provide guardrails and guidance, and describe what success looks like. The model, based on a military tool called "Commander's Intent," is outlined in *The Leadership Decade*.

"I Hate Consultants"

Luis, a savvy financial wizard, decided he could make hay in the construction industry and in the early 2000s bought a family-run construction firm. He was mocked by most in the industry regionally as he set out to rebuild the company from what had been a big fall from its earlier heyday.

He had one rule: No consultants.

"I hate consultants, no offense," Luis said matter-of-factly. "They either tell you what you already know, or they create another problem you have to pay them to solve."

Luis had been spending less time around the business as he pursued other ventures, and it showed. His lack of attention, combined with a team not yet ready to step up, resulted in some lost business, missed deadlines, and hefty fines due to cost overruns. While he had created a culture of problem-solving, he underestimated just how much the organization followed his day-to-day lead.

When he decided to do a deeper dive into what ailed the company, he realized that much of the work was getting done, and done well. The rest — the big organizational stuff that drives growth — was a mess.

"So I called you."

Entrusting us with his team, Luis gave us a year to help the organization get in shape. We made a strategic plan, helped the organization to reorganize and rebuild its meeting cadence, and set new cultural norms. The executive team and two other groups of high-performing leaders engaged in leadership development and coaching.

"You might be the first consultants that were actually helpful," Luis admitted. "It took about two years, but the team now largely runs without me. And they're doing the things we outlined when we first talked."

He didn't hesitate to end our discussion with honesty. "I still hate consultants, though." ▶

"You do not rise to the level of your goals. You fall to the level of your systems.

Your goal is your desired outcome. Your system is the collection of daily habits that will get you there."

That's the conundrum of leadership: No matter how much energy and effort we can spend to achieve a goal, the difference-maker tends to be what we've developed as rote behavior.

My strongest recommendation?

Don't try to go it alone.

There's a reason that consultants have built entire businesses and franchises on helping businesses implement an operating model.

It's hard to do your job and build new habits at the same time.

Sometimes *you're* the one who needs the accountability.

Be humble enough to recognize when you need outside support and get it.

The Relationship

It doesn't end at goodbye.

The relationship between the predecessor and successor has a long-tail effect on the business even after the transition.[97]

That's why, no matter how many wildfires have raged, how much damage has been repaired, or the extent to which you're now running the show, the predecessor still matters.

I'm not going to tell you how to win friends and influence people — someone else has a corner on that — but here are a few useful approaches to ensure your relationship stays strong and the impact on the business continues to be positive.

Judge Softly

In 1895, Mary T. Lathrap published a poem named "Judge Softly."

The suffragette and minister advocated for a compassionate perspective on others. This work is believed to be the origin of a slightly edited modern statement used to encourage empathy: "Walk a mile in his moccasins."

Much of this book provides you with context about the predecessors — their pressures, fears, goals, and mindset — in the moments of transition. Once the transition is happening or has happened, you're nurturing a completely different relationship.

Judge softly.

Some Background: I texted with a predecessor president of a construction firm on the Monday after his retirement the previous week. After a series of conversations about his transition over three years, I suspected he would be having a rough time. The exchange went as follows:

Me: How do you feel?

Predecessor: Mixed. Last week was hard.

Me: I bet — why?

Predecessor: There are so many terrific people there that I deeply care for. Sharing "war" stories was awesome but also heart-tugging. You know I'm a softy.

The predecessor was known to be a hard-charging, tenacious, conflict-comfortable leader. Few of his colleagues would have described him as a "softy."

This reputation affected his transition. Many of his colleagues were worried he would be unable to let go of significant tasks despite his repeated attempts to hand out parts of his job to the rest of the team. Even the business owner assumed, 90 days from his retirement date, that the predecessor was bluffing. Given those assumptions, the successors only partially planned to step into the role. It wasn't until a few weeks prior to his retirement that the executive team took the handoff seriously.

When challenged on why the team hesitated, they universally assumed the predecessor wouldn't be able to leave the role behind. He never "seemed" like he was leaving, they would say.

The predecessor was mystified. He gave two-plus years of notice and yet the organization was completely unprepared. No one else saw him as the softy.

Digging Deeper: In 2012, Mark Appel, a no-doubt, consensus first-pick pitching prospect out of Stanford, was drafted in the first round by the Pittsburgh Pirates, falling to their eighth pick after concerns about his salary demands. Three months later, Mark announced that an agreement had not been reached and he'd be reentering the draft the following year. As a long-suffering Pirates fan, I hated[xl] Mark Appel.

The next year, he was drafted by the Houston Astros and, with a few successes sprinkled in, largely struggled through the minor leagues. Eventually traded to the Philadelphia Phillies, he retired in 2018. After trying a comeback in 2021, he made his major league debut in 2022, ten years after being drafted for the first time. Injuries and performance pushed him out of the league the following year.

xl. Sports hate is a different and more permissable kind of hate. IYKYK.

As a sometimes mean-spirited sports fan, I hate-followed Mark Appel's career. I'm embarrassed to say I rooted against him because of his Pirates snub.

Then, on March 22, 2023, I changed my mind. He wrote a thread on X[98] that started with the following: "On Monday, I was released by the Phillies. Tomorrow, I am sharing the most vulnerable piece I've ever written."

Then, in the next tweet: "What if grief should be a regular part of life? What if I see grief like I do joy, as a part of the normal rhythms of being human? What if I stop resisting grief? What if I see grief as the cost of being emotionally and spiritually alive?"

I stopped in my tracks.

Knee-deep in interviews and writing about succession, I had just started looking at grief as a model to understand predecessors. Instead of sports-hating an athlete because of a petty grievance due to my fealty to a down-trodden franchise, I read his blog post,[99] full of openness and vulnerability and grief — as he experienced it in nearly real time. The most impactful line?

"Grief is the natural response to loss in life."

It hit me out of embarrassment. In my early 20s, I had served on a board that focused on supporting people in grief. "There is no wrong way to grieve" was a mantra. In that moment, I felt for Mark Appel.

Digging Even Deeper: It's so easy to judge the predecessor, much like it's easy (for me) to sports-hate Mark Appel.

At different scales, most predecessors (like Mark) have some notoriety. They've achieved financial success. They've achieved things others could only dream of. Why should I feel empathy for *that* person? Judge softly.

The Twist: You're a predecessor.

As a successor, you're stepping out of a job, right? Someone else must step in. You're a predecessor to that person. How many CEOs say, "On day one, you're looking for your replacement?" You're a predecessor from day one.

Perhaps you miss your prior responsibilities. Maybe you wish you could go back to the "easy stuff." Welcome to the emotional turmoil of a predecessor. The more you understand the emotional challenge of the predecessor, the better you will be at playing the successor role.

Bottom Line: Judge softly.

Connection and Communication

You're transactional or you're not.

While at a dinner with a group of current and future succession candidates, one person started badmouthing his predecessor.

The story went like this: Once connected at the hip, the relationship soured as the succession plan progressed. While they used to talk daily, and text each other nearly hourly, their relationship had ruptured to the point that the only communication between the two happened through the grapevine, none of it good.

I asked him what used to be a point of connection. "We used to golf together."

The solution wasn't a better succession plan or productive conflict or usurping power. It was a couple of beers on a Saturday away from the office.

He texted me a couple of months after our serendipitous chat.

"[Redacted] and I just got off the course. It was the best decision I ever made. It's all water under the bridge."

Connecting later, he shared that the two hashed out their differences and the predecessor started to engage in the process. A year later, the succession candidate was now successor, and the predecessor was a key supporter through some rough waters. Without that relationship, things would have gone sideways.

"I'm so happy to have him as an ally rather than an enemy. It made all the difference as I stumbled through my first few months."

Why It Matters: No matter how close, vulnerable, or connected we are, relationships can fall apart with just a hint of doubt and resentment. That disconnect can have huge implications for the individuals and the business.

Digging Deeper: We are in an epidemic of social isolation, so much so that the U.S. surgeon general sounded the alarm in a major research study in 2023.[100] The conclusions?

- The lack of social connection poses a significant risk for individual health and longevity. Loneliness and social isolation increase the risk for premature death by 26% and 29%, respectively.
- A lack of social connection can increase the risk for premature death as much as smoking up to 15 cigarettes a day.
- It is associated with increased risk for anxiety, depression, and dementia.

Given that the predecessor is in some stage of grief, social isolation and disconnectedness just pile on to already hurt feelings.

The next thought is almost inevitable.

"What if the successor was only doing all of this for the transaction?"

More to the Story: It is exceptionally rare that the predecessor steps away to the degree that they have zero contact with the business ever again. Current and former employees will keep in touch, and most predecessors will stay at least loosely connected to their professional network.

Beyond the benefits to the business and your reputation, keeping the relationship alive is just being a good person.

Isn't that part of what leadership is all about?

Bottom Line: Keep lines of communication open with the predecessor. You don't know when you might need it or, perhaps more importantly, when they might need you.

Honor the Legacy

Don't lose sight of who got you there.

For successors transitioning in the midst of a what-have-you-done-for-me-lately culture, it's all too easy to blow past opportunities to celebrate the predecessor.

That's a mistake.

The predecessor looms large, and keeping their brand around is both a useful leadership tool and an opportunity for you to be kind and humble to predecessors and their experience.

Quick Story: Joyce spent her career in administrative work, leading the office staff for a mid-sized professional services firm. She had a dynamic personality that lit up a room that was only surpassed by her passion for filling the office with plants.

Joyce's green thumb was legendary, even through the pandemic. While offices worldwide were shut down, Joyce would go to work when no one else was there, carefully tending to everyone's flowers and succulents in their cubicles. When hybrid workers returned a year-plus later, they were greeted by their thriving plant companions.

When Joyce retired, the employees got together to do something a little different. They pooled their money and sponsored a community garden where she lived, naming it after her. The employees committed to dedicating a volunteer day each year to clean up the space in Joyce's honor.

Some Ideas: Celebrating and honoring the predecessor's legacy isn't difficult. Here are some of the best examples:

▶ Naming a conference room or piece of equipment after the predecessor.

▶ Creating a scholarship fund in the predecessor's name in a chosen field or at their alma mater.

▶ Framing the predecessor's one-liners and hanging them throughout the office.

▶ Establishing an endowment for a cause that that predecessor cares about.

▶ Getting a street named after the predecessor.

▶ Creating an employee award that celebrates a value or behavior that the predecessor prioritized.

While these actions might seem like relatively small tokens of appreciation compared to the predecessor's impact, the gesture has staying power for both the predecessor and the organization.

Why It Matters: Funerals are for the mourners, not the deceased.

Similarly, celebrating the predecessor's legacy honors those who followed the predecessor, too. That communicates a profound respect for the work and sacrifices the followers of that predecessor made to get the organization to where it is today.

Bottom Line: Honoring that legacy is an exercise in humility.

The Bottom Line on Chapter 7: It's Go Time

TL;DR:

This is the moment you've been preparing for—stepping into your new role with confidence and clarity. Focus on practical tools and strategies to ensure your success as you take charge. From aligning vision with organizational goals to mastering the art of leadership, this is your playbook for hitting the ground running and sustaining momentum. You'll learn how to navigate the complexities of your new position, build strong relationships, and lead with purpose and impact.

The Hits:

▶ **Embrace the Challenge:** Recognize that taking on a new leadership role is challenging but also an opportunity for growth and impact.

▶ **Align Vision and Goals:** Ensure your vision aligns with the organizational goals to create a unified direction.

▶ **Master Leadership Skills:** Develop essential leadership skills such as decision-making, strategic thinking, and effective communication.

▶ **Build Strong Relationships:** Foster strong relationships with your team, stakeholders, and community to support your leadership.

▶ **Sustain Momentum:** Implement strategies to maintain momentum and drive continuous improvement in your organization.

Thought-Starter Questions:

▶ How can you ensure the vision aligns with the overall goals of the organization?

▶ What leadership skills do you need to develop further to excel in your new role?

▶ How will you build and maintain strong relationships with your team and stakeholders?

▶ What strategies can you use to keep up the momentum and drive continuous improvement?

▶ How can you effectively communicate your vision and goals to inspire and motivate your team?

Successor Strategies for Success:

▶ Reflect on your vision and ensure it aligns with the organization's goals to create a clear, unified direction.

▶ Create a leadership development plan that focuses on enhancing your decision-making, strategic thinking, and communication skills.

▶ Invest time in building relationships with your team and stakeholders through regular meetings and open communication.

▶ Create a plan to sustain momentum by setting short-term goals and celebrating small wins to keep the team motivated.

▶ Practice transparent and inspiring communication to ensure your team understands and supports your vision.

The Bottom Line

It's a Wrap

A few parting thoughts as you embrace your leadership role.

Don't go the process alone.

Great work.

I've mentioned a few times that people tend to be terrible at celebrating their achievements. Instead of relishing in the positive feelings of glory, they move on quickly to focus on the next burden, hurdle, or problem.

Don't do that. Life's too short. Celebrate accomplishment. It's deserved and contributes to momentum and success.

Harvard started a research project in 1938 to understand happiness and longevity.[xli] Following 268 participants throughout their lives, the study's objective was to understand what contributed to a long, happy life.

To quote an article about the research: "Good relationships lead to health and happiness. The trick is that those relationships must be nurtured."

Beyond the processes and balance sheets are people — they're what matters.

---

xli. Learn more about this incredible study at https://www.adultdevelopmentstudy.org/

The predecessor relationship is likely one of the most consequential in your world.

Your family and friends are on that list, too.

Every successor has a coach or confidant they can rely on. Who is that for you?

If you don't have one, here's an offer.

Reach out to me. I'm happy to help.

I make a joke in workshops that working with me is like Olive Garden, "Once you're here, your family."

That's true for those who read this book. Best of luck.

Albert Ciuksza Jr.
Solutions 21

Email: aciuksza@solutions21.com
LinkedIn: https://linkedin.com/in/AlbertCiuksza
Mobile: +1 (412) 419-1461

Image Credits

Throughout

- Various Emoji, pages 45, 67, 69, 73, 74, 84, 86, 88, 89, 91, 94, 96, 98,
- 100, 102, 104, 106, 109, 158, 179, 181, 183, 186, 196, 247, and 259. Copyright (c) 2013, Google LLC (Google.com), with Noto Color Emoji.

Chapter Introduction Images

- **Chapter 1:** EpicStockMedia / DepositPhotos.com
- **Chapter 2:** NewAfrica / DepositPhotos.com
- **Chapter 3:** nature78 / DepositPhotos.com
- **Chapter 4:** motortion / DepositPhotos.com
- **Chapter 5:** lapandr / DepositPhotos.com
- **Chapter 6:** BrianAJackson /DepositPhotos.com
- **Chapter 7:** joesive47 / DepositPhotos.com

Chapter 1

- **Fig 1.1:** U.S. Population by Generation, page 5. Percheron Publishing with data from the U.S. Census Bureau. 2023. Generations defined by Solutions 21.
- **Fig 1.2:** Worldwide GDP Per Capita in 2023 Dollars, page 8. Percheron Publishing with data from Bradford J. De Long. "Estimates of World GDP, One Million B.C.-Present." 1998.
- **Fig 1.3:** Not in the Labor Force and Retired (16+), page 11. Percheron Publishing, adapted from Joshua Montes, Christopher Smith, and Juliana Dajon. "'The Great Retirement Boom': The

Pandemic-Era Surge in Retirements and Implications for Future Labor Force Participation," Finance and Economics Discussion Series 2022-081. Washington: Board of Governors of the Federal Reserve System. 2022.

▶ Sponge, page 15. stevanovicigor / DepositPhotos.com

Chapter 3

▶ **Fig 3.1:** The Grief Process, page 45. Percheron Publishing.
▶ Danger Gauges, pages 46-52. Percheron Publishing.
▶ **Fig 3.2:** The Stages at a Glance, page 53. Percheron Publishing.
▶ **Fig 3.3:** Prisoner's Dilemma, page 55. Percheron Publishing.
▶ **Fig 3.4:** Maslow's Hierarchy of Needs, page 60. Percheron Publishing.
▶ **Fig 3.5:** The Exit Iceberg, page 61 — Percheron Publishing, composite of images from vlad_star / DepositPhotos.com, MazziB / Pixabay, RDNE Stock project / Pexels, Berend de Kort / Pexels, and Ben Mack / Pexels.
▶ **Fig 3.6:** The Learning Model, page 64. Percheron Publishing, adapted from model developed by Noel Burch. "Conscious Competence Ladder." 1970s.
▶ **Fig 3.7:** Sparks vs. Conditions, page 67. Percheron Publishing.
▶ **Fig 3.8:** Predecessor Grief Wildfire Process, page 69. Percheron Publishing.
▶ **Fig 3.9:** Behavior Chain, page 73. Percheron Publishing.
▶ **Fig 3.10:** Behavior Chain Example, page 74. Percheron Publishing.
▶ **Fig 3.11:** The Trust Triangle, page 77. Percheron Publishing, adapted from Frances Frei and Anne Morriss. "Begin with Trust." *Harvard Business Review.* May-June 2020

Chapter 4

▶ Shows, pages 46-52
  › damrong8899 / DepositPhotos.com
  › saravuth / DepositPhotos.com
  › jakkapan / DepositPhotos.com
  › ZeRatis / DepositPhotos.com

> stoonn / DepositPhotos.com
> jpkirkun / DepositPhotos.com
> sirikornt / DepositPhotos.com
> Title images for *Survivor, The Great British Bake Off, The Bachelorette, Jeopardy!, Wipeout, What Would You Do?, and Family Feud* property of their respective copyright holders, published under fair use.

▶ Hippo, page 127. wastesoul / DepositPhotos.com

Chapter 5

▶ Panda, page 139. lifeonwhite / DepositPhotos.com
▶ Student Driver Bumper Sticker, page 142. Seetwo / DepositPhotos.com
▶ **Fig 5.1:** Using the "Student Driver" Label, page 143. Percheron Publishing.
▶ Tape Measurer, page 146. hsagencia / DepositPhotos.com
▶ Mask, page 149. Jirsak / DepositPhotos.com
▶ Parachutist, page 153. Jamal1977a / DepositPhotos.com
▶ Saxophone, page 156. Firststar / DepositPhotos.com
▶ **Fig 5.2:** Brubeck vs. Bach at a Glance, page 158. Percheron Publishing.
▶ Sheriff Badge, page 161. mbongo / DepositPhotos.com
▶ Siren Light, page 164. JingleMarket / DepositPhotos.com
▶ Signal, page 169. lipsky / DepositPhotos.com

Chapter 6

▶ **Fig 6.1:** Role Mindset Theory, page 179. Percheron Publishing, adapted from model developed by Albert Ciuksza Jr.
▶ **Fig 6.2:** Role Mindset Theory and the Tripping Point, page 181. Percheron Publishing, adapted from model developed by Albert Ciuksza Jr.
▶ **Fig 6.3:** Role Mindset Interactions, page 183. Percheron Publishing.
▶ **Fig 6.4:** Role Mindset at a Glance, page 186. Percheron Publishing.

▶ **Fig 6.5:** Help Wanted: CEOs Who Are Good with People, page 188. Percheron Publishing, adapted from Raffaella Sadun, Joseph Fuller, Stephen Hansen, and PJ Neal. "The C-Suite Skills That Matter Most." Harvard Business Review. July 2022.

▶ **Fig 6.6:** Emotional Intelligence, page 189. Percheron Publishing, adapted from Daniel Goleman. "Emotional Intelligence: Why it Can Matter More than IQ." 1995.

▶ **Fig 6.7:** Decision Process, page 196. Percheron Publishing, adapted from Buster Benson. "Cognitive Bias Cheat Sheet." September 1, 2016.

▶ **Fig 6.8:** Same as figure 3.6, page 200.

▶ **Fig 6.9:** Eisenhower Matrix, page 205. Percheron Publishing

▶ **Fig 6.10:** The Cynefin Framework, page 214. Percheron Publishing, adapted from Cynefin framework. Wikipedia. 2022.

▶ Phone, page 217. Svstudioart / Freepik.com, composite with Percheron Publishing.

Chapter 7

▶ Whistle, page 230. Fotofabrika / DepositPhotos.com.

▶ **Fig 7.1:** Operational-Political Continuum, page 247. Percheron Publishing.

▶ **Fig 7.2:** Organizational Fitness Principles (Spine), page 250. Percheron Publishing, composite of image with illustration by msanca / DepositPhotos.com. Adapted from model developed by Rob Salome.

▶ **Fig 7.3:** Cadence Development Process, page 259. Percheron Publishing.

▶ **Fig 7.4:** Organizational Fitness Principles (Muscles), page 262. composite of image with illustration by msanca / DepositPhotos. com. Adapted from model developed by Rob Salome.

▶ Baseball, page 269. Willard / DepositPhotos.com.

▶ Checkered Flag, page 275. serezniy / DepositPhotos.com.

About the Author

Albert Ciuksza Jr. is a forward-thinking entrepreneur, leadership consultant, and community advocate with a passion for driving innovation and sustainable growth. As Vice President of Leadership Development at Solutions 21, Albert leads the design and implementation of transformative leadership programs, equipping high-potential leaders with the strategies and skills needed to excel in complex, dynamic environments.  He also works closely with executives, helping them develop and refine strategies that address their most pressing challenges and drive sustainable growth.

Albert's entrepreneurial journey reflects a deep commitment to innovation. He co-founded Eyenavision Inc., bringing cutting-edge optical products to market, and Draft Dynamics, where he secured a patent for a pioneering portable draft system. His experience in economic development includes managing technology-driven growth projects at the Idea Foundry and directing the Pittsburgh Impact Initiative for the Allegheny Conference on Community Development, where he played a key role in advancing regional growth.

Beyond his professional endeavors, Albert is dedicated to making a positive impact on his community. He co-chairs Food Assistance Match (FAM), an initiative that enhances access to locally grown food by doubling the benefits of food assistance programs like SNAP.[xlii] He also serves on the boards of several organizations, leveraging his expertise to drive both business success and community revitalization. Recognized as one of Pittsburgh's "40 Under 40," Albert is known for seamlessly blending innovation, leadership, and social impact.

Albert holds a degree from St. Vincent College and an MBA from the University of Pittsburgh's Katz Graduate School of Business. He resides in Bellevue, Pennsylvania, with his wife, Mallory, and their two dogs.

xlii. Learn more at foodassistancematch.org.

Book References

1. America Counts Staff. "2020 Census Will Help Policymakers Prepare for the Incoming Wave of Aging Boomers." Census.gov. December 10, 2019. https://www.census.gov/library/stories/2019/12/by-2030-all-baby-boomers-will-be-age-65-or-older.html.
2. Konish, Laurie. "As baby boomers hit 'peak 65' this year, what the retirement age should be is up for debate." CNBC. February 8, 2024. Baby boomers hit 'peak 65' in 2024. https://www.cnbc.com/2024/02/08/baby-boomers-hit-peak-65-in-2024-why-retirement-age-is-in-question.html.
3. U.S. Bureau of Labor Statistics. Charts related to the latest "State Employment and Unemployment" news release. Accessed July 31, 2024. https://www.bls.gov/charts/state-employment-and-unemployment/employment-by-state-bar.htm.
4. Routch, Kris, Monahan, Kelly and Doherty, Megan. "The holy grail of effective leadership succession planning." Deloitte Insight. September 27, 2018. https://www2.deloitte.com/us/en/insights/topics/leadership/effective-leadership-succession-planning.html.
5. ATD Research. "Succession Planning: Preparing Organizations for the Future" ATD. August 2022. https://www.td.org/product/research-report--succession-planning-preparing-organizations-for-the-future/192205
6. PeopleScout. "Gen X in the Workplace: Has Gen X Been Overlooked at Work?" Accessed July 31, 2024. https://www.peoplescout.com/insights/gen-x-in-the-workplace/.
7. PeopleScout. "Millennials in the Workplace: Keeping Millennials Motivated." Accessed July 31, 2024. https://www.peoplescout.com/insights/keeping-millennials-in-the-workplace-motivated/.
8. Principal. "Principal Financial Well-Being Index℠ 2023 Wave 1." Accessed July 31, 2024. https://secure02.principal.com/publicvsupply/GetFile?fm=EE12576A-0&ty=VOP.
9. Michael J. Urick, Elaine C. Hollensbe, Suzanne S. Masterson, Sean T. Lyons. "Understanding and Managing Intergenerational Conflict: An Examination of Influences and Strategies." OUP Academic. March 18, 2016. https://academic.oup.com/workar/article/3/2/166/2623784.

10. International Monetary Fund Research Dept. "THE WORLD ECONOMY IN THE TWENTIETH CENTURY: STRIKING DEVELOPMENTS AND POLICY LESSONS." IMF. April 12, 2000. https://www.imf.org/-/media/Websites/IMF/imported-flagship-issues/external/pubs/ft/weo/2000/01/pdf/_chapter5pdf.ashx.

11. De Long, J. Bradford. "Estimates of World GDP, One Million B.C. – Present." 1998. https://delong.typepad.com/print/20061012_LRWGDP.pdf.

12. FRED. "Real Gross Domestic Product." Accessed July 31, 2024. https://fred.stlouisfed.org/series/GDPC1.

13. The Investopedia Group. "US Recessions Throughout History: Causes and Effects." Investopedia. May 31, 2024. https://www.investopedia.com/articles/economics/08/past-recessions.asp.

14. S&P 500 Data. "Stock Market Returns Since 1964." Accessed July 31, 2024. https://www.officialdata.org/us/stocks/s-p-500/1964#:~:text=Stock%20market%20returns%20since%201964,%2C%20or%2010.31%25%20per%20..

15. CPI Inflation Calculator. "Value of $16,250 from 1964 to 2024." Accessed July 31, 2024. https://www.in2013dollars.com/us/inflation/1964?amount=16250.

16. Cerulli Associates. "Cerulli: Press Release: Cerulli Anticipates $84 Trillion in Wealth..." January 20, 2022. https://www.cerulli.com/press-releases/cerulli-anticipates-84-trillion-in-wealth-transfers-through-2045

17. Cfp.net. "About CFP Board History." Accessed July 31, 2024. https://www.cfp.net/about-cfp-board/history.

18. Abril, Danielle. Washington Post. "Zoom returned to office so employees feel your hybrid workplace pain." The Washington Post. October 5, 2023. https://www.washingtonpost.com/technology/2023/10/05/zoom-return-to-office-hybrid-remote-work/.

19. De Smet, Aaron, Dowling, Bonnie, Hancock, Bryan and Schaninger, Bill. "The Great Attrition is making hiring harder. Are you searching the right talent pools?" McKinsey & Company. Accessed July 31, 2024. https://www.mckinsey.com/capabilities/people-and-organizational-performance/our-insights/the-great-attrition-is-making-hiring-harder-are-you-searching-the-right-talent-pools.

20. Haynes, Taylor. "Why Is Gen Z So Unhappy at Work?" Indeed.com. August 31, 2023. https://www.indeed.com/career-advice/news/gen-z-unhappy-at-work.

21. Exit Planning Institute. "Become a Certified Exit Planning Advisor." Accessed July 31, 2024. https://exit-planning-institute.org/.

22. Thatcher, Kaitlinn. "Valuation Expectations - Buyers vs. Sellers." Axial. November 30, 2023. https://www.axial.net/forum/valuation-expectations-buyers-vs-sellers/t.

23. Pilat, Dan and Krastev, Sekoul. "IKEA effect." The Decision Lab. July 31, 2024. https://thedecisionlab.com/biases/ikea-effect.

24. Gambardella, Alfonso. "Policy Brief." Bocconi University. Accessed February 15, 2024. https://www.unibocconi.it/en/wps/wcm/connect/5123cfb7-cae5-4d90-8418-66fdb2e0d7f3/Policy+Brief+Gambardella+&+Co_rev5.pdf

25. Amazon.com. "The Leadership Capital Index: Realizing the Market Value of Leadership." Accessed July 31, 2024. https://www.amazon.com/Leadership -Capital-Index-Realizing-Market/dp/1626565996.

26. Ulrich, Dave. "Realizing the Market Value of Leadership." Thinkers50. Accessed July 31, 2024. https://thinkers50.com/blog/realizing-the-market-value -of-leadership/.

27. Sadun, R., Fuller, J., Hansen, S. and Neal, P. "The C-Suite Skills That Matter Most." Harvard Business Review. August 2022. https://hbr.org/2022/07/the -c-suite-skills-that-matter-most.

28. Pelham, B. W., Mirenberg, M. C., & Jones, J. T. "Why Susie sells seashells by the seashore: Implicit egotism and major life decisions." American Psychological Association. 2002. https://psycnet.apa.org/record/2002-12744-001?doi=1.

29. American Economic Review. "Eponymous Entrepreneurs." Accessed July 31, 2024. https://www.aeaweb.org/articles?id=10.1257/aer.20141524.

30. Statz, Tamara. "Resilience Through Retirement." ASA Generations. Accessed July 31, 2024. https://generations.asaging.org/resilience-through-retirement.

31. WFCA. "What Causes Wildfires?" July 5, 2022. https://wfca.com/wildfire -articles/what-causes-wildfires/

32. Inc.com. "Closely Held Corporations." Inc.com. February 6, 2022. https:// www.inc.com/encyclopedia/closely-held-corporations.html.

33. Neufeld, Dorothy. "The Influence of Family-Owned Businesses, by Share of GDP." Visual Capitalist. December 20, 2023. https://www.visualcapitalist.com/ family-owned-businesses-by-share-of-gdp/.

34. American Psychological Association. "APA Dictionary of Psychology." Accessed July 31, 2024. https://dictionary.apa.org/identity.

35. Adams, Linda. "Learning a New Skill is Easier Said Than Done." Gordon Training International. Accessed July 31, 2024. https://www.gordontraining.com/ free-workplace-articles/learning-a-new-skill-is-easier-said-than-done/.

36. Statz. "Resilience Through Retirement"

37. Bradberry, Travis. "Are You Emotionally Intelligent? Here's How to Know for Sure." Inc.com. March 24, 2015. https://www.inc.com/travis-bradberry/are-you -emotionally-intelligent-here-s-how-to-know-for-sure.html.

38. Lieberman, MD, Eisenberger, NI, Crockett, MJ, Tom, SM, Pfeifer, JH and Way, BM. "Putting Feelings into Words: Affect Labeling Disrupts Amygdala Activity in Response to Affective Stimuli." Psychological science, 2007. https:// pubmed.ncbi.nlm.nih.gov/17576282/.

39. Frei, Frances and Morriss, Anne. "Begin with Trust." Harvard Business Review. May 11, 2020. https://hbr.org/2020/05/begin-with-trust.

40. Barker, Eric. "4 Secrets to a Good Apology, According to Research." Barking Up The Wrong Tree. Accessed August 5, 2024. https://bakadesuyo.com/2012/07/ you-screwed-up-what-are-the-four-secrets-to-a/.

41. Dungan, James and Epley, Nicholas. "Surprisingly good talk: Misunderstanding others creates a barrier to constructive confrontation." APA PsycNet, March 2024. https://psycnet.apa.org/buy/2024-43827-001.

42. Amazon.com. "Wait: The Art and Science of Delay" Accessed August 5, 2024. https://www.amazon.com/gp/product/1610390040/ref=as_li_ss_tl?ie=UTF8&-camp=1789&creative=39095

43. Barker, Eric. "The 4 Most Common Relationship Problems — And How to Fix Them." Barking Up The Wrong Tree. December 21, 2014. https://bakadesuyo.com/2014/12/relationship-problems/.

44. Gravois, John. "You're Not Fooling Anyone." The Chronicle of Higher Education. November 9, 2007. https://www.chronicle.com/article/youre-not-fooling-anyone/.

45. Meacham, John. "Destiny and Power: The American Odyssey of George Herbert Walker Bush." Random House Publishing Group. 2016. Destiny and Power: The American Odyssey of George Herbert Walker Bush - Jon Meacham - Google Books

46. American Psychological Association. "Impostor Phenomenon." APA Dictionary of Psychology. Accessed August 5, 2024. https://dictionary.apa.org/impostor-phenomenon.

47. Harrell, Eben. "Impostor Syndrome Has Its Advantages." Harvard Business Review. May 2022. https://hbr.org/2022/05/impostor-syndrome-has-its-advantages.

48. Barthel, Christiane, Halvachizadeh, Sacha, Gamble, Jamison G., Pape, Hans-Christoph and Rauer, Thomas. "Recreational Skydiving-Really That Dangerous? A Systematic Review." National Library of Medicine. January 10, 2023. https://www.ncbi.nlm.nih.gov/pmc/articles/PMC9859333/

49. Sitter, Paul. "Malfunction, Malfunction, Malfunction—The 2017 Fatality Summary." Parachutist. April 2, 2018. https://parachutist.com/Article/malfunction-malfunction-malfunctionthe-2017-fatality-summary.

50. Psychology Today. "Dunning-Kruger Effect." Accessed August 5, 2024. https://www.psychologytoday.com/us/basics/dunning-kruger-effect.

51. Treacy, Michael and Wiersema, Fred. "Customer Intimacy and Other Value Disciplines" Harvard Business Review. February 1993. https://hbr.org/1993/01/customer-intimacy-and-other-value-disciplines

52. Latham, Gary P. "The Motivational Benefits of Goal-Setting." The Academy of Management Executive (1993-2005) 18, no. 4 (2004): 126–29. http://www.jstor.org/stable/4166132.

53. Merriam-Webster Dictionary. "Career ladder Definition & Meaning." Merriam-Webster.com. Accessed August 5, 2024. https://www.merriam-webster.com/dictionary/career%20ladder.

54. Leavitt, Harold J. "Why Hierarchies Thrive." Harvard Business Review. March 2003. https://hbr.org/2003/03/why-hierarchies-thrive.

55. The Colour Works. "Hippocrates, Galen & The Four Humours." Accessed August 5, 2024. https://www.thecolourworks.com/hippocrates-galen-the-four-humours/.

56. Sadun, Raffella, Fuller, Joseph, Hansen, Stephen and Neal, PJ. "The C-Suite Skills That Matter Most." Harvard Business Review. https://hbr.org/2022/07/the-c-suite-skills-that-matter-most.

57. Bradberry, Travis. "Emotional Intelligence – EQ." Forbes.com. January 9, 2014. https://www.forbes.com/sites/travisbradberry/2014/01/09/emotional-intelligence/?sh=435832ea1ac0.

58. Tversky, Amos and Kahneman, Daniel. "Belief in the Law of Small Numbers." stats.org.uk. Accessed August 5, 2024. http://stats.org.uk/statistical-inference/TverskyKahneman1971.pdf.

59. Markowsky, George. "Physiology." Britannica.com. Accessed August 5, 2024. https://www.britannica.com/science/information-theory/Physiology.

60. Matias, J. Nathan. "Bias and Noise: Daniel Kahneman on Errors in Decision-Making." Medium.com. October 17, 2017. https://natematias.medium.com/bias-and-noise-daniel-kahneman-onerrors-in-decision-making-6bc844ff5194.

61. Soll, Jack B., Milkman, Katherine L., and Payne, John W. "Outsmart Your Own Biases." Harvard Business Review. May 2015. https://hbr.org/2015/05/outsmart-your-own-biases.

62. Bellezza, Silvia, Paharia, Neeru and Keinan, Anat. "Conspicuous Consumption of Time: When Busyness and Lack of Leisure Time Become a Status Symbol." OUP Academic. December 27, 2016. https://academic.oup.com/jcr/article-abstract/44/1/118/2736404.

63. Celniker, J. B., Gregory, A., Koo, H. J., Piff, P. K., Ditto, P. H., and Shariff, A. F. "The moralization of effort." APA PsycNet. 2023. https://psycnet.apa.org/record/2022-85298-001.

64. Mind Tools Content Team. "Eisenhower's Urgent/Important Principle - Using Time Effectively, Not Just Efficiently." Mindtools.com. Accessed August 5, 2024. https://www.mindtools.com/al1e0k5/eisenhowers-urgentimportant-principle.

65. Zhu, Meng, Yang, Yang and Hsee, Christopher K. "Mere Urgency Effect." OUP Academic. February 9, 2018. https://academic.oup.com/jcr/article-abstract/45/3/673/4847790.

66. CognitiveEdge. "The Cynefin Framework." YouTube.com. Accessed August 5, 2024. https://www.youtube.com/watch?v=N7oz366X0-8.

67. Voigt, Julian, Marius Jais and Hugo M. Kehr. "An Image of What I Want to Achieve: How Visions Motivate Goal Pursuit." Current Psychology. April 17, 2024. https://link.springer.com/article/10.1007/s12144-024-05943-4.

68. Oettingen, Gabriele and Gollwitzer, Peter M. "Making Goal Pursuit Effective: Expectancy-Dependent Goal Setting and Planned Goal Striving." Researchgate.net. January 2009. https://www.researchgate.net/publication/43193998_Making_goal_pursuit_effective_Expectancy-dependent_goal_setting_and_planned_goal_striving.

69. Oettingen, Gabriele, Grant, Heidi, Smith, Pamela K., Skinner, Mary and Gollwitzer, Peter M. "Nonconscious Goal Pursuit: Acting in an Explanatory

Vacuum." ScienceDirect. September 2006. https://www.sciencedirect.com/science/article/abs/pii/S0022103105001216.

70. Reitman, Annabelle and Benatti, Sylvia. "Mentoring vs Coaching." Association of Talent Development. March 26, 2021. https://www.td.org/content/atd-blog/mentoring-versus-coaching-whats-the-difference.

71. Grant, Adam. "A Better Way to Ask for Advice." Behavioral Scientist. October 25, 2023. https://behavioralscientist.org/a-better-way-to-ask-for-advice-learn-from-the-best/.

72. International Coaching Federation. "Global Coaching Study: 2023 Executive Summary." 2023 https://coachingfederation.org/app/uploads/2023/04/2023ICFGlobalCoachingStudy_ExecutiveSummary.pdf

73. Grant, A. M., Curtayne, L., and Burton, G. "Executive coaching enhances goal attainment, resilience and workplace well-being: A randomised controlled study." APA PsycNet. 2009. https://psycnet.apa.org/record/2009-12395-008.

74. Future Market Insights Inc. "Leadership Development Program Market Outlook from 2024 to 2034." Accessed August 5, 2024. https://www.futuremarketinsights.com/reports/leadership-development-program-market.

75. Zenger, Jack. "We Wait Too Long to Train Our Leaders." Harvard Business Review. December 17, 2012. https://hbr.org/2012/12/why-do-we-wait-so-long-to-trai.

76. Leimbach, Michael. "2021 Leadership Development Survey: The Times They are a Changing..." Trainingmag.com. May 18, 2021. https://trainingmag.com/annual-leadership-development-survey-the-times-they-are-a-changing/.

77. Michaels, Philip. "Best family cell phone plan in 2024" Tom's Guide. July 15, 2024. https://www.tomsguide.com/best-picks/best-family-cell-phone-plan.

78. Gnepp, J, Klayman, J, Williamson, IO and Barlas, S. "The future of feedback: Motivating performance improvement through future-focused feedback." National Library of Medicine. June 19, 2020. https://www.ncbi.nlm.nih.gov/pmc/articles/PMC7304587/.

79. Industry Research. "Global Self-Paced E-Learning Market Research Report 2024." Industryresearch.biz. January 23, 2024. https://www.industryresearch.biz/global-self-paced-e-learning-market-26638338

80. Practical Psychology. "Ebbinghaus Forgetting Curve (Definition + Examples)." Accessed August 5, 2024. https://practicalpie.com/ebbinghaus-forgetting-curve/.

81. New Level Work. "The ROI of Leadership Development." 2023. https://21464110.fs1.hubspotusercontent-na1.net/hubfs/21464110/NLW%20-%20ROI%20Files/nlw-roi-of-leadership-development-study-2023-full-report-1.pdf.

82. Hobart, Buddy. *The Leadership Decade: A Playbook for an Extraordinary Era*. Novato, California: Select Press. 2020.

83. Carufel, Richard. "New research finds 85 percent of companies lack the ability to implement strategy they've developed—wasting millions and falling behind." Agility PR Solutions. October 10, 2023. https://www.agilitypr.com/

pr-news/public-relations/new-research-finds-85-percent-of-companies-lack-the-ability-to-implement-strategy-theyve-developed-wasting-millions-and-falling-behind/

84. Wheeler, S., Wipf, J., Staiger, T., Deyo, R. and Jarvik, J. "Evaluation of low back pain in adults." UpToDate. May 26, 2022. https://www.uptodate.com/contents/evaluation-of-low-back-pain-in-adults/print.

85. Collins, Jim and Porras, Jerry I. "Building Your Company's Vision." Harvard Business Review. October 1996. https://hbr.org/1996/09/building-your-companys-vision.

86. Southwest Airlines. "About Southwest." Accessed August 5, 2024. https://www.southwest.com/about-southwest/.

87. IKEA. "The IKEA vision, values and business idea." Accessed August 5, 2024. https://www.ikea.com/us/en/this-is-ikea/about-us/the-ikea-vision-and-values-pub9aa779d0.

88. Neilson, Gary, Estupinan, Jaime and Sethi, Bhushan."10 principles of organization design." Strategy-business.com. March 23, 2015. https://www.strategy-business.com/article/00318.

89. Harter, Jim. "Disengagement Persists Among U.S. Employees." Gallup. April 25, 2022. https://www.gallup.com/workplace/391922/employee-engagement-slump-continues.aspx.

90. Crestcom. "5 reasons people don't perform at work, and how YOU can change that!" Accessed August 5, 2024. https://www.crestcomsocal.com/articles/leadership-development/non-performance.

91. Atkins, Isaiah. "Setting Clear Expectations for Employees." Business News Daily. October 24, 2023. https://www.businessnewsdaily.com/9451-clear-employee-expectations.html.

92. Fierce Inc. "86 Percent of Employees Cite Lack of Collaboration for Workplace Failures." Accessed August 5, 2024. https://fierceinc.com/wp-content/uploads/2020/06/PR__2011_Workplace_Collaboration_Survey__Fierce_Inc__.pdf.

93. Fierce Inc., *Workplace Failures.*

94. Chui, M., Manyika, J., Bughin, J., Dobbs, R., Roxburgh, H.S,, Sands, G., Westergren, M. "The social economy: Unlocking value and productivity through social technologies." McKinsey & Company. July 1, 2012. https://www.mckinsey.com/industries/technology-media-and-telecommunications/our-insights/the-social-economy.

95. Serenko, Alexander, Bontis, Nick and Hardie, Timothy. "Organizational size and knowledge flow: a proposed theoretical link." Emerald Insight. October 23, 2007. https://www.emerald.com/insight/content/doi/10.1108/14691930710830783/full/html.

96. Clear, James. "3-2-1: On systems vs. goals, identity-based habits, and the lessons of life." Jamesclear.com. January 2, 2020. https://jamesclear.com/3-2-1/january-2-2020.

97. Caykoylu, Sinan. :Post-succession predecessor-successor interactions and their relational and organizational outcomes." Simon Fraser University. May 7, 2013. https://summit.sfu.ca/item/13516.

98. Appel, Mark. "Grief and Goodbyes." X. March 23, 2023. https://x.com/markappel26/status/1638586837810683906?lang=en.

99. Appel, Mark. "Grief and Goodbyes." MarkAppel.com. March 23, 2023. https://markappel.com/journal/grief-and-goodbyes.

100. Health and Human Services. "Our Epidemic of Loneliness and Isolation." HHS.gov. 2023. https://www.hhs.gov/sites/default/files/surgeon-general-social-connection-advisory.pdf.

Printed in the USA
CPSIA information can be obtained
at www.ICGtesting.com
LVHW010923250924
791668LV00038B/129